THE ROLE OF REGIONS?

TASSILO HERRSCHEL – PONTUS TALLBERG (EDS.)

THE ROLE
OF REGIONS?

NETWORKS, SCALE, TERRITORY

© Contributing Authors
Editors: Tassilo Herrschel and Pontus Tallberg
Graphic Form: Christer Wigerfelt
Cover Illustration: Kerstin Holmstedt
Printed by Kristianstads Boktryckeri, Sweden 2011

ISBN 978-91-7261-222-8

TABLE OF CONTENT

Introduction –
Regions, 'Fuzziness' as Opportunity?

Regions and regionalisation seem to have become buzzwords in current debates on the 'best' spatial level of governance vis-à-vis the challenges of global competitiveness and, especially in an EU context, cohesion and convergence. Much of this discussion revolves around 'best' forms and the 'right' scale of governance, implying changes to the ways in which the conventional main variables institutions, hierarchy and territoriality interact to produce and operate regions as part of hierarchical arrangements of territories   Yet current debates are not merely a continuation of previous enthusiasm for regionalisation. The main focus now is on the distinction between 'old' and 'new' regionalism, i.e. in particular the degree of flexibility and responsiveness to policy challenges which, mostly, refer to economic competitiveness. And this shift towards a new understanding of regions as variably defined policy spaces, rather than centrally implemented fixed units of administration, has raised conceptual and practical questions about territoriality and boundedness of 'new' regions. Evidence 'on the ground' among policy makers suggests that the changes from 'old' to 'new' may go further than a varying emphasis on territory and scale (Brenner, 2000, 2003).

All this has made the region an interesting and increasingly popular subject of academic and political discussions. Yet ideas vary about the nature of regions and their role in existing governance structures. The repeated experimentation in the UK with regionalization for England, moving between all-out localism and notions of devolution, is a case in point. In both academic debate and political practice, the term 'region' refers to two quite different positions on the scale between the endpoints 'global' and 'local' respectively. On the one hand, 'region' is presumed to sit somewhere at the sub-national level, linking the local and national scales by offering an 'intermediate' platform to negotiate between different scale policies. On the other hand, the term refers to a framework for cooperation between sovereign nation states; a cooperation driven mostly by concerns about economic competitiveness in a globalised environment, and strategic considerations about security (Hentz, ed 2003). Thus, apart from their sheer differences in scale, the two dimensions of regionalisation represent varying underlying rationales, and ways of operation towards a "regionalised world" (Moller and Spindler, 2002, p 8). This lack of clarity in meaning, however, may well have aided the growing popularity of the regional level in debates on the best effective level of governance *vis-à-vis* global, increasingly economic, challenges of maintaining competitiveness.

It is against this background that regions are increasingly understood as rather more virtual constructs on the basis of shared agendas and policy objectives between actors. The latter understanding of 'regions' has, over the last decade or so, become increasingly labelled with the prefix 'new' to mark a conceptual and practical departure from the conventional association of 'region' as administrative-governmental and planning-related territoriality, defined by using specific criteria and indices. The NUTS system used in, and by' the European Union is one such example of drawing up geographic divisions of its territory. This serves the purpose of applying policies and dispensing subsidies on the basis of centrally defined criteria. Here, 'regions' are perceived as a set level in a spatial hierarchy, situated between the 'local' and the 'global', albeit with national variations, and usually defined 'top-down'. By contrast, the 'new version' of regionalisation focuses much more on the strategic, instrumental side of regions as flexible, dynamic spaces circumscribed by shared policy agendas 'from within' – and that means collaborations between localities and their actors and policy makers in an often *ad hoc*, 'bottom-up' process.

By its nature, such a 'new' understanding, with its greater emphasis on actor networks and policy agenda-driven collaborations as the main drivers of regionalisation, is inherently variable, time-limited and, in its bordering often less clear. Such 'fuzziness' has been identified by Markusen (2003) as a key characteristic of the concept of (new) regionalism and, indeed, appears as its particular strength. On the other hand, Lovering (1999) views this fuzziness as an indication for insufficiently developed theoretical underpinning, which may, in fact, have aided the growing popularity, even 'hype', as he puts it, of discussions on 'new regionalism', as it encourages the development of new ideas on this phenomenon. Yet the proof of the pudding of the actual relevance of such regionalism is in the evidence 'on the ground'. Are there really 'new' ways of 'making regions' (Herrschel, 2005) and utilising them as part of policy making, or is it primarily about a body of ideas that simply mirrors particular language and political discourse (Moller and Spindler, 2002)?

Process, rather than fixed structure, in region building means that negotiations between actors are the main mechanism behind such network-based, relational territorialisation. Regions in this understanding are understood as shaped through varying collaborative alliances, i.e. forming linkages and building networks in policy-making and economic governance. It seems also important for regions to establish strategic cooperation with other regions (Rylander and Tallberg 2011). Such openness and flexibility is credited with providing a good platform for greater policy responsiveness to such challenges as economic changes, and may involve emerging 'innovative networks' (Cooke and Morgan, 1998), or even 'intelligent regions', developing and distributing ideas and innovation through their particular institutional and operational architecture (Storper and Wharf, 1997). This type of regions is in effect virtual, permitting actors to join and leave without having to surrender powers or being tied in institutionally. But the details of their workings remain rather less clear, so that putting 'new regionalism' into practice has been likened to a 'black box'. It is here, that case studies, such as those brought together in this book, offer the opportunity to gain further insights into different ways of 'doing regions'.

In this 'new' sub-national regionalism, economic pressures are considered the main drivers of these changes, pushing for cooperation between localities across jurisdictional and administration-internal departmental borders, as the following case studies illustrate. What also became evident is a progressing 'adjustment' of actors to the new conditions and, indeed, their way of operation, albeit with considerable variations. Yet, despite a possible impression to the contrary, this does not necessarily mean a wholesale replacement of established mechanisms and ways of doing things or, indeed, the type and range of actors involved. Instead, it is about extension of the former 'old' by the 'new', leading to a form of 'composite' regionalism (Herrschel, 2009). Accordingly, 'new' regions take shape and operate by combining both engagement in varying, informal arrangements, which define a region through the territories represented by the participating actors, while simultaneously also working through existing structures with their associated clearly defined portfolios of power, responsibility and, crucially for effective policy making, finances. In essence, such collaboration is possible for a group of either weaker (actual or perceived) actors seeking to 'gang up' to improve their joint prospects in a wider political (strategic) and economic context. From that angle, regions are, and increasingly seem so to be so, policy-making vehicles. A sense of connectivity across boundaries, a connectivity that needs matching policy responses, is at the centre of this meaning of regionalisation.

Often, municipal or key business leaders play an instrumental role in establishing the necessary 'connectivity' through networks of shared interests. Following regional arrangements are thus essentially time limited and project specific, and, importantly, have no specific administrative structures attached. This matters, as administrative structures tend to be seen as irreversible commitments and potential sources of competing political interests. Instead, they prefer to operate through the institutional structures and legitimation of the participating actors. This contrasts with ambitions at the international level, where administrative fixtures are seen as important underpinnings of agreed international trading areas. But then, the participants there are autonomous nation states. At the sub-national level, institutionally 'thin' arrangements for regions are generally favoured by local and central governments, because they are less 'threatening' as potential competing power bases, and also are likely to look to the electorate less like 'profligate' bureaucracy. Being represented by effectively little more than an office, a website and a secretary is unthreatening to established 'power brokers' and acceptable to the tax-paying public.

Given their institutionally 'thin' nature, these new arrangements for sub-national 'new' regionalisation cannot replace 'old' established practices altogether. Ultimately, 'new regions' need to prove their utility. Envisaged and promised projects and developments need to happen 'on the ground' to give the 'virtual' a reality and thus credibility. But the situation is not as clear cut. Differences between national contexts, for instance, matter for scope and purpose of regions. It is here that comparative analyses of regionalisation in different national contexts promise to provide useful insights.

In this collection of essays, regions are understood to be located at the sub-national level, i.e. between the local and national tiers of administration. The precise location on this vertical scale varies between countries, and also with the nature and role of regions themselves. There are differences in institutional and governmental purpose and capacity in reflection of national state structures. Federal Germany and centralised England (as one of the historic four national entities of the UK), where all regions have just been abolished leaving just national and local government, are just one such example of contrast. Given the combination of fixed administrative regions and variable, time-limited, virtual policy regions, the actual number and shape of such units varies over time. Lidström (in this volume) counts a total of 1400 sub-national regions across the EU, although this includes all the various regional entities located between the national and local level. Taking into account only the immediately sub-national entities, he still counts some 700 units. Against this background of a plethora of national subdivisions into regional entities of varying scope, size, purpose and 'realness', the concept of a 'Europe of the Regions' emerged during the 1990s, seemingly challenging the primary role of the nation state. There was thus talk about a potential 'hollowing out' of the state (Jessop, 2004), challenges 'from above' by globalisation' and supra-national region building, and from 'below' by sub-national regionalization

In some cases, driven by political agenda and ideology, there has been a form of fight-back by national governments, seeking to re-assert their supremacy in national politics and policy making. In the UK, both a new emphasis on localism, as well a continuous lamenting about loss of sovereignty 'to Brussels' in all its somewhat stereotypical argumentation, illustrate such responses. Similarly, in the Nordic states, centralisation is firmly embedded in national political discourse, too (Gidlund and Jerneck, 2000), with regions portrayed as something 'alien' and superfluous. For some time now, over the last ten or so years, Sweden has been witnessing some debate on regionalization and also two pilot cases of devolving policy responsibilities. This was accompanied by establishing a degree of political autonomy through newly installed, directly elected regional parliaments (an attempt that failed in England) in two regions, *Västra Götaland* and *Region Skåne*. The experiment has been successful insofar, as the status quo of devolution has become a permanent arrangements since its legislative approval in January 2011. Other regions may well follow these examples sooner, rather than later. Norway has been studying these developments in neighbouring Sweden and seems to have concluded that it, too. ought to follow the path to more regionalization St Meld nr 12 2006-2007). Currently, there are 14 *fylke* (equivalent to counties as lower tier regions), based on historic administrative structures. But these possess few powers. Yet, based on more recent evidence, the announced regionalisation agenda se3ems to have been somewhat moved to the back burner. process seems to have ground to a halt.

This seeming stop-go approach may reflect a degree of ambivalence about adding a further layer of administration with devolved powers and responsibilities. Such concerns tend to follow a neo-liberalism-inspired, 'efficiency'-driven, lean state approach, competing with traditional Keynesian-inspired views of government-led regional policies. In both cases, 'regions' is understood in the conventional, territorial-administrative sense, rather than the 'new' meaning of virtual spaces where form follows function (Herrschel, 2007). This inherent vagueness, however, irritates those who focus on fixed, bounded political-administrative geographies. The picture is slightly different, however, when it comes to policy implementation. Here conventional administrative structures matter for managing expenditure and budgets, and provide democratic legitimacy. In fact, therefore, it takes both forms of regions, 'real' and 'virtual' to be used for policy strategies and administration tasks respectively.

This book brings together a selection of papers which seek to address the complex and multifaceted nature of 'regions' from different angles: The question of scale, creation of network-based marginalisations, questions of legitimacy and identity, the difference between 'real' and 'virtual' regions, and the role of the European Union as facilitator of different forms of region building and regionalization. Admittedly, this variety may give the impression of a somewhat eclectic set of paper topics, but such hint of eclecticism is in the very nature of the object of study. The papers evolved out of presentations and discussions had a two day workshop at the University of Gothenburg (Cefos) in April 2010. They provide comparative views of regions and regionalization methods and processes in different national contexts, including contrasts between Europe and North America. One of the main objectives of the workshop was to bring together practitioners and academics to illuminate theory and practice of regionalization in different national contexts, and thus contribute to current discussions on this topic in Norway and Sweden, but also a wider European level.

The following sections provide an overview of the main arguments offered by the contributions contained in this volume. In the first contribution, Lidström raises questions about the degree of democratic representativeness and, ultimately, legitimacy, of regions as a result of their inherent vagueness in conceptual role, functional purpose, and scalar position in a governmental-administrative hierarchy. In particular, he points to the question of self-government as part of regionalisation. This is especially, and increasingly so, the case for city-regions as the growing focus of collaborative (and virtual) regionalised local governance. Yet the success, i.e. the acceptance of such regional constructs by international investors, which is a main purpose of competitive city-regionalism, depends, according to Stegman McCallion, on attitudes and priorities among national policy makers towards to such projects. These do ultimately require statutory 'backup' to allow concept s and policy strategies to turn into projects 'on the ground'.

Their growing push for more national independence in shaping and using their policy networks and framing agendas, may challenge existing formalised sources of legitimacy and democratic accountability. Such concerns are also addressed in Nergelius's (in this book) examination of the relationship between the Swedish state and its regions. Here, too, possible challenges are noted to 'official' hierarchical structures of communication as 'backbone' of visible democratic legitimacy, as they get bypassed through informal linkages. And it is these developments which, as Hepburn argues, are leading to a multi-level citizenship, where different senses of belonging are attached to each level of state administration - above and below national government, especially in a European context.

These shifts to a more clearly multi-level form of governance may well, as Mc Ewen points out, affect the very operation of the welfare state. Regionalising the responsibility for social policy may lead to inefficiencies through a proliferation of actors and associated agendas, as organisational structures and lines of communication and responsibility become less institutionalised and accountable. And this may thus mean a greater need to co-ordinate policy responses, especially with regard to longer-term strategic decisions. Yet this, in itself, uses up resources, while, on the other hand, may also allow better targeting of initiatives through greater flexibility and innovativeness in policy making. Further study on this is required. There is a danger, as Herrschel (2009), and, later in this book, Grindheim and Manga respectively, argue a danger of creating and/or reinforcing inequalities through the creation or reproduction of inclusions and exclusions in the wake of a growing role of networks. These can take the form of spatially 'virtual' inter-actor linkages (Herrschel), or more physically visible manifestations as a network of high-speed railways (Grindheim and Manga). Such differentiation reflects a shift from viewing regions as all-embracing containers of policies, where territories are contiguous and include all those within specified territories, to a much more linear, selective approach to implementing regions. Such inherent unevenness may also reinforce differences in economic opportunities, as networks have also been viewed as crucial for facilitating innovation and thus economic competitiveness.

The societal manifestations and implications of these general perceptions require more detailed appraisals, so as to allow role and impact of specific local conditions and actor constellations to be taken into account. Using the example of the Skåne region, Boye's contribution to this book examines the appropriateness of such generalizations as used by the OECD, vis-à-vis the realities of regional specificities found in more detailed examinations. Such broader international comparative perspective, applied to the societal manifestations and implications and exclusions are the focus of Lidström and Seller's discussion of inequalities in regions around metropolises. In particular, the authors investigate scope and efficacy of policies by metropolitan governments in addressing societal divisions and social exclusions. And this, they demonstrate, requires adopting a comparative perspective, so that inter-local as well as inter-national differences and particularities can be identified and assessed in their impact. And responding to such differences requires a more flexible, collaborative, rather than formalised and technocratic approach to planning. Using two examples from Norway, Amdam demonstrates the importance of learning by actors and institutions when engaging in collaborative planning arrangements, so that these can remain sufficiently flexible and responsive to rapidly changing circumstances and requirements. And this involves allowing regional actors to define and shape policies in response to particular local and regional conditions and requirements, rather than merely implementing centrally defined policies. It is such learning as the basis of flexible policy making, that, as Uyarra concludes, ought to be underpinning the approach to fostering innovation clusters. Instead, there is evidence, she points out, that innovation is seen as a suitable subject for top-down management. In the form of an increasingly instrumental view among policy makers of innovation networks has shifted the focus on using networks to facilitate innovation from the outside, that is higher tier government., and use network linkages as vehicles to distribute 'good practice' in building innovative capacity.

Such more variable and network-based approach to viewing and defining regions applies in particular to metropolitan areas as the increasingly more acknowledged – in academia and public policy – drivers of national economic competitiveness and development. In effect, as Knieling discusses for the example of the Hamburg metropolitan area, there are different layers and institutionally shaped 'strands' of regionalization, of both the virtual and conventionally territorialised kind. And these challenge existing, territorially-based and bounded, fixed forms and practices of planning and regulation. Instead, he argues, and thus affirms the tenor of many of the contributions in this book, there is a need for more relational, network-based planning and ways of governance. This includes an increasingly modular approach to spatial planning and governance, based on variable, and temporally limited, alliances and thus networks between actors. With the growing range and diversity of their search for participation in spatial governance, there is a growing task in bringing together and co-ordinating an equally growing range of interests and agendas and ways of doing things.

The need for combining theory – indeed, several theories - and practices in regionalization policies and projects, if they are to be used as drivers of economic development, is highlighted by Lykk (later in this book) in her account of developments around the Øresund Bridge between Denmark and Sweden. Based on the effects of high-profile projects, she concludes that projects of physical connectivity, such as transport links, need to be accompanied by relevant social and cultural policies to change mindsets and perceptions about the changes. Only then, relations between previously separate regions may result in approximation and, eventually, new, combined, regional spaces, even if more at the virtual than 'real' level. This example is also very interesting, because it shows the production of an international trans-border region which, at the same time, entails local divisions and collaborations at city-regional level. This trans-border regionalism around the Øresund aims in particular at an international audience of investors. And this includes such projects which are sponsored by thy European Union, such as the euroregions. The focus remains on the institutional side of regions and regionalisation in Herodes's comparative study of evidence of 'new institutionalism' in the wider London region (South East England) and the Stockholm region. Her main interest rests in the effect of external factors, such as EU policies, on regional governance arrangements, and thus the interaction between the sub-national and the supra-national. And given the centralised state structures in both countries, informal communication between regions and the EU proved very important as a means of circumnavigating the respective central governments. Even when successful by the set targets, such as on the German-Polish border, their future rationale and purpose needs, as Belof suggests, reconsideration and clarification. Otherwise, they may eventually 'run out of steam'. Such concerns raise bigger, more fundamental questions, inter alia the generalising policy conceptions of regions and regional development at the international level.

Lindeborg addresses the differing scales covered by 'regions', stretching from international macro-regions to small regional groupings of localities. In a number of countries, the regional level of administration distinguishes between an upper and lower tier, with the former sitting immediately beneath the level of national government, while the latter takes the lower, near local, end of the regional scale. This 'scalar fuzziness' is very well illustrated by the international and multi-scalar cross-border Baltic Sea Region, as it embraces many variations of regional scale: inter-national to inter-local, and also combines features of both 'old' and 'new' regionalism. And seeking empowerment may also involve collecting and sharing information across the regional level and across boundaries and borders, such as reported by Josefsson for the Skåne region . And this need not necessarily involve the central state.

With this overview of the multifaceted nature of regions and their governance, the editors and the publishers; *Region Skåne, Region Västra Götaland*, Regionplanekontoret vid *Stockholms läns Landsting* (Office of Regional Growth and Planning, Stockholm County Council), *Sveriges Kommuner och Landsting*, SKL,

(Swedish Association of Local Authorities and Regions) and *Kommunesektorens Interesse- og Arbeidsgiverorganisasjon*, KS, (The Norwegian Association of Local Authorities and Regions) hope to initiate further discussions within Europe and also beyond, about the role and purpose of regions, and also encourage additional research on the role of regions. This includes providing materials and answering questions concerning the respective regions. Some of the research presented here covers the regions in southern Sweden, represented by the publishers, while the rest extends to a much bigger geographic area, thus offering a range of comparative perspectives. Rooted in different academic traditions, varying conceptual and practical approaches to investigating regions have provided further comparative-analytical perspectives.

Concept and practical implementation of regions will continue to attract attention and interest in political and academic debates, and they are likely to gain further in relevance within individual countries. Regions are an integral part of democratic representation and governance within states, including different geographic scales and institutional-governmental capacity: provinces, municipalities and states. The large number of sub-national units of governance in Europe – as provided in Anders Lindström's chapter in this book – shows the diversity of political bodies in Europe, yet also different political traditions.) As such, regions make important contributions to multi-level governance, in all their varying formats. It is this diversity and complexity of the role and nature of the regional scale of governance that highlight the questions which require further attention. This includes in particular the role regions can play in delivering national political agendas between neo-liberal and Keynesian ideologies.

REFERENCES

Cooke, Ph and Morgan, K (1998): *The Associational Economy Firms, Regions, and Innovation*. Oxford: Oxford University Press

Gidlund, J and Jerneck, M (2000): *Local and regional governance in Europe: evidence from Nordic regions*. Cheltenham: Edward Elgar

Hentz, J (ed 2003): *New and critical security and regionalism: beyond the nation state*. Aldershot–Ashgate

Herrschel, T (2005): *Creative Regionalization*: Making Regions for 'Upscale' and 'Downscale' consumption – Experiences from Post-socialist eastern Germany. In: GeoJournal, Vol. 62, No. 1. (January), pp. 59–70.

Herrschel, T (2009): *Regionalisation, 'virtual' spaces and 'real territories. A view from Europe and North America*. In International Journal of Public Sector Management, vol 22, no 3, pp 261–272

Jessop, B (2004): *Hollowing out the 'nation-state'*. In: P Kennett (ed): A handbook of comparative social policy. Cheltenham: Edward Elgar, pp 11–25

KS, The Norwegian Association of Local and Regional Authorities

Lidström, A, 2004. *Kommunerna – idag och imorgon*. I Studieförbundet Vuxenskolan, 2004: Att styra eller styras. En bok om demokrati och federalism.

Loughlin, J (1996): *"Europe of the Regions" and the Federalization of Europe*. In: Publius, vol 26; number 4, pages 141–162

Lovering, J (1999): *Theory led by policy: the inadequacies of the 'New Regionalism'* (illustrated from the case of Wales). In: International Journal of Urban and Regional Research, Vol 23; Number 2, pages 379-396.

Markusen, A (2003): *Fuzzy Concepts, Scanty Evidence, Policy Distance*: The Case for Rigour and Policy Relevance in Critical Regional Studies. In: Regional Studies, Vol 37; Part 6/7, pages 701–718

Moller, J and Spindler, J (2002): *Language games played in the processes of co-construction*. In: Change. Transformations in Education. Vol 5.2.

SKL, Swedish Association of Local Authorities and Regions (SALAR)

Storper and Wharf (1997): *The Regional World: Territorial Development in a Global Economy*. Economic Geography, Vol 76; Part 1, pages 101

Rylander, D and Tallberg, P *Strategic Cooperation between regions:* Building and utilizing transnational relations

Remark: This Chapter will appear in forthcoming book Jan Bucek, J., and Ryder, A. eds. (2011). *Growth and Change*: Public Policy, Administrative Reforms and Economic Development. Bratislava: Geografika.

Stortingsmeld nr 12 2006–2007

ANDERS LIDSTRÖM, UMEÅ UNIVERSITY, SWEDEN

Regional Self-government and Democracy

During the last few decades, regions have become increasingly important units for territorial self-government in the European countries. This coincides with strong tendencies of globalization, a questioning of the role of the Westphalian nation state and the gradual development and strengthening of the European Union. The regional level of government is now a part of the modern multi-level system of government that characterizes most European countries (Lidström 2007). The particular strength of the regional level is that it has a population size that is usually sufficiently large to provide economies of scale in the provision of services and functions with relative closeness to the citizens. Regions are generally more socially diverse than municipalities, often containing strong within-regional differences and preconditions. Strengthening the regions has also been an efficient way of preventing states with strong sub-national identities, such as Spain and Belgium, from breaking up.

Although regions appear in different sizes and forms, they have certain features in common. This chapter discusses how democratically legitimate regions may be defined and delineated from other units of territorial governance. In addition, it provides an overview of the wide variety of different types of regions that are contained within this common definition. Regions vary not only in size but also in terms of powers and functions. Finally, regions are discussed in terms of their democratic qualities. Although regions have elected representatives their democratic vitality can often be questioned.

The European regional map

In its declaration of regionalism in Europe, the Assembly of European Regions (AER) defines regions as units of democratic decision-making at the intermediate level: "The region is the territorial body of public law established at the level immediately below that of the State and endowed with political self-government". An additional criterion is that regions should have a representative, directly elected decision-making assembly and executive bodies (AER 1996). It is also made clear that the lowest tier of self-government, i.e. municipalities, cannot be regions.

Regions are a contested concept in a European setting. The emphasis on the regional level in the EU, codified by the Maastricht Treaty from 1992, has made it important for sub-national units to be recognized as regions in order both to be able to exert influence through various organizations and to receive resources targeted at regions by the EU. Hence, there are many ways of defining regions. However, we will take our starting-point in the definition established by the AER, not only because this is the largest network of regions in Europe but also as it is logically consistent and relevant for the regions that exist in Europe today.

On the whole, the AER definition is clear, although the AER is not consistent when it applies it as a criterion for membership. First, it is not obvious whether the second level in federal states, such as *länder* and *cantons,* should be regarded as regions. These have a constitutional status as parts of states, not as bodies in an intermediate position between the state and the municipalities (Swenden 2006). However, the AER has chosen to accept *länder* and *cantons* as members. Second, although the definition allows for states to have several regional levels, the AER tends to favour the highest of these levels. For example, French and Italian regions are AER members, but not the next levels – the departments in France and the provinces in Italy. Third, although being strict with the criterion that regions should have a directly elected assembly, the AER grants membership status to Finnish indirectly elected assemblies. This is a bit surprising as it could easily open up for other indirectly elected units to claim the right to be members.

When using the AER definition as a criterion for delineating European regions, we need to apply it a bit more consistently. In common with the AER, we will include the second level authorities in federal states. However, contrary to the AER practice, we will accept that there may be several levels of regions in a state and be strict with the line of demarcation against indirectly elected bodies. Using these principles as a guideline when identifying the regions in the European countries (outside of Russia, Belarus and Ukraine) leads to the identification of a total of 1374 units. These are listed for each country in Table 1 (next page).

Table 1 Overview of the regional levels in Europe (2007)

Country [1][2]	Total number of tiers [3]	Regions		
		Label	No	Average population size
Albania	2 (1)	Rrethe	36	88 900
Austria	2	Bundesland	9	922 000
Belgium	3	Région Communauté/Gemeenshap Provins	3 3 10	3 533 000 3 533 000 1 060 000
Bosnia-Hercegovina	3 (2) 2	Entiteta Kantona	2 10	1 900 000 380 000
Czech Republic	2 (3)	Kraje	14	736 000
Croatia	2	Županija	21	210 000
Denmark	2 (1)	Region	5	1 100 000
Finland	1 (2)	Åland, Kainuu	2	27 000
France	3 (4)	Région Département	22 96	2 805 000 643 000
Germany	3 (2)	Bundesland Kreise	16 323	5 144 000 255 000
Greece	2 (3)	Nomarxia	51	220 000
Hungary	2 (3)	Megye	19	532 000
Irish Republic [4]	1 (2)	County/city council	34	129 000
Italy	3 (4)	Region	20	2 965 000
		Provins	102	581 000
Norway	2 (1)	Fylkeskommun	19	247 000
Poland	3 (2)	Wojewodztwo Powiat	16 373	2 381 000 102 000
Portugal [5]	1 (2)	Madeira, Açores	2	245 000
Rumania	2	Judeti	42	514 000
Serbia	1 (2)	Belgrad, Vojvodina	2	1 801 000
Slovakia	1 (2)	Kraj	8	680 000
Spain	2 (3)	Comunidades Autonomas	17	2 665 000
Sweden	2 (1)	Landsting/region	20	455 000
Switzerland	2	Kanton	26	288 000
The Netherlands	2	Province	12	1 367 000
Turkey [6]	2	Vilayets	4	2 843 000
United Kingdom	1 (2)	County council, GLA	35	893 000
		Total	1374	536 000

Notes to table:

1. There are no regions in the smallest states (Andorra, San Marino etc) and in Bulgaria, Cyprus, Iceland, Luxembourg, Slovenia, Estonia, Kosovo, Latvia, Lithuania, FYR Macedonia, Malta, Moldavia and Montenegro.

2. The overview does not include Russia, Belarus and Ukraine.

3. The number of self-governing, directly elected levels of government below the state. Länder and cantons in federal states are counted as separate levels of government. The figure in parenthesis represents the deviation from this principle in parts of the country.

4. County/City Councils have been regarded as regions although Ireland lacks a municipal level in the five largest cities and in the rural areas.

5. Apart from these levels Portugal also has a parish level (freguesias) that is sometimes regarded as having municipal status.

6. These figures represent the European part of Turkey including the Istanbul city-region (that partly also extends into Asian territory).

Main source: AER (2006).

As the table indicates, there are considerable differences between countries in terms of the very structure of their regions. The largest countries tend to have two levels of regions, although the United Kingdom stands out as the remarkable exception where England (apart from Greater London) lacks a regional level of government. Further, most states are asymmetrical with a regional structure that varies between different parts of the country. For example, Portugal has only two self-governing regions (Madeira, Açores) although there is constitutional provision for a country-wide regional level of government. In Finland, the island of Åland and now on experimental basis, the region of Kainuu, have directly elected regional assemblies. The United Kingdom has recently introduced regional self-government in Scotland, Wales and Northern Ireland.

The average European region has 536 000 inhabitants but countries vary extensively with regard to the average sizes of their regions. The largest regions are generally found in the federal states and the largest states, e.g. Germany, Belgium, Spain and Italy. Although federal, both Austria and, in particular, Switzerland have fairly small regions. Belgium is a special case with two partly overlapping upper levels of regions – regions and language communities. The smallest regions are found in some of the smallest countries – Albania, Finland and the second regional level (Powiat) in Poland. Of course, many countries are too small to have any regions at all. The largest of the countries with no regions at all is Bulgaria, with 7.7 million inhabitants.

There are considerable variations between different regions. The largest region in Europe is the German land Nordrhein-Westphalen with 18 million inhabitants. If this had been a sovereign state, it would have been the 10th largest in Europe. Other large regions are Bavaria (12.4 million inhabitants), Ile-de France (Greater Paris, 10.9 millions), Baden-Württemberg (10.7 millions), Istanbul (10.0 millions), Lombardy (9 millions) and London (7.5 millions). At the other end we find the smallest regions, such as Delvine in Albania (11 000 inhabitants), Appenzell Innerrhoden in Switzerland (15 000), Sejnenski in Poland (21 000), Leitrim in the Irish Republic (26 000) and Åland in Finland (27 000). These regions correspond to medium-size municipalities in countries such as Sweden and Denmark.

The powers and functions of regions

Another important distinction between different regions concerns their powers and functions. European regions are (to a varying degree) responsible for legislation; planning and development; public welfare and education, and coordination of public functions (Hopkins 2002).

Regions with *legislative functions* have the most far-reaching powers of all regions as they are entitled to decide on laws, albeit within the limits set by the constitution or the national parliament. The second level in the federal states of Germany, Austria, Switzerland and Belgium has such powers, but also the regional levels in Italy and Spain. In addition, the two Portuguese regions, Åland, Scotland, Wales and Northern Ireland belong to this group. In total, there are 99 regions with such powers.

Regions with legislative powers within the EU have a direct link to the union as they implement EU directives. The European Council has recognized their importance in the Laeken-declaration of 2001. A network of these regions was formed in 2001 – The Conference of Regions with Legislative Powers (REGLEG) – with the purpose of promoting their interests in the EU decision-making processes.

A major task for regions in most countries is responsibility for *planning and regional development*. During the last few decades regions have replaced national governments in most European countries as the key actors in regional policies. National regional policies have become less redistributive and regions are instead expected to take responsibility for their own development. Regions are seen as living in a competitive, globalized world in which they have to struggle to keep their positions. The regional development role is reinforced by the EU which allocates resources from its structural funds to the regional level of government. Functions such as responsibility for public transport, infrastructure, tourism and cultural institutions also enhance the role of regions in creating conditions for economic development.

In the deeply divided Belgium, the three regions of Brussels, Wallonia and Flanders have key functions with regard to economic development. In France, the regional level that was established in 1964 and that has been directly elected from 1986 is also a major development actor and makes five-year development agreements with central government. New regions in Poland, Greece and the Czech Republic have tasks as receivers of funding from the EU and as users of these for the purpose of developing their regions.

Many regions have functions in *public welfare and education*. Typically, many of these tasks are fairly specialized and have been allocated to regions as they require a larger population than the municipalities can provide. Functions may include upper secondary and vocational education, public health care and care for the disabled. In Poland, which has two regional levels, such functions are allocated to the lower (powiat) level, but in France, they are divided between regions and departments. In Sweden the main task for county councils is the responsibility for public health care.

A fourth type of regional function involves the *coordination of public sector activities at intermediate level*. The typical pattern in most European countries is that there are a large number of different types of public sector units at the regional level – self-governing regions, central government agencies and inter-municipal associations. Central government agencies often have a role as coordinator of these various units, but in Belgium and the Netherlands, this coordinating task is a function of the provinces. However, in a sense, these are also delegated from central government, as the presidents of the provinces in these countries are appointed by the state.

Regional democracy

One crucial defining criterion for regions is that they should have a directly elected and representative assembly. All the 1374 regions are democratically legitimate in the sense that they are units of representative democracy. They have multi-party systems which regularly compete for the support of the voters in general elections. However, despite these formal requirements, the regions have certain features that make them vulnerable as units of democracy.

Firstly, regions lack the closeness to the citizens that municipalities enjoy. As regions are larger than municipalities, their politicians have to rely to a much greater extent on indirect means of communication, such as through the media and the internet. This makes it difficult for elected representatives to connect directly with citizens. To some extent, this may be different in a situation where regions have significant powers or where there are strong common identities among the citizens in the regions, as this would make it easier to create an interest in regional politics.

Secondly, the regional level has turned out to be less willing than the municipal level to develop new means for public participation. A recent overview of the state of local and regional democracy in Europe has clearly indicated that regions are not attempting to experiment with new means of democracy as a way of improving their relationship with their citizens (Loughlin, Hendriks and Lidström

2011). For example, directly elected mayors, the use of referendums and more deliberative forms of democracy are usually developed in municipalities rather than regions. This is paradoxical as regions, as previously mentioned, already have problems with a greater distance between citizens and their elected representatives.

Thirdly, there has generally only been limited support among citizens for setting up the new regions that have been established in recent years. This is likely to give them a bad start and limit their chances to become legitimate as units for democracy. On the rare occasions when referenda have been arranged to determine whether or not to introduce a new level of regional government, such suggestions have mostly been turned down. In 1998, a majority of the Portuguese rejected a proposal to set up new regions, although there are provisions for these in the constitution. Two referenda were required in Scotland and Wales before a popular majority for devolution was secured. In Greater Newcastle in the UK, a considerable majority rejected the proposal to introduce a directly elected regional government for the city-region. Instead, reforms have been pursued by the political elites at national or sub-national levels. It is among the politicians that regions are seen as solutions to problems that require an intermediate scale. However, it is likely that citizens are supportive of regional self-government in regions with their own languages, distinctive identities and strong regional political parties. Such regions include Catalonia and Basque in Spain and Wallonia and Flanders in Belgium.

Fourthly, the territorial structure of the regional level is mainly based on traditional patterns and borders and is not adjusted to one of the most important contemporary trends with relevance for regionalism – the expansion of cities to city-regions and in particular the growth of metropolitan areas. In 1950, 50 percent of the European population lived in cities and this is has now increased to 75 percent. By 2050, the share is expected to have increased further to 84 percent (UN 2008). In addition, most major cities are now functionally integrated metropolitan areas that have expanded far beyond their territorial borders. Commuting over long distances turns cities with suburbs into large city-regions. Hence, the future Europe will be predominately urban or suburban.

City-regions have their specific problems and challenges (OECD 2010). For example, they are becoming increasingly socially diverse. Although the European metropolis is dominated by the middle class, differences are increasing between the areas for the very wealthy and those for the more socially vulnerable. In addition, they suffer from congestions and environmental problems. In the metropolitan areas, there is a need for democratically legitimate governments that can take decisions about priorities in the city-region as whole, with regard to planning, infrastructure, public transport, environmental protection and perhaps also welfare services.

However, very few such units exist in Europe. One exception is the Greater London Authority, although this only covers half the commuting area of London. Generally, priorities about the city-region as a whole are either not taken at all or are handled by units appointed by the municipalities and hence lack the legitimacy that directly elected governments enjoy (Heinelt & Kübler 2005, Hoffmann-Martinot & Sellers 2007).

The regional level in Europe has a number of very important challenges to address if it wants to retain and further develop its democratic legitimacy. Regions must be more willing to experiment with new ways of linking with their citizens. The division into regions must be better adjusted to the city-regional challenge in order to establish more democratically legitimate forms of decision-making.

Citizens and regions in Sweden

Swedish citizens are also skeptical about establishing new regions. At the end of the 1990s, a number of county councils were amalgamated into the two new regions of Västra Götaland and Skåne, and these were given functions mainly in areas of health care and economic development. Such regions have also been proposed in other parts of the country (Lidström 2010). The main proponents of these regions have been local and regional politicians and, at least initially, they lack popular support (Lidström 2009, Nilsson 1999, Wadbring et al 2002). Research also indicates that Swedes differ with regard to their views on regions. Those in favour of larger regions tend to live in the largest city in the region, are interested in politics at regional level and take an interest in European matters. In addition, those that support other types of territorial reforms, such as municipal mergers, are also more positive to establishing larger regions (Lidström and Johansson 2009).

On the other hand, and contrary to the overall European pattern, there are indications of Swedes being in favour of directly elected governments for city-regions. A recent citizen survey carried out in the city-regions of Göteborg and Umeå suggests that there is a very clear majority in both these regions for setting up an elected assembly with responsibility for matters affecting the city-region as a whole (Lidström, Eklund, Westin 2010). In the larger Göteborg region, the majority in favour is 40 percent and in the smaller Umeå region there is a majority of 25 percent in favour of such an assembly. Today, most of the city-regional matters are handled through inter-municipal cooperation. These results challenge the traditional position of the municipalities as the key actor in local politics.

Conclusions

Regions are now an established level of government in most large and medium-sized countries in Europe, although there are still states of considerable size that lack such a level. This includes the English part of the United Kingdom, Portugal, Finland and Bulgaria, which are perhaps the most obvious candidates. Hence, in the future, additional regions may be added to the 1374 that now exist, although there are no immediate signs in that direction.

It remains to be seen whether the regional model will be applied to the growing city-regions in Europe. At the moment, the most common form for governing the city-regions is the indirectly elected inter-municipal association. However, as metropolitan areas become increasingly important, it seems likely that the question of how the metropolis can be governed in a just and legitimate way will come high on the agenda. Hence, we would expect that the regionalization debate will change, from a focus on comprehensive solutions for a country as a whole to specific solutions for city-regions. These may be more adjusted to the particular local circumstances that exist in each city-region.

All types of regions lack the closeness to the citizens that municipalities enjoy. In order to improve their position as democratically legitimate units of decision-making, they need to be much better in connecting with their citizens. All regions should be more willing to experiment with new forms of links to their citizens.

REFERENCES

AER, 1996. Deklaration om regionalism i Europa.

AER, 2006. AER Regionalism Report, Part 3: Country Reports. For adoption at the general Assembly, Palma de Mallorca, 2-10 November 2006. Assembly of European Regions.

Heinelt, Hubert and Kübler, Daniel (eds), 2005 *Metropolitan Governance. Capacity, democracy and the dynamics of place.* ECPR Studies in European Political Science. London and New York: Routledge.

Hoffmann-Martinot, Vincent and Sellers, Jefferey, 2007. Metropolitan Governance. In United Cities and Local Governments, *World Report on Decentralization and Local Democracy*, pp. 255-279. Barcelona: United Cities and Local Governments.

Hopkins, John, 2002. *Devolution in Context.* London: Cavendish.

Lidström, Anders, 2007. Territorial Governance in Transition. *Regional and Federal Studies*, vol 17 (4), pp 499-508.

Lidström, Anders (ed.), 2009. *Kan norra Sverige regionaliseras? Beslutsprocesser och medborgarperspektiv.* Forskningsrapporter i statsvetenskap vid Umeå universitet 2009:2. Statsvetenskapliga institutionen, Umeå universitet.

Lidström, Anders, 2010. The Swedish model under stress. Waning of the Egalitarian, Unitary State? Rose, L., and Baldersheim H. (eds) *Territorial Choice. The Politics of Boundaries and Borders.* Basingstoke: Palgrave Macmillan.

Lidström, Anders; Eklund, Niklas och Westin, Kerstin, 2010. Stadsregioner – nya enheter för lokal och regional politik? *Tvärsnitt*, nr 3.

Lidström, Anders and Johanson, Susanne, 2009. Citizens' attitudes to regionalization in Sweden – territorial and individual variations. Paper prepared for The 18th Nordic Local Government Research Conference, Turku 26-28 November 2009

Loughlin, John; Hendriks, Frank and Lidström, Anders (eds), 2011. *The Oxford Handbook on Local and Regional Democracy in Europe.* Oxford: Oxford University Press.

Nilsson, Lennart (ed), 1999. *Region i omvandling.* Göteborg: SOM-institutet, Göteborgs universitet.

OECD, 2010. *Trends in Urbanisation and Urban Policies in the OECD Countries: What Lessons for China.*

Swenden, Wilfried, 2006. *Federalism and Regionalism in Western Europe.* Basingstoke: Palgrave Macmillan.

UN, 2008. *World Urbanization Prospects. The 2007 Revision.* United Nations

Wadbring, Ingela, Weibull, Lennart & Bergström, Annika, 2002. *Efter arbetet. Synen på nedläggning och dess konsekvenser.* Göteborg: Institutionen för journalistik och masskommunikation, Göteborgs universitet.

MALIN STEGMANN MCCALLION – KARLSTAD UNIVERSITY, SWEDEN

Paradiplomacy – *Competing, Reinforcing or Coexisting Regional Action?*

Introduction

Over the years, we have seen an increase in the number and diversity of regional actors in the international arena (see for example Duchacek *et al*, 1988, Hocking, 1993, Aldecoa and Keating, 1999); and this phenomenon has been described as *paradiplomacy*. Paradiplomacy can be understood as 'a broadening of the universe of international affairs, in which states are no longer the sole actors' (Keating, 1999:6). This *sharing of the international stage* by central governments, in their roles as the 'traditional' state actors, has coincided:

> *with the new thinking on economic development, which places less emphasis on central state policies and more on factors rooted in the regions themselves. So the old dyadic exchange between the state and the regions, with the state mediating regions' relations with the global market, has given way to a more complex set of relationships, in which regions operate within the state, but also within transnational regimes and the global economy (Keating 1999:3).*

Not only has the relationship between national and sub-national levels[1] such as regions[2] and local authorities changed within, but also part of, the current economic globalisation process. For countries in 'EU'rope, this relationship has also been transformed through membership in the European Union.

As a consequence of these changed relationships, and taken as axiomatic in this chapter, the role of the region within the welfare state has changed. A second assumption is that the nation state is part of a fused system of governance.[3] However, in order to provide a more holistic depiction of paradiplomacy, it is necessary to provide a brief overview of how the regional level has changed.[4] Thus, in order to understand the 'complexities of international politics' (Hocking 1993:1), one has to have a greater understanding of not only the domestic frameworks regions are working within, but also their ability to *act* within these frameworks.

It is now, within European integration studies, widely recognised that regions within the European Union are involved in paradiplomatic activities. Examples of these activities can be found in the increased importance of regional actors as recognised within the *new regionalism* academic literature (see for example Keating 1998; 1999; Gren 1999; 2002) and, more practically, with the, for example, establishment of regional offices in Brussels. These also participate in networks, such as *RegLeg*, and/or the involvement of regions in international trade fairs or trade missions in order to represent their regions and its interests on the international stage. There are, of course, several possible explanations for these activities, although within the EU, this can be traced back to the *'Europe of the Regions'* debate in the early to mid-1990s as well as the *new regionalism* literature. However, as Benz *et al.* (2000:7) argue regionalisation/ devolution – can and does – prompt new or changed administrative structures and/or new procedures. These changes then become *fora* for mobilisation, co-operation, participation and democratic self-determination. One could thus, as with Lindh *et al.* (2009:14),, define *regional action* as 'the consciously, rationally-taken political measures taken by regional actors [in order to] ... seek to ... promote regional interests'. Regions then, as Lindh *et al.* (2009:18) assert, are acting more often and do so increasingly for themselves. This increased regional action could be viewed as a *win-win* situation for the nation, illustrated by a quote from a speech by Cecilia Malmström from 2007, when she was Swedish EU Minister, 'if Sweden wants to be in the core of EU-policymaking, we need active regions that build international alliances, formulating strategies and priorities' (as cited in Lindh 2010).

If one accepts that actors operate in a 'melded' (fused) system (Hooghe and Marks 2001:27) then this 'melding process' is, according to Warleigh (2006:79), 'partly – [and] perhaps mainly – the result of deliberate choices made by national elites to delegate powers "upwards" (to the EU) and "downwards" (to the regions/ localities) in order better to achieve the policy objectives' as set out by central governments. One could here draw the conclusion that the national (central) level, at least in some instances, sees regional action as positive and welcoming.[5] Our interest now turns to *how* regions can engage internationally.

Paradiplomacy

In order to gain an understanding of *how* regions engage on the international arena, the arguments of Duchacek are highly pertinent. According to Duchacek (1990:14-15) regions can establish permanent offices in foreign capitals or centres of commerce and industry abroad. Examples of this could be the Welsh Assembly Government's offices found in say, Bangalore, Beijing, Brussels, Chicago, Dubai, Dublin, Hong Kong, Houston, New York, Seoul, Shanghai, Singapore, Sydney, Taipei and Tokyo (EEAC 2006:5). The size of the respective representation in these offices can, of course, vary; it could be as little as one person working from home, or at a desk in a shared office, or as large as a fully equipped Welsh International Centre office with sizable manpower. The level of representation is adapted to the different markets (EEAC 2004:7). The key argument is that these International Business Wales offices act as the 'face' of Wales internationally. They may be primarily responsible for attracting inward investment and trade to Wales, yet, they can also be described as 'ambassadors' for Wales. Politicians and other significant actors of the regions can participate in extensively promoted and well-publicised trips abroad; such as, in fact-finding missions to explore possible inward investment and/or, alternatively, by promoting export from the region through participation in trade and investment shows; by involvement in the creation of trade zones; as part of national delegations and/or in helping to represent the national government. For example, the national government can be represented by a regional minister in the Council of European Union (Council of Ministers) if a sub-national matter is on the agenda.

Duchacek (1990:18; 24-25) further divides the paradiplomatic activities of regions into three geo-political areas; more specifically these are trans-border, trans-regional, and global paradiplomacy regions. Trans-border paradiplomacy refers to the networks of communication, both implicit and explicit rules, as well as informal and formal procedures. Thus, trans-border paradiplomacy can be illustrated through a regional government's relationship with a bordering region's government. These relationships are predominantely formed as a result of geographic proximity between the respective actors/ and or regions, such as, for example, the Värmland-Østfold-Hedmark region or the Öresund/Øresund region. Trans-regional paradiplomacy concerns the relationships developed and sustained by a regional government with non-neighbouring regions. Here, the regional government is separated by 'other provincial/state jurisdiction from the international border which, in order to establish and maintain their links, they have, as it were to leapfrog' (Duchacek 1990:25); the Baltic Sea Region is an example of such paradiplomatic activity. Global paradiplomacy, the third geo-political area, represents the relationships that regional governments have with, for example, other non-central governments, central governments, and/or international actors in order to influence trade, investment or other policies or actions of the region. Global paradiplomacy can be illustrated by the abovementioned International Business Wales Offices or the global network nrg4SD.[6]

The discussion above is a brief introduction to *how regions engage in the international arena*, as well as a rationale for such engagement. Yet, it is essential to be aware of the preconditions that the respective regions can operate within and which constraints are placed upon the regions international actions. These preconditions are usually, formally, set out in legislation of various kinds. For example, the

Swedish Constitution Instruments of Government (SFS 1974:152) states that '[a]greements with other states or with international organisations are concluded by the Government (Article 1, Chapter 10), and that '[t]he Government may not conclude an international agreement which is binding upon the Realm without Riksdag approval' (first sentence, Article 2, Chapter 10). Another example can be the Concordat on International Relations as in the UK. It is, for example, the UK Government which is responsible for *foreign policy* in order to 'ensur[e] consistency between foreign policy and the full range of policies of the United Kingdom Government, Northern Ireland Executive Committee, Scottish Ministers, and the Assembly' (Foreign and Common wealth Office 2001:35). Although *foreign policy* is not defined, it can be taken, in this UK context, to include all international, that is to say external, relations of the devolved administrations which are not EU policy related (as there is a separate *Concordat on Co-ordination of European Union Policy Issues*). These two examples represent instances from one decentralised unitary state and one devolved state and would differ from the constraints experienced by, for example, regions in a federal state. Although in order to appreciate all possible constraints of a regional government engaging in international relations, as well as provide a more holistic picture, it is necessary to explore the preconditions, and how these influence the actions of regional government for each region as these can vary within nations as well. Such an exploration lies, however, outside the remit of this chapter.

Paradiplomacy – Competing, Reinforcing or Coexisting Regional Action?

As illustrated in the discussion above, one of the most traditional areas of national/central government's policy-making has been shared with other levels, namely that of international relations. The regionalism/regionalisation literature highlights an increased international regional activity as well as awareness of regional action; one example is the increased number of regional offices in Brussels, since the early 1990s, with the aim to influence EU policy/policies affecting the regions. One could thus argue that this support Hill's (1998:48-49) argument that '[t]his has produced a pattern of multi-level diplomacy in which the various elements sometimes compete, sometimes reinforce each other, and sometimes merely coexist'.[7] What is of interest then is how regions act on the international stage and to what extent these actions are 'accepted' by the national level, i.e. how much they are seen as competing, reinforcing or coexisting. What becomes vital, in relation to generating an understanding of regional action and paradiplomacy, are the 'attitudes and priorities of national policy-makers towards regional cross-border activities, the composition of national discourses on the EU, [and] general characteristics of national-regional relations' (Lindh *et al.* 2009:29). Thus the answer to the question if international regional action, i.e. paradiplomacy, is competing, reinforcing or coexisting with national policy, has to be examined and evaluated on a policy by policy basis. It also depends on who gives the answers to the questions. A national actor's perspective may be different from that of a regional one. One relatively new policy area, which would be interesting to examine further, would be that of the Baltic Sea Strategy, especially as the European Parliament has called for '[r]egional and local authorities [to] be more extensively involved in implementing the EU Strategy for the Baltic Sea Region' (European Parliament 2010). Would participating regions face different constraints depending on the national level's attitude towards the Baltic Sea Strategy and recourses (made) available for implementation of the policy? These resources can be influenced by the national-regional relations as well as the ability of regions to *mobilise* resources (not only economic ones) but also, as Stegmann McCallion and Miles argue (2010) 'the acquisition of the 'know-how' needed in order to implement and influence the policy successfully'.

NOTES

1. Sub-national levels are here referred to as any administrative level below national (central) level.

2. A region in this text is to be understood as the *meso* level, i.e. the level(s) between the national/central and local levels. The type of region would depend upon what kinds of classification of the state, i.e. if it is a federal or unitary state, see for example Loughlin (2001) or von Bergmann-Winberg (2010).

3. The changed political environment have been described as fused by (Miles 2005, 2006, 2008, 2009, and Wessels 1997, Romtech and Wessels 1996, Wessels *et al.* 2003), *sammanlänkat* (*interlinked* or alternatively *connected*) by Blomgren and Bergman (2005); *invävd* (interweaved) by Jacobsson and Sundström (2006); or also more commonly described as a system of multi-level governance see Bache (2008), Bache and Flinders (2004), Hoohge and Marks (2001), Marks (1993), Marks, Hooghe and Blanks (1996).

4. This chapter will restrict itself to regions and the *meso* level in 'EU'rope due to limited space in which the discussion can be held.

5. However, the central government can – and does – act as 'gate-keeper' in certain policy areas (see for example Bache 1998; 2008) in order to constrain regional action.

6. nrg4SD is a global network, formed at the Johannesburg Summit on Sustainable Development in 2002. The nrg4SD's mission is to be both a voice and representative for regional governments at the global level when it comes to promoting sustainable development (nrg4SD 2005).

7. It has been concluded elsewhere that this is 'even more appropriate when the regional level is included' (Lindh *et al.* 2009:29).

REFERENCES

Aldecoa, F. & Keating, M. (eds.) (1999) Paradiplomacy in Action: The Foreign Relations of Subnational Governments, London: Frank Cass

Bache, I. (1998) *The Politics of European Union Regional Policy Multi-Level Governance or Flexible Gatekeeping? Sheffield: Sheffield Academic Press*

Bache, I. (2008) *Europeanisation and Multilevel Governance. Cohesion Policy in the European Union and Britain,* Lanham: Rowman & Littlefield Publishers

Bache, I. & Flinders, M. (eds.) (2004) *Multi-level Governance,* Oxford: Oxford University Press

Benz, A., Fürst, D., Kilper, H. & Rehfeld, D. (2000) *Regionalisation Theory, Practice and Prospects in Germany,* Östersund: SIR

Blomgren, M. & Bergman, T. (eds.) (2005) *EU och Sverige – ett sammanlänkat statsskick* Malmö: Liber

Duchacek, I., Latouche, D. & Stevenson, G. (eds.) (1988) *Perforated Sovereignties and International Relations. Trans-Sovereign Contacts of Subnational Governments*, New York, NY

Duchacek, I. (1990) 'Perforated Sovereginties: Towards a Typology of New Actors in International Relations' in Michelmann, H. J. & Soldatos, P. (eds.) *Federalism and International Relations: The Role of Subnational Units* Oxford: Clarendon Press

EEAC (2004) EUR(2) 09-04(p4) Wales, A World Nation – A Strategic Framework 9 December 2004

EEAC (2006) EUR(2) 06-06(p3) Wales in the World 12 July 2006

European Parliament (2010) European Parliament Press Release 6 July 2010 EU's Baltic Sea Strategy: more local input needed URL Address http://www.europarl.europa.eu/en/pressroom/content/20100705IPR77800 Date accessed October 2010

Foreign and Common wealth Office (2001) *Devolution Memorandum of Understanding and Supplementary Agreements* CM 5240

Gren, J. (1999) *The New Regionalism in the EU. The lessons to be drawn from Catalonia, Rhône-Alpes and West Sweden*, Östersund: SIR

Gren, J. (2002) *Den perfekta regionen?: en nyregionalism i Europa och samspelet mellan staten, regionen och den europeiska integrationen*, Lund: Studentlitteratur

Hill, C. (1998) 'Convergence, Divergence and Dialectics: National Foreign Policies and the CFSP'in Zielonka, J. (ed.) *Paradoxes of European Foreign Policy* The Hauge: Kluwer

Hocking, B. (1993) 'Introduction' in Hocking, B. (ed.) *Foreign Relations and Federal States* London: Leicester University Press

Hooghe, L. & Marks, G. (2001) *Multi-Level Governance and European Integration*, Lanham: Rowanfield & Little

Jacobsson, B. & Sundström, G. (2006) *Från hemvävd till invävd* Malmö: Liber

Keating, M. (1998) *The New Regionalism in Western Europe: Territorial Restructuring and Political Change*, Cheltenham: Edward Elgar

Keating, M. (1999) 'Regions and International Affairs: Motives, Opportunities and Strategies' in Aldecoa, F. & Keating, M. (eds.) *Paradiplomacy in Action: the foreign relations of subnational governments* London: Frank Cass Publishers

Lindh, M., Löden, H., Miles, L., Räftegård, C. & Stegmann McCallion, M. (2009) *Fusing Regions? Sustainable Regional Action in the Context of European Integration* Nordic Research Programme 2005-2008: Internationalisation of regional development policies – Needs for demands in the Nordic countries. Report 8

Lindh, M. (2010) 'Fusing Regions? Nordic Regional Action in a Fused Europe', *Paper presented* at *The Road to Europe: main street or backward alley for local governments in Europe?*, Centre for Local Politics, Ghent University, Belgium, 29-30 April 2010

Loughlin, J. (ed.) (2001) *Subnational Democracy in the European Union: Challenges and Opportunities,* Oxford: Oxford University Press

Marks, G. (1993) Structural Policy and Multilevel Governance in the EC, in Cafruny, A. W. & Rosentahl, G. G. (Eds.), *The State of the European Community – The Maastricht Debates and Beyond* Harlow: Longman

Marks, G., Hooghe, L. & Blank, K. (1996) European Integration from the 1980s: State-Centric v. Multi-Level Governance, in *Journal of Common Market Studies,* Vol. 34, No. 3, pp. 341-378

Miles, L. (2005) *Fusing with Europe? Sweden in the European Union,* Aldershot: Ashgate

Miles, L. (2006) Making Sense of the Fusion Perspective for Regional Studies: Placing the Fusion Literature in the Regional Context, FUSE-EUROPA programme, Discussion Paper No 3, Karlstad: Karlstad University, Dept of Political and Historical Studies

Miles, L. (2008) *Future of a Fusing Europe* Karlstad: Karlstad University Studies

Miles, L. (2009) A Fusing Europe? Insights for EU Governance, in Dougan, M. & Currie, S. (Eds.), *50 Years of the European Treaties,* Oxford: Hart Publishing, pp. 19-42.

nrg4SD (2005a) *nrgs4SD Strategy 2005-2011* Available online http://www.nrg4sd. org/sites/default/files/content/file/documentation/en/ESTRATEGIA2005_EN.PDF

Rometsch, D & Wessels, W. (Eds.) (1996) *The European Union and Member States: Towards Institutional Fusion?,* Manchester: Manchester University Press

SFS 1974:152 *Instruments of Government* available online http://www.riksdagen. se/templates/R_Page____6307.aspx Date accessed October 2010

Stegmann McCallion, M. & Miles, L. (2010 *Forthcoming*) 'Baltic Sea Strategy – Värmland's Experience' in Compendium *European Union Strategy for the Baltic Sea Region – a new challenge for knowledge-based regional and local governance and cooperation* Tallinn University

von Bergmann-Winberg, M-L (2010) Flernivåstyrning i ett jämförande EU-perspektiv: nätverkssamverkan för effektivitet och demokrati' i Tallberg, P. & von Bergmann-Winberg, M-L. (red.) *Flernivåstyrning för kommuner, regioner och staten* Region Skåne, Västra Götalandsregionen, Regionplanekontoret vid Stockholms läns Landsting och Sveriges Kommuner och Landsting

Warleigh, A. (2006), Multi-Level Governance and Policy Networks: Conceptual Combinations and the Study of the Euro-Policy, in M. Cini and A. Bourne (eds), European Union Studies. Basingstoke: Palgrave Macmillan

Wessels, W. (1997) An Ever Closer Fusion? A Dynamic Macropolitical View on Integration Processes, in *Journal of Common Market Studies,* Vol 35, No. 2, pp. 267-99

Wessels, W., Maurer, A. & Mittag, J. (2003) *Fifteen into One? The European Union and its Member States,* Manchester: Manchester University Press

JOAKIM NERGELIUS – UNIVERSITY OF ÖREBRO, SWEDEN

The Swedish State and Its Subdivisions

Distribution of Powers Between the State and the Municipalities

The traditionally very centralized Swedish state has during the last ten years, in particular after joining the European Union in 1995, been severely affected by what we may here call a vertical separation of powers, upwards in relation to the European Union, and downwards in relation to a gradually increasing development towards stronger regionalization, which is accompanied also by the traditional strong autonomy of the Swedish municipalities.

Concerning the latter question, the point of departure is that Swedish democracy, according to the Instrument of Government (IG) Chapter 1, Article 1, Section 2 is based and realized, among other values, upon local self-government. Somewhat more detailed rules are to be found in Chapter 1, Article 7, which used to state that Sweden has municipalities and county councils (*landsting*). However, as from 1 January 2011, it will instead only state that municipalities exist at the local and regional levels, a change that will undoubtedly benefit future regionalisation. This rule also used to state that the decision-making power in these local authorities is exercised by elected assemblies and that the local authorities may levy taxes in order to perform their tasks[1], but this rule is now moved to a new chapter 14 that deals exclusively with the municipalities (without really increasing their autonomy, unfortunately). Chapter 1, Article 8 also reveals that central and local government adminis-

45

trative authorities exist for 'the public administration', which may thus be either national or local.[2]

Still, all those rules are rather general and vague. Some more precise rules may be found on the topic, like Chapter 8, Article 2, Section 1 point 3 IG, according to which the principles governing changes in the division of the Realm into local government districts, as well as the principles governing the organization and working procedures of the local authorities and their competences are laid down in law,[3] but a further analysis of the legal conditions for local and the recently so much discussed regional autonomy in Sweden definitely seems to be necessary to conduct here.

Concerning municipal and local elections, it may be noted that the same parties that are known from national elections dominate also at local and regional level, where some variations are however possible. Also at those levels, the same electoral rules apply, though in a slightly modified form; exact details on this are to be found in the lengthy Electoral Law (*Vallagen*, 1997:157), in particular Chapter 18. It may be noted that according to the new chapter 5, article 5 a of the Municipal Law (*Kommunallagen*), municipal assemblies starting from 2011 may decide, with a two-thirds majority of its present members, to organise new elections between the general elections to be held every fourth year. Such an election will however not change the date of the next general election. Municipal referendas, of a purely advisory nature, are in the future to be held whenever ten percent of the registered voters in a certain municipality ask for it (chapter 5, art. 23 of that same law).

Sweden is, as mentioned above, a unitary, highly centralized nation-state, where federalism has never been a realistic alternative and regionalization is a very recent phenomenon. Two attempts of regional autonomy have been implemented between 1998 and 2010, but now continuing also after that (mainly in Skåne, the southern part of Sweden, and Västra Götaland, centred around Gothenburg in the west-part of the country).4 Alongside this centralized tradition, a high degree of local autonomy has existed since 1862, when an important reform in that respect took place. The extent of the local and, to be more precise, municipal autonomy, is however a highly contested issue. It must be noted that regardless of which rules really apply here, the competences may be shifted between the state and the municipalities; thus, the organization of the police force used to be local, but became national in the 1960s. And conversely, the school system turned into a local, or rather municipal affair in the early 1990s. It is obvious that the municipal autonomy is not strong enough to be a real obstacle for major reforms of this kind.[5]

In the constitutional doctrine, opinions are very divided, ranging from old-fashioned state-oriented professors who truly believe that the state (Parliament, Government) may limit the municipal autonomy as it wishes, to younger constitutionalists (like myself) who believe that the above-mentioned constitutional provisions must, after all mean something and that they do thus offer a minimum of constitutional protection to the municipal autonomy. When the IG was enacted in the 1970s, the former opinion undoubtedly prevailed,[6] but on this, like on many other issues, opinion(s) have since then changed somewhat. That new, contrary opinion has, above all, been advanced by the Law Council (*Lagrådet*) when examining a number of law proposals in the late 1990s and in the beginning of the 21st century, concerning transfer of money through a system for re-distribution of taxes between rich and poor municipalities (*inomkommunal skatteutjämning*), a prohibition for municipalities to sell their housing companies, for county councils to let certain hospitals be organized privately, or an obligation for municipalities to organize agencies for housing transfer. In all those cases, when the Law Council has recommended that the laws in question should not be enacted due to their lack of constitutionality, Parliament has nevertheless approved them anyway.

From a legal point of view, maybe the first question to ask here is whether the provisions of IG as outlined above are really legally binding or not. The situation varies. Thus, while Chapter 1, Article 1 IG contains general, non-binding provisions. On the other hand it is clearly binding, this means little more than that but this does in fact mean nothing else than that Parliament may decide certain things concerning municipal activities through law. The former Chapter 1, Article 7, Section 2 (now Chapter 14, article 4) was open to different interpretations about local powers anf funding, but seemed to mean that local authorities may only levy taxes from their inhabitants for the fulfilment of tasks aimed solely at that specific municipality, an interpretation that is supported by the Municipal Law (*Kommunal-lagen*) Chapter 2, Article 1. This would seem to make transfers of money from one municipality to the other, such as from richer to poorer parts of the country. [7] However, the new Chapter 14, Article 5 expressly permits such transfers. The question has, unfortunately, never really been examined by the Swedish courts, since both the Supreme Court, and the Supreme Administrative Court, in 1998 and 2000, refused to admit similar cases brought forward by local authorities against the new fiscal arrangements.[8] From many points of view, it is regrettable that the courts refused to deal with the case, which, when seem in its wider context and implications, could be seen as amounting to a case of *déni de justice*.[9]

In fact, it would also be almost impossible for the municipalities to fulfil the main part of the tasks that they statutorily required to execute (cfr IG Chapter 8, Article 2, Section 1 point 3) without being allowed some freedom to raise local tax revenue and spend it according to locallyu-defined priorities. If they were not able to control and plan their budgets themselves, they would not be autonomous in the way that IG stipulates, so that they follow the principles and spirit of the Swedish democracy. Thus, a minimum constitutional protection of their rights needs to to exist. However, in particular during the late 1990s, but also now, the limits of this autonomy have been a hotly contested issue. This may, in pure political terms, be explained by the fact that when the Social Democratic Party stayed in power for so long at the national level, that the possibility of using the local level to challenge national politics at the national level, gained in appeal to the main opposition party Government then became increasingly interested in stopping doscourage debatechange, in line with its political logic.[10] Such a reaction may, outside purely political terms, also be justified the aim of assuring that citizens are treated equally in all parts of the country.[11] In purely political terms, this perspective is the one that has prevailed discussions leading to the big constitutional compromise that has now become a reality in 2010.

Thus, both changes that could have been put into practice before 2010, i.e. more precise provisions in the Constitution guaranteeing autonomy for the municipalities. This includes keeping the dates for local and national elections separate, and has thus now partly become reality – although the autonomy of the municipalities per se, in legal terms, has not grown, as we shall see below.

The Legal Position of the Swedish Regions – Towards Autonomy or Not

As mentioned above, in recent years a vivid debate has started in Sweden concerning future regionalization, which is noteworthy and also slightly surprising as such in this old nation-state. One reason for this is the weakness of the old county councils (*landsting*), which are not considered serious political actors at a time when regions in many other European states such as Germany and Spain, are becoming ever more important, and co-operation across traditional national frontiers is onthe increase, as shown by examples from southern, western and northern Sweden.

Against this general background, two important things that have happened in recent years, which contributed to raising the political profile attempts need to be seen introduce regional autonomy in the southern part of the country (Skåne) and in a western area around Gothenburg (Västra Götaland). This arrangement has now become permanent the end of 2010. Regionalisation was also favoured in the end report of February 2007. Then, the national committee examined the future division of the country and the organization of welfare and social services[12] (the so-called *Ansvarskommittén*).[13] This report suggests a division of Sweden into between six or nine regions, even though their organization and boundaries have been much contested, by the many different regional interests vested in such a big reform. Those regions would then be responsible for the organization not only of hospitals and medical care, but also for transportation and environmental issues. What then happened, however, is that the regions of Västra Götaland and Skåne have been given a kind of permanent licence to continue their activities, while no decisions have yet been made concerning other parts of the country (except for Halland on the west coast, between Skåne and Gothenburg, and the island of Gotland in the Baltic Sea), both of which will be allowed to carry on as "regions", although this a change to the status quo in name only.[14]

It should however be noted that there is still no political consensus on those issues. Under the current, right-wing government, the suggestions made by Ansvarskommittén are not supported by the dominant, conservative party, which is currently larger than the three other governmental parties together. Thus, the issue has been left for future decision-making. The position of the (opposition) Social Democratic party and the left-wing opposition, on the other hand, has, over the last few years, moved in a more region-friendly direction.

The arguments raised in the debate in favour of increased regionalization, in particular have to do in particular with how, and to what extent, regions do, in fact, today affect the lives of individuals who increasingly tend to commute, work and live at a regional level beyond the boundaries of individual municipalities. The regions also are becoming increasingly actors in their own right at the international level for place marketing purposes, such as evident in the regions' own offices in Brussels. That is true both for regions which want to be active and visible internationally, such as Skåne, and regions that are more concerned aboutr a stronger voice within the country, like the so-called *Mälardal* area around Stockholm. Apart from that, strengthened regional identities among individuals, wishes for increased democracy and new means to organize, provide and distribute welfare services, are other well-known arguments from the debate in the last few years. It remains to be seen which impact they will have on the final reform proposals in this respect. What seems certain, however, is that the issue is here to stay and that some further reform, including perhaps both municipalities and regions, is likely eventually to take place some time after 2010.

The new Chapter 14, of the Swedish constitution

On the 1ˢᵗ of January 2011, a new chapter 14 of the IG entirely devoted to the municipalities will enter into force. The six articles of this chapter will replace certain rules that are today to be found in chapters 1 and 8, but the chapter also contains some new rules.

Articles 1-2, state that the decision-making powers within the municipalities are to be exercised by popularly elected assemblies and that the municipalities handle, and are responsible for, local and regional matters of public interest, all in accordance with Swedish law, and on the basis of the principle of local autonomy. Article 6 then adds that any changes concerning the division of the Swedish realm into municipalities (of which today some 290 exist) must be regulated by law. Those rules are not very complicated or difficult to understand.

As stated above, the former Chapter 1, Article 7, Section 2 (now Chapter 14, article 4) was open to different interpretations concerning its binding force, but clearly seemed to indicate that local authorities may only levy taxes from their inhabitants for the fulfilment of tasks within that specific municipality. This is an interpretation that is supported by the Municipal Law (*Kommunallagen*) Chapter 2, Article 1, and that would seem to make transfers of money from one municipalitiy to another. This would include inter-regional transfer payments, such as the ones that have been decided by Parliament since 1995.[15] However, the new Chapter 14, Article 5 makes clear that such transactions or contributions from rich municipalities to poorer ones are now to be considered legal and constitutional, although a contradiction thus seems to exist between the new articles 4 and 5.

The main difficulty, or complication, in the new chapter, however, is to be found in its article 3. The background to this new rule, which states that a limitation of the municipal autonomy should never go beyond what is absolutely necessary, given its reasons (a kind of proportionality principle, in other words), as mentioned above. During the late 1990s, but also now, the limits of municipal autonomy have been hotly contested, which may in pure political terms be explained by the fact that when the Social Democratic Party was in government for a long period of time, (1932–76, 1982-91 and 1994–2006), the opposing Conservatives discovered, and used, the local level as a proxy counter-government to challenge the centre. Such a reaction may, as mentioned above, be justified by with the aim of seeking to ensure that citizens are treated equally in all parts of the country. In purely political terms, it is this understanding that has ultimately prevailed in the discussions leading to the big constitutional compromise that has now been enacted and turned into reality at the beginning of 2011.

At the same time, as part of this process, Parliament overruled the Law Council's concern about constitutionally protected local autonomy. In other words, Parliament took the opportunity to directly intervene in municipal affairs and even changed democratically made municipal decisions. This meant a far-reaching shift in local;national power relations, indeed.

However, the legal solution chosen to address this problem does not seem very satisfactory from a municipal point of view. According to the new chapter 8, art. 21, sect. 2 p. 5 of the IG, the Law Council shall henceforth always examine new law proposals concerning municipal taxations or other obligations for the municipalities, concerning their legality, constitutionality and practical applicability (cfr chap. 8, art. 22). But as we have already seen, Parliament has repeatedly disregarded the legal opinions of the Law Council in this respect. And things are in fact even more problematic, if we take the *travaux préparatoires* of the new rule in chap. 14, art. 3, into account, under which[16], the opinion of the Parliament prevails the legislative body, when it comes to statutory findings on municipal autonomy.

Here, however, it may be questioned whether this legal line of reasoning – that is not given any prominent place in the bill presenting the constitutional reform – is actually legally valid.[17] None of the new constitutional rules regulating judicial reviews (chap. 11 art. 14 and chap. 12 art. 10) or their *travaux préparatoires,* mention the existence of any exception for the kind of laws that may be subjected to judicial review. Neither does the tradition of Swedish judicial reviews in all their limitations, know of any attempt to exclude specific types of law(s) from such review, simply on the ground of their topical political relevance. Thus, it remains to be seen which impact those new rules and governmental statements will really have.

An example or illustration of the difficulties that is both practical and theoretical may be given from the Swedish political debate in the spring of 2010. The left-wing opposition then decided, in the run-up to the Parliamentary elections in September, to not stop a recent governmental decision to build a new motorway around Stockholm, but, instead, call for, should they have won the majority of parliamentary seats in the election, a special referendum in the affected 26 municipalities around Stockholm. However, such a parliamentary decision, though formally speaking possible to effect, would have been contrary to all traditional views in Sweden which stipulate that there is a scalar division in statutory entitlement: Parliament decides on national referende, and local government on those at the local level/. The fact that the Law Council would probably have reached that very conclusion would then not have amounted to much, since the parliamentary majority is never bound to follow the Council's opinion (and has, as we have seen, been particularly unwilling to do so in this policy field). But would it then really make sense not to allow any judicial review of the constitutionality of the new law, in such a specific and controversial case? That would indeed seem very strange, to say the least.

Some final remarks

The area discussed in this article has been one of the most contested constitutional topics in Sweden over the last two decades and may well continue to remain so for a few more years. This is due not only to the above-mentioned lack of clarity concerning the future limits of judicial review of laws that concern municipal autonomy, but also to the currently very lively development at the regional level, which historically was less significant in Sweden than the municipal and the national levels. Thus, the interested observer should study both those two issues in order to get a good unerstanding of the development in the years to come.

A new constitutional reform, like the one decided in 2010, looks unlikely to occur. Instead, what will be crucial now, is for once, the legal situation concerning judicial reviews of laws relating to municipal autonomy, whenever legally clarified through jurisprudence, and, on the other, the proposal, that will be presented before 2014, on how to organise Sweden into new regions, concerning both their size and numbers. As stated above, the new formulation of chap. 1, art. 7 IG will make such a "territorial transformation" of Sweden easier. The effect of these changes, however remain to be seen.

NOTES

1. Here, once again, it may be noted that the Government may never adopt provisions which relate to local taxation, according to IG Chapter 8, Article 7, Section 2, 2nd sentence. On the other hand, municipalities or the Government may under certain conditions make decision concerning burdensome charges that should otherwise be made by the Parliament, as follows from Chapter 8, Article 9 IG.

2. Something that does in fact also follow from IG Chapter 12, Article 4, Section 2, which specifically states that administrative functions may be entrusted to a local authority.

3. Also a few other provisions may be noted here. Thus, whenever the Parliament has authorized the Government to adopt provisions in a particular matter under Chapter 8 IG, it may also according to its Article 10 authorize the Government to delegate the power to adopt regulations in the matter to an administrative or local authority (so-called sub-delegation). Finally, it should be noted that administrative functions may be entrusted to local authorities according to Chapter 12, Article 4, Section 2 IG.

4. A sign of the new times and the new climate in the debate, where it is now possible to seriously discuss also federalism, is the anthology *Federalism på svenska* (Federalism in Swedish), ed. by N. Karlson/J. Nergelius, Stockholm 2007 (Ratio).

5. In both cases it may be noted that many critics want to turn the system back the other way around once again, which is at least not constitutionally impossible.

6. This is perhaps most clearly expressed in a governmental bill (*proposition*) from 1973, which contains much of the principled reasoning that is included in the IG (prop. 1973:90, here on p. 190).

7. *See more* in detail Nergelius, Svensk statsrätt, 2nd ed., Lund 2010., p. 354 ss with further references.

8. *See* NJA 1998, p. 656 (II) and RÅ 2000 ref. 19.

9. For legal reasons, the municipalities, formally being components of the State, were also unable to bring their cases to the Strasbourg court, who dismissed it in June 2001 (case *Danderyd v. Sweden*).

10. Cfr Nergelius, *op. cit.*, in particular p. 360 s.

11. This issue is particularly dealt with and analysed in the anthology edited by Karlson and Nergelius, mentioned *above*.

12. Concerning welfare issues, those were dealt with in a previous report from 2003 (SOU 2003:123, Utvecklingskraft för hållbar välfärd).

13. The official title of which is SOU 2007:10, Hållbar samhällsorganisation med utvecklingskraft.

14. The situation concerning the rest of the country is now subject to review of special experts, according to the governmental instructions (*Direktiv*) 2009:62. See also the governmental bill 2009/10:156.

15. *See more* in detail Nergelius, *op. cit.*, p. 289 ss with further references.

16. That are to be found in the governmental bill 2009/10:80 p. 210 ss, in particular p. 212 s.

17. Cfr Nergelius, op.cit. p. 363.

REFERENCES

Litteraturlista: Karlson, N.´/Nergelius, J. (red.): *Federalism på svenska*, Stockholm (Ratio) 2007

Nergelius, J.: Svensk statsrätt, 2:a uppl. Lund 2010

Prop 2009/10:80, *En reformerad grundlag*

Prop 2009/10:156, *Regionalt utvecklingsansvar i vissa län*

SOU 2003:123, *Utvecklingskraft för hållbar välfärd*

SOU 2007:10, *Hållbar samhällsorganisation med utvecklingskraft*

Direktiv 2009:62, Översyn av statlig regional förvaltning m.m.

EVE HEPBURN – UNIVERSITY OF EDINBURGH, SCOTLAND

Between Region and State:
Rescaling Citizenship in a Multi-level System

Introduction

Citizenship is usually regarded as the exclusive domain of the state, whereby the rights, duties and responsibilities of citizens form part of a relationship with the state – which since the nineteenth century has been perceived as an indivisible and territorially bounded entity (Brubaker 1992; Benhabib 2005; Bauböck 2007a). However, the rescaling of political authority, resulting from decentralization and globalization, has also led to the rescaling of citizenship, so that the rights, duties and responsibilities of citizens are re-aggregated at different territorial levels (local, regional, state, supranational).

When examining these processes, most scholars have focused on the level above the state as a new arena for citizenship, tracing the emergence of transnational, postnational or even global citizenship (Bauböck 1994, 2007a,b; Soysal 1994; Shaw 2007a,b). These studies have broadened our understanding of citizen rights and participation in a globalizing world where principles of human rights sit alongside common notions of citizenship rights. This chapter, however, is interested in the exercise of citizenship at the level *beneath* the state, which has until recently been largely neglected by social scientists. This is a key omission, as the continual decentralization of states has empowered substate regional governments with considerable control over social, cultural and economic policy that determines and differentiates citizens' access to rights and public services. Thus, whilst supranational integration and globalization have resulted in the relocation of certain rights at a higher level, the parallel decentralization and federalization of states means that certain aspects of citizenship have been moved downwards. As such, this chapter focuses on the exercise of citizenship at the interstices of the regional and state political communities.

A recent study by Marks, Hooghe and Schakel demonstrates that 'regional authority' – including regional-level democratic institutions, policy competences, tax-raising powers and input into central government policy-making – has increased and strengthened dramatically across OECD countries since 1945 (Marks et al 2008). Devolution and federal reforms have endowed regions with political legitimacy and authority over a wide range of policies including health, education, and planning. This has provided regions with the capacity to become the key actors in the formulation and delivery of often innovative public services (Keating 2002; Greer 2005; Wincott 2005). The devolution of legislative powers to regions, along with other forms of spatial rescaling such as the allocation of powers upwards to the EU, may be explained by a desire to 'offload' state functions whilst retaining sovereignty (Keating 1988).

Regions have also become important sites for identity and belonging and 'containers' of social attitudes and values – especially if the region has claims to nationhood (Keating 1996; Guibernau 1999; Berg 2007; Henderson 2007). The question of who does or does not belong to a region is becoming a highly important and politicized question, and one that is not as easily resolvable as that of state membership due to the relative openness of regional borders. Regional membership has also taken on a new significance in the face of international migration, which has altered the composition of regional populations. Immigration raises important questions for the future prospect and survival of regional cultures (Carens 1995; Kymlicka 2001). It also challenges regional actors to develop new understandings of regional membership (Hepburn 2009).

This chapter begins by analysing some theoretical contributions to the study of multi-level citizenship, before turning specifically to the concept of regional citizenship. Within this section, it examines the effects of state decentralization (including the creation of regional governments and policy communities, and the growth of regional identity) on the three main dimensions of citizenship: the exercise of rights (civil, social and political), participation (in a polity, society and economy) and membership (in terms of identity and belonging) in a multi-level state. The paper then assesses whether 'regional citizenship' complements to state (and indeed, supranational) citizenship.[1]

Different spheres of citizenship

Citizenship is generally viewed as a relationship between an individual and the state. To be a citizen means to enjoy certain rights and obligations, guaranteed by the state, and to owe that state loyalty (Jenson 1997). This conception of citizenship as exclusively conferred by the state has existed for over two hundred years as part of the 'sovereignty norm of the Westphalian system' (Jenson 2007: 55). Unpacking this conception of state citizenship, Marshall (1992 [1950]) distinguished between three main components: civil rights, political rights and social rights, which the state successively conferred in response to demands for participation and minimum welfare standards from the eighteenth century onwards. For Marshall, these rights should act as a force for statewide integration and nation-building. However, many scholars have argued that we now live in a post-Westphalian system in which sovereignty is shared and identities, powers and rights are distributed across multiple levels (Keating 2001). This means that it is no longer the state alone that 'confers' rights of citizenship. Moreover, this classical understanding of citizenship links national integration with state-building, whereby the state and the nation are considered the same thing. This is problematic, however, given that people have been shown to have strong attachments to more than one political community, or nation, in states of a multi-level nature (Moreno 1999).

State-centric understandings of citizenship have come under fire by a large number of scholars who have proclaimed the emergence of suprastate and substate forms of citizenship. At the global level, Benhabib (2005) has argued that the state has undergone a number of 'crises' of citizenship and sovereignty as a result of globalization, the movement of people across territory boundaries and the rise of multicultural movements. She maintains that as a result of these external pressures the divisions or lines between citizens and residents, nationals and foreigners have fundamentally shifted, thereby creating new spaces for citizenship within a transnational context (Benhabib 2005: 674). From a similar perspective, Soysal (1994) argues that international migration has eroded the link between nationality, national identity and citizenship. This has led to the development of new forms of postnational citizenship anchored in a universal discourse of human rights, which are divorced from narrow understandings of national belonging.

The European Union has developed the world's most advanced supranational citizenship project. The EU first became involved in developing citizenship practices in 1957, though it was not until the Treaty of Maastricht (1992) that a citizenship of the European Union was formally established. The Treaty granted EU citizenship to all nationals of member states, which was later conferred as a personal status in the Amsterdam Treaty of 1997 (Jenson 2007). Legal rights include the right to travel and reside anywhere in the EU, the right to vote and stand in some local and European elections, the right to petition the European Parliament, and to have consular protection from another EU member state whilst abroad (Painter 2008: 6). These rights were intended to enable people living in Europe to consider themselves as citizens of the same political community. At a theoretical level, Bauböck (2007a: 453) has defined European citizenship as 'a nested membership in a multilevel polity that operates at member state and union levels', which confers a variety of benefits including non-discrimination, access to nationality and voting rights. In particular, EU nationals are now allowed to vote for local, regional and European elections (though not state elections) as well as regional referendums in some member states (Shaw 2007a). European citizenship has therefore created new rights for people living in EU states.

At the level beneath the state, scholars have made a strong case for disconnecting local from state citizenship, and endowing local governments and city regions with powers to confer citizenship status (Bauböck 2003; Sassen 2003). It has been argued that citizenship has a particularly strong urban heritage: it originated in the city-states of Athens and Rome, was reinvented in the Italian city-republics during the Renaissance, and its modern form arose in the urban revolutions that swept across Europe in the late eighteenth century (Bauböck, 2003: 156). Cities have long provided alternative spaces for political community, and the global city has become a new site for social, economic and political processes and identity (Sassen 2003). Unlike the birth, descent or naturalization requirements of the state, membership of provinces, municipalities and cities is acquired through residence, creating new forms of citizenship practice. As such, Bauböck (2003: 150) argues that cities should be able to assert their autonomy and unique heritage, by granting full local citizenship to all residents within their jurisdiction. However, while there has been a focus on the local level as a sphere of citizenship, there have been surprisingly few analyses of another significant substate level for the exercise of citizenship; that of the region.

Regional Citizenship

The decentralization of states has led to the rescaling of powers and authority to substate levels of government. Regions are now responsible for large areas of the welfare state, for organizing elections to regional assemblies, and for cultural policy and integration. This has had a significant impact on the nature of citizenship, as regional governments and parliaments take over citizenship responsibilities that were previously exercised by the state. This includes the rescaling of public services, the devolution of resources, and the re-definition of the 'sharing community' from the statewide political community to the regional political community (McEwen 2002; Béland and Lecours 2009; Greer and Mätzke 2009; Jeffery 2009). Furthermore, substate regions may impose requirements such as residency or language, which enables citizens to access services and participate in the political life of the region. This has been the case in regions and provinces such as Quebec and Catalonia, which require immigrants to learn the language of the stateless nation (i.e. French and Catalan, respectively) to access public services (Hepburn 2011). As such, substate regions have emerged as important spaces for democratic attachments, identity and citizenship (Benhabib 2005: 674; Guibernau 2006). The politics of belonging and citizen allegiance, far from moving to the suprastate level, have been shifted down to the regional level (Bellamy 2008: 602). The EU, for instance, has failed to attract any degree of citizen belonging and identity comparable to that of regions (ibid).

However, there has been something of a normative objection amongst social scientists to enabling regions to develop their own forms of citizenship. There is a widespread perception that regions cannot be trusted with such an important issue, as they will favour particularist policies that include some groups whilst excluding others (Castles and Davidson 2000: 209). Scholars have refrained from engaging in regional geographies of citizenship, as they are suspicious of potential exclusionary appeals to regional cultural identity (see Painter 2008). Part of the explanation for this caution is that regionalism, and minority nationalism have been powerfully portrayed as throwbacks to the past, and associated with ethnic exclusivism (Hobsbawm, 1990). Such broad assertions ignore the complexity of regionalisms, of which many are seen as progressive, democratic forces (Keating, 2006). Many regionalist parties, for instance, support diversity and multiculturalism (Hepburn 2009). Moreover, such objections neglect evidence of policy divergence within federal and devolved states, which has created different sets of entitlements to public services (Greer 2009). The following section explores what a number of scholars have argued are the central components of citizenship – rights, membership and participation (Shaw 1998; Bellamy et al 2004) – from a regional perspective.

Rights

The main understanding of citizenship relates to rights (Bellamy 2008: 603). Most famously, Marshall (1992 [1950]) distinguished between three types of citizenship rights – civil, political and social. *Civil rights* include personal liberties such as freedom of speech, movement, assembly and the right to own property. *Political rights* refer to those rights which enable citizens to participate in the political process, by voting or standing for election. *Social rights*, which arrived just as Marshall was completing his theory in 1950, consisted of minimum welfare standards such as protections against the risks of ill-health, old age and unemployment. For Marshall (and others), these rights were all guaranteed by the state. However, this is no longer the case in states that contain multiple territorial levels, such as federal, devolned or regionalised states.

Citizenship rights are territorial 'because they come from governments and governments are territorially delineated' (Greer and Mätzke (2009: 7). Therefore, when the powers and responsibilities of states are redistributed across different territorial levels, the rights associated with these functions are also rescaled. As regions now control a large number of policy areas, many public services and freedoms are now regionally-based. We can illustrate this argument by exploring the three types of citizenship rights Marshall identified through a devolved lens. First, decentralization has generally had few consequences for civil rights. Indeed, this can be contrasted with the considerable accumulation of powers at the European level, which now guarantees many of the civil rights that were once strongly attached to the state – such as freedom of movement and freedom to trade without restrictive practices. However, decentralization has had some effects on civil rights, especially given that some regions have control over criminal law (such as in Scotland and Northern Ireland) and thus citizens' access to justice various across states. Furthermore, in the case of the UK, whilst the Westminster Parliament can opt out of the European Convention for the Protection of Human Rights and Fundamental Freedoms, the devolved assemblies in Scotland, Wales and Northern Ireland cannot. This 'detaches considerable areas of civil rights from British membership and makes possible the development of distinct forms of Scottish and Northern Irish civil rights, within a European framework' (Keating 2009: 102). Civil rights have therefore undergone a process of extensive Europeanization and limited regionalization.

Second, decentralization has had an enduring impact on political rights. According to Marshall (1992 [1950]), political rights to vote or stand in elections emerged in the nineteenth century. At this point, elections in the UK were to Westminster, and suffrage was decided by the actions of that parliament. However, in the late twentieth century, with states decentralizing across Europe and elsewhere, political rights began to vary across state territories. Political citizenship came to be exercised at the regional level, through rights of participation in regional electoral processes for residents living in the Spanish autonomous communities, Canadian provinces, Belgian regions, German Länder, American states, Italian regions and so on.

Yet, it is the regionalization of social rights of citizenship that has received the greatest scholarly attention (Keating 2002, 2009; Greer 2005, 2009; Wincott 2005; Jeffery 2009). As theorized by Marshall (1992), citizens have since the nineteenth century been entitled to equal access to social rights guaranteed by the welfare state, such as health, education and housing. However, this situation no longer pertains in states of a devolved, federal or multi-level nature. Whilst social security rights (i.e. pensions, unemployment benefits) remain firmly entrenched at the state level, the vast majority of social rights have been devolved to the regional level (including health, education, social work, housing). Moreover, there is substantial evidence that, as policy in these areas diverges, so does access to social services (Keating 2002; Greer 2005; Wincott 2005). Due to differentiated access to welfare provision, social citizenship has become distinct in different parts of multi-level states. This development has been met with concern, and sometimes envy, by those who live in regions that have 'fewer' social rights. For instance, in the UK, news editors looking for sensationalist headlines have cast growing social policy divergence as a new form of 'apartheid' between the different regions (Devlin 2007; Greer and Mätzke 2009; Jeffery 2009). Residents of Scotland have access to free eye care, a tuition fee waiver, free personal care for the elderly and a number of drugs not available in England, whilst Welsh residents enjoy free prescriptions and Northern Ireland's elderly residents have free access to public transport (Keating 2005; Keating et al 2009). One unofficial ballot conducted for the *Tonight* programme on UK television found that over 60% of UK citizens living on the English border were favourable to redrawing regional boundaries to give them access to benefits provided in Scotland that were not available in England (Kelly and Madeley 2008).[2] Regions are therefore developing their own standards of welfare provision, leading to uneven development of access to social rights (Painter, 2008: 9). This has not led to the much-feared 'race to the bottom' in welfare standards; instead, some regions have proved more solidaristic than states, offering a greater range of social services (Keating 2009: 111).

Participation

Not only does the decentralization of states alter the structure of citizenship rights; it also creates new opportunities for citizen participation. This is most obvious in states of an asymmetrically decentralized nature (whereby the constituent units of the state exercise different degrees or types of powers), whereby citizens in a region that has greater political autonomy (such as an elected assembly or parliament) have more opportunities for political participation than those who do not (Grahl 1996). The UK case is instructive here. Citizens living in Scotland, Wales, Northern Ireland and Greater London enjoy greater political representation through the devolved assemblies than those living in England outside London, which do not have devolved institutions (Painter 2008: 14). The same is true of Italian citizens living in the five 'special regions' which have legislative powers over areas such as health and education, compared to those living in 'ordinary regions'; or Spanish citizens living in Catalonia, the Basque Country or Galicia, constitutionally acknowledged as 'historic nationalities' with special rights and privileges, than those living in other regions of Spain, which have less powers.

On a different note, it is not only nationals that have differentiated access to political rights across states, but also non-nationals. Shaw's (2007b: 2561) analysis reveals that EU citizens have a right to vote not only in local and European elections across the whole of the UK, but also the right to vote in the regional elections of Scotland, Wales and London, as well as regionally based popular referendums such as those held in 1997–9 to decide whether or not to have devolved assemblies in Scotland, Wales and Greater London. This is because regional elections are governed within the same framework as local elections. Shaw (2006: 4) calls this a '"mini" version of the West Lothian question' for the field of electoral rights for non-nationals, whereby EU citizens living in regions with devolved institutions can influence the election of representatives dealing with issues that affect them, such as housing and healthcare, whilst those living in other regions cannot.

Yet citizenship is not restricted to the passive conferral of rights – it also implies active engagement, not only in political processes but also civil society (Bellamy 2008). On a practical basis, citizenship participation may include becoming a member of a political party, labour union, interest group or civil society organization. In decentralized states, citizenship participation may be circumscribed at a regional level. Scholars have demonstrated that some regions (in particular, those with claims to nationhood such as Catalonia, Quebec, Wales, the Basque Country and Scotland) have historically maintained distinct civil societies, which constitute the primary social and political communities for citizens of that region (Keating 1996: Guibernau 1999). Civil society organizations and trade unions may operate on a regional-only basis to serve that regional community. Moreover, recent research has shown that decentralization has led to the creation of territorial policy communities, whereby interest groups now articulate their policy platforms at a regional level (Keating et al 2009). Citizen participation in social, political and policy processes may now be achieved within a narrower regional frame. This shows that citizenship participation has also become regionalized.

Membership

Along with rights and participation, membership is the third basic building block of citizenship (Bellamy et al 2004: 7). This dimension is more difficult to measure that rights and participation, as it relates to a citizen's more nebulous sense of identity and belonging (Painter and Philo 1995; Painter 2002). Membership refers to an allegiance and belonging to a given political community, and in particular, citizenship is often made synonymous with nationality (Brubaker 1992). As was discussed above, this correlation is problematic as nations are rarely congruent with states. Indeed, there are only a handful of states in the world – such as Iceland or Japan – that are not multiethnic or plurinational in nature. As such, citizens ordinarily consider themselves to be members of several political communities. This is most evident in countries such as Switzerland and Italy, where political allegiance lies first with the city or canton, next with the region, then the province, and finally with the state (not to mention to European dimension of identity). Citizens tend to have multi-level attachments (Berg 2007), which must be understood as plural, contested and changeable (Jenson 2007).

Furthermore, according to some authors, decentralization has promoted a re-definition of the territorial scale of belonging, and strengthened citizen identification with, and attachments to, the region (Guibernau 2006; Henderson 2007; Jeffery 2009). This is especially true if there are claims to nationhood based on the existence of historical traditions, cultures and languages. In these cases, attachments to the regional community are even stronger than those to the state (Moreno 1999; Guibernau 2006). In Spain, for example, a large percentage of residents in the 'historic nationalities' of Catalonia (40%), the Basque Country (44%) and Galicia (32%) identify more strongly with their region than with the state, with only 8% of Catalans and 3% of Basques prioritizing their identification with Spain (Guibernau 2006: 66).[3] Regional attachments are also very strong in Canada, where the vast majority of inhabitants of Newfoundland and Labrador (97%), British Columbia (88%) and Quebec (85%) feel attached to their province (ibid: 68).[4] Meanwhile, in the UK, few residents of Scotland (5%) and Wales (10%) identify themselves as 'more British than Scottish/Welsh'; instead they express strong regional identities, with 30% of Scots and 21% of Welsh identifying themselves as 'more Scottish/Welsh than British' (Jeffery 2009: 87).[5] Clearly, decentralization has contributed to the consolidation of territorial identities, whereby the region has – for many citizens – become the primary political community of allegiance and belonging.

Conclusion: Multi-level citizenship

This paper has demonstrated that, owing to decentralization, European integration and globalization, we are seeing the reconstruction of citizenship at different territorial levels. In particular, there is compelling evidence to suggest a consolidation of citizenship at the regional level. Regions have become particularly important arenas for the exercise of political and social rights (especially relating to voting and access to public services), participation in social and political processes (such as civic society engagement), and identification with, and membership of, a political and cultural community.

There are a number of factors contributing to the emergence of regional citizenship. These include the decentralization of state powers to regional institutions in key areas of social welfare, the emergence of new forms of political representation and participation in devolved institutions, and the persistence of regional identities and political cultures that provide a framework for regional belonging. Together with the emergence of new forms of supranational and transnational citizenship, the development of regional forms of citizenship within the state has created a form of 'multilevel citizenship' (Delanty 1997; Painter 2002). In multi-level political communities, there are multiple sites of citizenship, as the status, rights and entitlements of a person may change depending on which state, region or municipality they inhabit. These different spheres of citizenship are by no means mutually exclusive; instead they may be seen as complementary. A useful analogy is the EU principle of 'subsidiarity', which implies that the locus of decision-making should be closer to the citizen (Moreno 1999: 71). Equally, we can say that the rights, duties and responsibilities of citizenship are now also being exercised at the most appropriate level. The rescaling of citizenship is reflective of the rescaling of political authority and functions, whereby there are now multiple sites of authority, identity and citizen engagement in multi-level political communities.

NOTES

1 This discussion is based on a similar argument found in Hepburn (2011).

2 The poll turnout was 1,957 votes (out of a possible 12,000 residents in Berwick upon Tweed). It followed a similar online survey held by a local newspaper, *The Berwickshire Advertiser*, one week before, which revealed that 78% of residents backed unification with Scotland. Historically, the town has changed hands between Scotland and England at least 13 times, but has been part of England for the last 500 years.

3 This data was taken from the Centro de Investigaciones Sociológicas (CIS), Datos de Opinión in 2003.

4 This data was taken from Opinion Canada (2003) 5(17). 8 May. Accessible at: http://www.cric.ca.

5 This data was taken from the British Social Attitudes Survey, Wales Life and Times Survey and Scottish Social Attitudes Survey in 2007.

REFERENCES

Bauböck, R. (1994). *Transnational Citizenship. Membership and Rights in International Migration.* Aldershot: Edward Elgar.

Bauböck, R. (2003). Reinventing Urban Citizenship. *Citizenship Studies,* 7(2), 139-60.

Bauböck, R. (2007a). Why European Citizenship? Normative Approaches to Supranational Union. *Theoretical Inquiries in Law,* 8(2), 452-88.

Bauböck, R. (Ed.) (2007b) *Migration and Citizenship: Legal Status, Rights and Political Participation.* Amsterdam: University of Amsterdam Press.

Béland, D. and Lecours, A. (2009). *Nationalism and Social Policy. The Politics of Territorial Solidarity.* Oxford: Oxford University Press.

Bellamy, R. (2008). Evaluating Union citizenship: belonging, rights and participation within the EU. *Citizenship Studies* 12(6): 597–611.

Bellamy, R., Castiglione, D. and Santoro, E. (2004). *Lineages of European citizenship. Rights, Belonging and Participation in Eleven Nation-States.* Basingstoke: Palgrave Macmillan.

Benhabib, S. (2005). Borders, Boundaries and Citizenship. PSOnline, www.aspanet.org.

Berg, L. (2007). *Multi-level Territorial Attachments. The Influence of Territorial Attachments on Political Trust.* Göteborg: Department of Political Science, Göteborg University

Brubaker, R. (1992) *Citizenship and Nationhood in France and Germany.* Cambridge, MA: Harvard University Press.

Carens, J. (1995) Immigration, political community and the transformation of identity: Quebec's immigration policies in critical perspective. In J. Carens (Ed.) *Is Quebec nationalism just?* Montreal: McGill-Queen's University Press.

Castles, S. and A. Davidson (2000). *Citizenship and Migration: Globalization and the Politics of Belonging.* London and NY: Routledge.

Delanty, G. (1997). Models of Citizenship: Defining European Identity and Citizenship. *Citizenship Studies,* 1(3), 285-303.

Devlin, K. (2007). Scotland plans to axe prescription charges. *Telegraph,* 24 October.

Grahl, J. (1996). Regional Citizenship and Macroeconomic Constraints in the European Union. *International Journal of Urban and Regional Research,* 20, 480-97.

Greer, S. (2005). The territorial bases of health policymaking in the UK after devolution. *Regional & Federal Studies,* 15(4), 501–18.

Greer, S. and Mätzke, M. (2009). Introduction: devolution and citizenship rights. In S. Greer (ed) *Devolution and Social citizenship in the UK.* Bristol: Policy Press.

Guibernau, M. (1999). *Nations without States.* Cambridge: Polity Press.

Guibernau, M. (2006) National identity, devolution and secession in Canada, Britain and Spain. *Nations and Nationalism,* 12(1), 51–76.

Henderson, A. (2007) *Hierarchies of Belonging National Identity and Political Culture in Scotland and Quebec.* Montreal-Kingston: McGill-Queen's University Press.

Hepburn, E. (2009). Regionalist Party Mobilisation in Immigration. *West European Politics,* 32(3).

Hepburn, E. (2011) '"Citizens of the Region": party conceptions of regional citizenship and immigrant integration', *European Journal of Political Research.*

Hobsbawm, E. (1990). *Nations and Nationalism since 1780,* 2nd edn. Cambridge: Cambridge University Press.

Jeffery, C. (2009). Devolution, public attitudes and social citizenship. In S. Greer (ed.) *Devolution and Social Citizenship in the UK.* Bristol: Policy Press.

Jenson, J. (1997). Fated to Live in Interesting Times: Canada's Changing Citizenship Regimes. *Canadian Journal of Political Science,* 30(4), 627-44.

Jenson, J. (2007). The European Union's Citizenship Regime. Creating Norms and Building Practices. *Comparative European Politics,* 5(1), 35–51.

Keating, M. (1996). *Nations Against the State: The New Politics of Nationalism in Quebec, Catalonia and Scotland.* London: Macmillan.

Keating, M. (2001). *Plurinational Democracy. Stateless Nations in a Post-Sovereignty Era.* Oxford: Oxford University Press.

Keating, M. (2002). Devolution and public policy in the United Kingdom:

divergence or convergence? In J. Adams and P. Robinson (Eds.), *Devolution in Practice. Public Policy Differences within the UK.* London: Institute for Public Policy Research.

Keating, M. (2005). *The Government of Scotland. Public Policy Making after Devolution.* Edinburgh: Edinburgh University Press.

Keating, M. (2006). Introduction. In J. McGarry and M. Keating (Eds.) *European Integration and the Nationalities Question.* London: Routledge.

Keating, M. (2009). Social citizenship, devolution and policy divergence. In S. Greer (ed.) *Devolution and Social Citizenship in the UK.* Bristol: Policy Press.

Keating, M., P. Cairney and E. Hepburn (2009) 'Territorial Policy Communities and Devolution in the United Kingdom', *Cambridge Journal of Regions, Economy and Society*, 2(1).

Kelly, T. and G. Madeley (2008). Berwick-upon-Tweed 'votes' to leave England and join Scotland for better public services. *Daily Mail*, 18 February.

Kymlicka, W. (2001). Minority Nationalism and Immigrant Integration. In W. Kymlicka (Ed.) *Politics in the Vernacular.* Oxford: Oxford University Press.

Marks, G., L. Hooghe and A. Schakel (Eds.) (2008). Regional Authority in 42 Countries, 1950-2006: A Measure and Five Hypotheses. *Regional & Federal Studies*, 18(2/3).

Marshall, T.H. (1992 [1950]). *Citizenship and Social Class.* Cambridge: Cambridge University Press.

McEwen, N. (2002). State welfare nationalism: the territorial impact of welfare state development in Scotland. *Regional and Federal Studies* 12(1): 66–90.

Moreno, L. (1999). Local and Global: Mesogovernments and Territorial identities. *Nationalism and Ethnic Politics*, 5(3/4), 61-75.

Painter, J. (2002). Multilevel Citizenship, Identity and Regions in Contemporary Europe. In J. Anderson (Ed) *Transnational Democracy. Political Spaces and Border Crossings.* London: Routledge.

Painter, J. (2008). European Citizenship and the Regions. *European Urban and Regional Studies*, 15(1), 5-19.

Painter, J. and C. Philo (1995). Spaces of Citizenship: an Introduction. *Political Geography,* 14, 107-20.

Sassen, S. (2003). The Repositioning of Citizenship: Emergent Subjects and Spaces for Politics, *CR: The New Centennial Review* 3(2), 41-66.

Shaw, J. (1998). Citizenship of the Union: Towards Postnational Citizenship. In Academy of European Law (Ed) *Collected Courses of the Academy of European Law.,* Vol. VI, Book 1. The Hague: Kluwer Law International.

Shaw, J. (2006). Migrants' Political Rights: What role for Scottish political institutions? Paper presented at the Scottish Policy Innovation Forum, Edinburgh, 24 November.

Shaw, J. (2007a). *The Transformation of Citizenship in the European Union: Electoral Rights and the Restructuring of Political Space*. Cambridge: Cambridge University Press.

Shaw, J. (2007b). E.U. Citizenship and Political Rights in an Evolving European Union. *Fordham Law* Review, 75, 2549-2579.

Soysal, J. (1994). *Limits of Citizenship. Migrants and Postnational Membership in Europe*. Chicago IL: University of Chicago Press.

Wincott, D. (2005). Reshaping public space? Devolution and policy change in British early childhood education and care. *Regional & Federal Studies*, 15(4), 453-70.

NICOLA McEWEN – UNIVERSITY OF EDINBURGH, SCOTLAND

Regional Government and the Welfare State

Can regional governments sustain systems of social welfare? Or does the spread of multi-level government weaken the welfare state? These are pertinent questions given the widespread development of multi-level government and the growth of regional authority across advanced capitalist democracies. Across Europe and North America, new regional institutions have been established while existing legislatures and governments have seen their power and responsibility extended (Keating, 1998; Keating, *et al.*, 2003). The regional authority index recently compiled by Hooghe, Marks and Schakel demonstrated that, between 1970 and 2005, 29 of 42 mainly EU and OECD states had become more 'regionalized', while only two had become marginally less regionalized (Hooghe, *et al.*, 2008). Regional institutions now make legislative, policy and spending decisions over a vast range of activities central to their populations, including policies that are key components of the welfare state.

And yet, the literature examining the welfare state is replete with the assumption that a centralised state structure is the optimal form of state for the delivery of social welfare. As such, the welfare state represented an advanced stage in the territorial integration of national communities, and of the evolution of the modern state as a *nation-state* (Rokkan, 1999; Bartolini, 2005). For Mishra, the idea of maintaining and consolidating the national community, economically, politically and socially, was 'the ideological underpinning *par excellence* of the welfare state' (Mishra, 1999: 12). Welfare states have been assumed to rest upon shared identities and shared solidarities (Miller, 1995; Canovan, 1995), and to represent the evolution of the rights of citizenship, from civil and political rights to social rights (Marshall, 1992). In T H Marshall's influential account of citizenship and social class, social rights uniquely granted an equalisation of status to members of the political community, as well as an equitable right to health care, education, social security and other public services. Such equitable access to social programmes allowed social rights to be the basis of social solidarity among the state's citizens (*ibid.*). Such accounts leave little room for the variation in social programmes, welfare systems or social citizenship rights which the regionalisation of the welfare state may imply, and indeed concern has been expressed that regionalising welfare may undermine the welfare state and the social solidarity upon which it rests (Miller, 1995; Jeffery, 2005).

This chapter considers the effect of the expansion of regional authority on the welfare state. It first considers whether regionalising constitutional and political responsibility for aspects of state welfare has a detrimental impact on the welfare state. It then considers some counter hypotheses which suggest that the regionalisation of welfare can have beneficial consequences for welfare state development by promoting social solidarity at the regional scale, as well as opportunities for social policy innovation and policy transfer. Although a thorough empirical examination of these hypotheses is beyond the scope of this brief chapter, some evidence is drawn from the experience of welfare development in multi-level states in Europe and North America.

1. Hypothesising the Impact of Regionalising Welfare

Providing an assessment of the impact of regionalisation on the welfare state will be heavily influenced by how we define the object of study. The term 'welfare state' is sometimes used to refer to a set of social programmes delivered by the state, while at other times it is considered to be a *form* of the state itself (Wincott, 2003;

McEwen, 2006). In this chapter, I adopt Asa Briggs definition of the welfare state as 'a state in which organised power is deliberately used (through politics and administration) in an effort to modify the play of market forces'. For Briggs, this has three distinctive dimensions: first, the welfare state guarantees a minimum income to its citizens, irrespective of the value of their work or property; second, it minimises insecurity by supporting individual citizens and their families in times of need (such as illness, unemployment, infancy or old age); and third, it provides 'an agreed range of services' to which all citizens are entitled, without distinction of class or status (Briggs, 2000: 18). The scope of each of these dimensions is of course open to political debate and ideological interpretation, leading to different configurations of welfare – distinctive welfare regimes – in different state contexts (Titmuss, 1974; Esping-Andersen, 1990). Moreover, the growth of regional political authority is likely to have a variable effect across these different dimensions of the welfare state, as a result of the division of welfare competencies.

Although considerable variation exists between cases, central governments within multi-level states have usually retained control over redistributive welfare and social security, but regional governments with competence in this area have often developed their own social assistance schemes and minimum income guarantee programmes associated with the development of 'safety nets' (Moreno, 2003). Regional governments also have considerable scope for developing a distinctive range of services and entitlements for citizens within their fields of policy jurisdiction, for example, in health care, education, child care and social services. This can give rise to the development of distinctive welfare regimes at the regional level, and variations in the recognition of social citizenship rights across regional boundaries of the same state. As a consequence, the regionalisation of welfare poses a challenge to the assumption in the literature that progressive welfare systems must be founded upon centralised and territorially homogeneous nation-states (see Keating, 2009).

Does the regionalising of welfare have a detrimental impact on the welfare state?

Three distinctive hypotheses have been developed within the literature to suggest that regionalising welfare undermines the welfare state. The first is centred upon institutional design. It has been argued that dispersing authority for welfare provision between levels of government inhibits progressive welfare development by increasing the number of institutional veto points within the system, creating more opportunities for 'veto players' (Tsebelis, 2002) to block coordinated policy change. This is particularly the case in federal states, where sovereignty is constitutionally divided between the federal and lower level (state, province, land). When welfare initiatives span jurisdictions, as has often been the case, inter-governmental consensus can be more difficult to secure and policy stalemate a common occurrence   (Banting, 1987; 1995; Huber, *et al.*, 1993; Swank, 2002). Federalism, and multi-level government more broadly, also promotes political fragmentation, making it more difficult for pro-welfare coalitions to mobilise and develop coherent strategies on a national scale (Swank, 2001; Pierson, 2001: 453; Obinger, et al., 2005: 35). Indeed, there is considerable evidence to suggest that federal states such Australia, the United States, Switzerland and (in some respects) Canada witnessed a slower pace of welfare expansion – whether measured in the level of social spending or the scope of social programmes – and that at least some of the explanation lies in the institutional configuration of federalism (Banting, 2005; Castles and Uhr, 2005).

Federal state structures may have impeded welfare expansion, but these same institutional constraints also make it more difficult to gain intergovernmental consent for welfare retrenchment. Obinger, *et al.*'s analysis of welfare development in six federal systems (2005) suggested that the institutional veto points built into federal systems produced a 'ratchet effect' that impeded welfare retrenchment, not least because weaker lower level governments had a vested interest in maintaining systems of redistributive welfare that promote transfers from richer to poorer regions. Thus, the Atlantic provinces in Canada and the eastern German länder successfully modified at least some of the federal efforts of the 1990s to limit both explicit inter-regional transfers and implicit transfers to residents in poorer regions via national social programmes, such as unemployment benefits (Banting, 2005; Manow, 2005). The Australian Senate, meanwhile, proved to be an influential veto player blocking the Commonwealth government from pursuing policies to limit the scope of social spending (Castles and Uhr, 2005: 84-86).

As well as promoting fragmentation among pro-welfare interest groups, multi-level government also promotes differentiated identities and fragmented solidarities. Indeed, the growth of regional authority in recent years has often been in response to demands for self-government from territorially distinctive communities. Strong regional institutions, especially when centred upon elected legislatures, reinforce that sense of difference vis-à-vis the rest of the state, and sustain the idea that such communities hold and should defend distinctive values and interests. This fragmentation of community identity has concerned those who regard a shared national identity as a necessary basis upon which state-wide systems of redistributive welfare must be based. Without the shared obligations and feelings of solidarity that a shared national identity embodies, membership of a political community would be based on rational self-interest and a strict reciprocity between individual contributions and benefits, rather than on the basis of need (Miller, 1995: 71-3; 2000: 105-6; Canovan, 1996: 27-35). The regionalisation of welfare, especially where it generates distinctive policies, social programmes and entitlements for citizens of the same state depending on the region in which they live, also poses a challenge to the principle of social citizenship and uniform social rights. Regional welfare systems promote policy variation such that citizens in one part of the country may be entitled to particular social services that are denied to their co-citizens in other regions, potentially threatening class and inter-regional solidarity ties. For example, in the post-devolution UK, there has been concern among the liberal left at the lack of common social citizenship rights (largely due to the absence of conditional central government transfers or framing legislation). Conservatives, meanwhile, have railed against disproportionately higher levels of spending transferred to Scotland not least when these are used to support more generous social programmes – such as reduced charges for medical prescriptions, free university tuition, and free personal care for the elderly – not offered to citizens south of the border (Jeffery, 2005; Andrews and Mycroft, 2008).

A third charge levelled at the regionalisation of welfare is that it promotes a 'race to the bottom' in welfare provision. Regional governments are, by definition, smaller than their national counterparts, and usually (though not always) less well-resourced. Regional economies are often more heavily dependent on a narrower range of industry and more vulnerable to the risk of capital and middle class flight. This may in turn make them less willing to impose additional burdens on business or higher earners, or to pursue generous welfare policies that involve raising taxes or impinging on the freedom and flexibility of the market (Piven, 1995; Pierson, 1995). Regional governments may thus be more inclined to depress welfare expenditures in order to maintain a competitive edge vis-à-vis other competitor regions, provoking an inter-regional 'race to the bottom' in welfare provision (Huber, et al., 1993; Peterson, 1995; Swank, 2002). The evidence for such a 'race to the bottom' outside of the United States is somewhat sparse, however (Schram and Soss, 1998). Some findings suggest that the effect of decentralisation depends upon the division of responsibility for revenue-raising and spending between the levels of government. Regions with a high level of fiscal autonomy appear less likely to have high welfare expenditures than regions with a high dependence on fiscal transfers from central government (Rodden, 2003; Obinger, et al., 2005). However, relative wealth, ideological preferences and political culture are clearly mediating factors.

The regionalisation of welfare: new solidarity communities?

There are a number of counter hypotheses which illustrate the potential for the growth of regional competence over key aspects of social policy to boost welfare state development, especially at the regional scale. First, in territorially heterogeneous states, regional governments may be better placed to draw upon shared identities and solidarities at the regional level to support progressive regional welfare systems. The state need not be the only appropriate level of social citizenship. Indeed, in periods characterised by state-wide welfare retrenchment and weakened social solidarity, multi-level government opens up opportunities for new forms of social solidarity to emerge at the regional level, where political rights, social rights and citizenship can be embedded in regional political communities and regional institutions (Keating, 2009: 504-6). Regional control over social policy can also facilitate a welfare system that matches regional needs and preferences, and provide a tool for identity construction and nationalist mobilisation. In Quebec, for example, family-oriented income support and child care policies have been utilised by all political parties to help define and reinforce Quebecers' cultural and national distinctiveness, while nationalists have utilised social policy objectives in campaigns for Quebec sovereignty, as in the 1995 referendum (McEwen, 2006; Béland and Lecours, 2008). Scottish social solidarity was frequently invoked by campaigners for Scottish self-government in the late 1980s, with a Scottish Parliament presented as a necessary pre-requisite for maintaining a social democratic welfare state (McEwen, 2006; Mitchell and Bennie, 1996). Of course, the ideological leanings of regional political elites matters here, but even regions where the dominant nationalist party is from the centre-right, as in Flanders, the Basque country and Catalonia, provide some evidence of nationalist elites utilising control over social policy to strengthen social provision within their territorial boundaries, and reinforce their community's distinctiveness (Keating, *et al.* 2003; Moreno, 2003; Béland and Lecours, 2008).

This leads to the second hypothesis. In multi-level states, in which the state's claim to represent a single national community is challenged by regional political leaders claiming nationhood for their regional community, the welfare state can be utilised as a nation-building tool. Elsewhere, I developed the concept of 'welfare state nationalism' to describe the distinctive ways in which the welfare state could serve a nation-building function: by providing an institutional focus for national solidarity, embodied in shared institutions (a health care system, for example); by strengthening the ties that bind citizens to the political institutions providing for their social and economic security; and by increasing the presence and relevance of political institutions overseeing these social programmes in the everyday lives of the citizens (McEwen, 2006: 62-79; see also Banting's notion of the welfare state as 'statecraft' [1995: 270-1]). It is not just central governments that engage in welfare state nationalism; regional governments with jurisdictional competence over social policy can also develop distinctive social policies in pursuit of their nation-building objectives. Where the welfare state becomes a tool deployed in the competitive nation-building strategies of state and regional governments, it can 'ratchet up' social welfare provision as each level of government competes for recognition in similar policy spheres. Such actions can also generate intergovernmental tensions over breaches of jurisdictional competence. For example, Canadian provinces, especially Quebec, have frequently objected to successive federal governments using their spending power to invest in social programmes in areas like education and health care, which are the constitutional responsibility of provincial governments (James and Lutszig, 2001; Banting, 2005).

Third, we can also identify more functional benefits of regionalising welfare. Granting regional governments autonomy over social welfare provision provides opportunities for policy innovation and experimentation. Indeed, just as the institutional complexities of multi-level government increase the number of veto points within a political system which could potentially inhibit welfare development, so too does it increase the number of access points for pro-welfare advocates, not just to defend existing social programmes but to get new policy ideas on the agenda and facilitate social policy innovation. (Of course, the proliferation of veto and access points can also assist the lobbying efforts of those opposed to progressive social welfare). The extent to which this exacerbates social policy divergence and variable citizenship rights across territories within the same state can be mitigated by policy transfer through 'demonstration effects' (Moreno and McEwen, 2005). For example, in 1988, the Basque country developed its own minimum income guarantee, the *Plan de Lucha contra la Pobreza*, a policy innovation which, by the end of the 1990s, had been adopted (with regional variations) by all 16 autonomous communities, each of which had devised their own regional minimum income guarantee scheme combining means-tested cash benefits with social inclusion programmes (Moreno, 2003; Gallego, 2005). In Wales, the Welsh Assembly Government pioneered the establishment of the post of children's commissioner to oversee children's services and advocate for children's rights, and similar positions were subsequently set up in Northern Ireland, Scotland and England (Birrell, 2009: 35-8).

Conclusion

There is no simple way to evaluate the impact of regionalising social policy responsibility on the development of the welfare state, not least because of a lack of systematic comparative data and analyses measuring the effects of regional autonomy and multi-level government in this sphere. One can find evidence to support the view that multi-level government, especially in federal systems where constitutional sovereignty is divided between levels of government, tended to have a braking effect on welfare expansion in the 'golden age' of welfare. Some of the institutional impediments contributing to that braking effect – the division of welfare responsibilities, the proliferation of veto points, and the need for intergovernmental consensus – remain evident in multi-level systems today, and can be invoked as a bulwark against retrenchment pressures. Multi-level government, too, provides greater opportunities to develop welfare systems suited to local preferences and needs, and can create an institutional environment which is conducive to social policy innovation.

Regionalising welfare has also led to new forms of social solidarity in some cases, especially in regions which represent national minorities whose citizens already share a strong sense of identity and mutual belonging which can lend support to redistributive welfare. Such societies often benefit, too, from greater solidarity – or 'institutional thickness' (Rhodes, 1996: 169) - between government, business leaders and the trade unions that can generate the mutual trust which underpins compromise between social partners. That is not to suggest that regions are necessarily better equipped to deliver social welfare than are states. It is merely to refute the claim that the central state is always the optimal level for the design and delivery of welfare systems.

There is, however, an important distinction to be made between intra-regional solidarity and inter-regional solidarity (Keating, 2009: 507). The former is based on the shared identity and solidarity found within regions, while the latter assumes a shared identity and mutual commitment between regions across a state's territory. Regional political institutions with responsibility for social programmes can capitalise on intra-regional solidarity while weakening inter-regional solidarity, or at least making it more difficult to maintain explicit or implicit inter-regional transfers from richer to poorer regions. There is ample evidence of political elites in relatively affluent strong identity regions (for example, Flanders, northern Italy, Catalonia) objecting to what they see as excessive cash flows from their region to other dependent parts of the country (Cattoir and Docquier, 1999; Dandoy and Baudewyns, 2005; Dupuy and Le Galès, 2006; Béland and Lecours, 2008). The fragmentation of territorial identities and relative economic disparities across regions within multi-level states are not the only factors which must be taken into account when examining the effects of regionalisation on systems of state welfare. Welfare development will also be shaped by the particular institutional configuration of the multi-level system and the degree of regional autonomy over social policies and revenue-raising, as well as the ideological preferences, political culture and nature of party competition within and between regions.

REFERENCES

Andrews, R and A Mycroft, 2008, 'Dilemmas of devolution: the "politics of Britishness" and citizenship education' *British Politics*, 3/2: 139-55.

Banting, K G, 1987, *The Welfare State and Canadian Federalism, 2nd edition* (Kingston and Montreal: McGill-Queen's University Press). 1995, 'The welfare state as statecraft: territorial politics and Canadian social policy', in Leibfried, S and P Pierson, *European Social Policy – Between Fragmentation and Integration* (Washington, DC: The Brookings Institute), pp269-300. 2005, 'Canada:

nation-building in a federal welfare state', in Obinger, *et al.*, *Federalism and the Welfare State*. 2005b,

Bartolini, S, 2005, *Restructuring Europe: centre formation, system building and political structuring between the nation-state and the European Union* (Oxford: Oxford University Press).

Béland, D and A Lecours, 2008, *Nationalism and Social Policy. The Politics of Territorial Solidarity* (Oxford: Oxford University Press).

Birrell, D, 2009, *The Impact of Devolution on Social Policy* (Bristol: the Policy Press).

Briggs, A, 2000, 'The welfare state in historical perspective', in Pierson, C and F Castles (eds), *The Welfare State Reader* (Cambridge: Polity Press), p.18-31.

Canovan, M, 1996, *Nationhood and Political Theory* (Cheltenham: Edward Elgar).

Castles, F G and J Uhr, 2005, 'Australia: federal constraints and institutional innovations' in Obinger, *et al.*, *Federalism and the Welfare State*.

Cattoir, P and F Docquier, 1999, 'Sécurité sociale et solidarité interrégionale', in Docquier, F (ed), *La solidarité entre les regions: bilans et perspectives* (Brussels: De Boeck Université, pp.227-53.

Dandoy R and P Baudewyns, 2005, 'The preservation of social security as a national function in the Belgian federal state', in McEwen, N and L Moreno, *The Territorial Politics of Welfare*, Routledge.

Dupuy, C and P Le Galès, 2006, 'The impacts of regional governments', in Greer, S (ed), *Territory, Democracy and Justice. Regionalism and Federalism in western democracies* (London: Palgrave).

Esping-Andersen, G, 1990, *The Three Worlds of Welfare Capitalism* (Cambridge: Poility Press).

Gallego, R, R Gomà and J Subirats, 2005, 'Spain: From state to regional welfare', in McEwen, N and L Moreno (eds), *The Territorial Politics of Welfare*

Huber, E, C Ragin and J Stephens, 1993, 'Social democracy, christian democracy, constitutional structure and the welfare state', *The American Journal of Sociology*, vol.99, no.3: 711-49.

Jeffery, C, 2005, 'Devolution and social citizenship: which society, whose citizenship?', in Greer, S (ed), *Territorial, Democracy and Justice* (London: Palgrave)

Keating, M, 1998, *The New Regionalism in Western Europe. Territorial restructuring and political change* (Aldershot: Edward Elgar). 2009, 'Social citizenship, solidarity and welfare in regionalized and plurinational states' *Citizenship Studies*, 13/5: 501-13.

Keating, M, J Loughlin and K Deschouwer, 2003, *Culture, institutions and economic development. A study of eight European regions.* (Aldershot: Edward Elgar).

McEwen, N, 2006, *Nationalism and the State: Welfare and Identity in Scotland*

and Quebec, Regionalism and Federalism Series. Presses interuniversitaires européennes/ Peter Lang, forthcoming.

Mannow, P, 2005, 'Germany: co-operative federalism and the overgrazing of the fiscal commons', in Obinger, *et al.*, *Federalism and the Welfare State.*

Marshall, T H (with T Bottomore), 1992, *Citizenship and Social Class* (London: Pluto Press).

Miller, D, 1995, *On Nationality* (Oxford: Clarendon Press). 2000, *Citizenship and National Identity*, Cambridge, Polity Press.

Mitchell, J and L Bennie, 1996, 'Thatcherism and the Scottish Question', in *British Elections and Parties Yearbook 1995* (London: Frank Cass), p.90-104.

Moreno, L., 2003, 'Europeanization, mesogovernments and safety nets', *European Journal of Political Research*, vol. 42, no. 2: 185-199.

Moreno, L and N McEwen, 2005, *The Territorial Politics of Welfare* (Routledge)

Obinger, H., Leibfried, S. and Castles, F. (eds.), 2005, *Federalism and the Welfare State. New World and European experiences*, Cambridge, Cambridge University Press.

Peterson, P., 1995, *The Price of Federalism*, Washington, D.C., Brookings Institution.

Pierson, P. (ed.), 2001, *The New Politics of the Welfare State*, Oxford, Oxford University Press.

Piven, F., 1995, 'Is it global economics or neo-laissez-faire?', *New Left Review*, no. 213: 107-114.

Rhodes, M, 1996. Southern European welfare states: identity, problems and prospects for reform. *South European Society & Politics*, 1/3: 1-22.

Rodden, J., 2003, 'Reviving Leviathan: fiscal federalism and the growth of government', *International Organization*, vol. 57, no .4: 695-729.

Rokkan, S, 1999, *State formation, nation-building and mass politics in Europe. The theory of Stein Rokkan* (Oxford: Oxford University Press).

Schram, S and J Soss, 1998, 'Making something out of nothing: welfare reform and a new race to the bottom', *Publius, the Journal of Federalism*, vol.28

Swank, D., 2001, 'Political institutions and welfare state restructuring. The impact of institutions on social policy change in developed democracies', in Pierson, P (ed), *The New Politics of the Welfare State.*

Titmuss, R, 1974, *Social Policy: an introduction* (London: George Allen & Unwin).

Tsebelis, G, 2002, *Veto players. How political institutions work* (Princeton: Princeton University Press).

Wincott, D, 2003, 'Shifting context, (national) states and welfare in the Veit-Wilson/Atherton debate', *Social Policy and Administration* 37/3: 305-15.

TASSILO HERRSCHEL, UNIVERSITY OF WESTMINSTER, ENGLAND

Regional Development, Peripheralisation and Marginalisation – *and the Role of Governance*

The challenges of peripherality have been a recurring theme in dis-cussions and policies on regional (usually economic) development. Much of this has focused especially on concerns about inequalities in such development, and the implications for the perceived legitimacy of state governments (Saunders, 1994). The European Union's long established regional policy is a particularly potent illustration of a policy seeking to counteract inequalities in the participation in , so the dominant paradigm, growing economic welfare. Results, however, have been mixed (Cappelen et al, 2003) In fact, there is evidence, that approximation in terms of economic development has largely been restricted to the inter-national level, while imbalances at the sub-national regional) level have been much less evident (Cappelen et al, 2003). This goes to the heart of the self-understanding of the European Union and the legitimacy of its Keynesian policies of a state-'managed' market economy.

Not being part of this equalisation process has been considered as questioning the legitimacy of policies and the very representativeness of democratic policy making (Radaelli, 2000).In this context, periph-erality has usually been conceptualised geographically as 'margin' or 'edge' of a territory, whether within member States, or the EU as a whole, based essentially on the notion of 'reachability', that is perceived and actual distance from a central 'core'. This distance may be simple geographic distance, or travel distance in terms of time needed and/or space covered to reach a point from the core which is usually being associated with the main metropolitan areas of the 'Blue Banana' (Hospers, 2003) reaching from London to Milan. It is in this context that the Nordic countries are usually seen, from a metropolitan western European perspective, as 'on the edge' or the continent, as inherently peripheral, This includes a close association with rurality, sparse-ness in population and remoteness, yet also, as a positive association, unspoiltness' and 'escape' and respite from urban hectic and overcrowding.

Yet, and that is the main argument here, it may also be based on variations in social connectivity among policymakers and other actors, within the increasingly more popular actor networks as the main determinants of governance (Albrechts and Mandelbaum, ed 2005). Yet, by the very nature of networks as linear linkages between points, rather than broader spaces, there may be more exclusions and marginalisations through the ways in which policies and power are implemented and defined. It is easier to 'miss' – or be missed – by a narrow line, than it is by a wider space. And this dimension of peripherality and marginality has gained in relevance with the observed (and propagated) 'new' patterns and practices in governance: open, flexible, non territorially defined, network based, informal (Herrschel, 2009; Jones, et al, 1997). This means that inter-personal and inter-institutional linkages, be they power relationships, dependencies, or trust, gain in importance, leading to a dissection of 'conventional' territoriality as contiguous, bounded spaces into linear avenues of preferred connectivity and thus relevance. In between these linear linkages sit actors who find themselves much less involved, and who find it more difficult to gain access to these networks and make their voices heard, and views and interests acknowledged. This can be either by choice or as a result of exclusion. The outcome is peripheralisation through 'in between-ness', that is exclusion from a network, rather than distance-based spatial edgeness or peripheral-ity. This distinction between geographic and social-communicative distance and marginality is at the centre of this chapter and will be examined in the following sections.

Policy-led, pragmatic and voluntary cooperation between policy-making actors that goes beyond formal governmental-administrative structures and territorial boundaries of institutionalised 'responsibilities' is considered the key driver behind the observed 'new' forms of governance with their associated 'background spatiality' (Herrschel, 2009). One such example, the recently more widely debated concept of 'new regionalism' (Cox 1997; Whitehead 2003; Keating, 1998; MacLeod, 2001; Hettne et al, 1999)), is portrayed as offering possible answers to the competitive pressures driven by globalization, These revolve around networks and linear inter-actor relationships. By their nature, such responses are more *ad hoc* and opportunistic and thus also variable and unpredictable. No longer is spatiality the main organising parameter alone, but rather linkages and connectivities through actor networks. These are defined through the reach, direction and distribution of linear relationships, rather than through boundaries drawn around contiguous spaces, where everyone belonging to that space is automatically included in the relevant policies. This linearity, however, by its nature, differentiates sharply between those actors who are connected to, and by, these linear connections, and those who find themselves outside, that is in between those lines. As a result, such 'in between spaces' find a more restricted access to, and scope to participate in, policy-making networks and thus opportunity to impact on the formulation and implementation of policy agendas.

The distribution of these connections and linkages varies, of course, with the differing relative functional importance and thus variety and 'reach' of linkages , leading to their clustering or grouping. And urban centres, especially larger metropolitan areas or city regions, may be expected to attract and generate more connections, that is a denser clustering of them, than smaller and more sparsely populated areas. In other words, metropoiltan areas as clusters of inter-urban functional relationships and policy and actor networks, will produce virtual regions (Herrschel, 2007) which underlie and, through their virtual boundaries, circumscribe, these network clusters and differentiate them from the other places and regions outside the urban clusters. A good example of this is the relationship between the conventional, administrative Skåne region in southern Sweden, with its large rural interior and concentration of cities along the coast line facing Denmark. It is around those, that the virtual Øresund region was built, reaching out to Copenhagen and the other urban centres along the opposite Danish coast, linked since 2000 by the Øresund Bridge as a clearly visible and usable symbol of connectivity. What can be observed, is the emergence of a dynamic, increasingly internationally oriented virtual region, successfully marketed as the Øresund Region. This is based around the main cities – all on the coast – and their respective functional interconnections. And the spatial manifestations of these circumscribe the spatial extent – and thus virtual boundary, of this virtual region. Within it, the cities all look at each other, so to speak, and, especially via Copenhagen, further afield to continental Europe and beyond. They do not look 'behind their backs' towards the interior, rural part of the Skåne region, or to Stockholm, much further beyond There is thus an invisible, but potentially very effective, dividing line manifesting itself within the Skåne region, *de facto* separating the dynamic, internationally connected urban-defined Øresund region from the rural, less dynamic and more inward-looking hinterland to the east. There is a danger, therefore, of the Skåne region, despite being administratively one entity, effectively falling into two halves, each developing its own dynamics and trajectory. And a similar process, albeit less strongly marked out, may also be expected for the Danish region Seeland, surrounding the Copenhagen Capital Region, which is part of the Øresund region.

As a consequence, therefore, new peripheries and exclusions may be created, whether deliberate or not, and they may be within as well as between the core areas. They embrace conventional geographic peripheral regions as well as, at a smaller scale, 'cores', that is city regions. They are therefore not merely the result of geographic distance from a core, but rather of communicative, participative distance to functional networks between policy-making actors. And this distance circumscribes the scope to participate in, and influence, decision making and outcomes. It is thus not merely about infra-structure alone shaping communication and reachability, although this does play an important role, permitting face-to-face contacts, as the Øresund Bridge clearly demonstrates. Some of these actors may participate in different networks at the same time, in the simultaneous pursuit of varying interests, and thus enhance their relevance and efficacy as part of that. These networks may be overlapping and overlaying, following variable geometries of engagement and prioritising, and thus producing differences in density across space. Some such actors, be they individuals, institutions or localities, may thus gain dominant roles in an emerging hierarchy of the nodes within such networks. Borrowing Amin and Thrift's (1995) term of 'institutional thickness', perhaps one could refer to 'communicative thickness', meaning the bundeling of connectivities in some areas, while avoiding others. Effectively, therefore, the two types of peripherality – spatial and social-communicative – may overlap and intersect, creating varying combinations of degrees of geographic and communicative (social) marginalities. This is referred to here as 'composite peripherality'. Conceptually, it combines conventional neo-cassical models of geographically defined distance-dependent costs and duration of conveying information and products, and the more recent behavioural approaches underpinning actor network theory with its relational perspective and emphasis on relationships between actors as nodes. In a wider, societal context, this has also been referred to as 'network society' (Castells, 2010).

Peripherality is thus a more complex phenomenon than merely the conventional notion of being 'on the edge' of a territory. Grabher (2006) points to the *connection* between the two concepts of peripherality – 'place' and 'flow' – that is the impact on inter-actor connectivities through variations in spatial economic competitiveness, when he refers to the forming of networks between economic sociology and economic geography. But he also points out that such a link is not a straightforward causal relationship between the variability of economic geography. For instance, a variation in the 'globalness' between localities alone not necessarily translates directly into 'more centrality', and thus more influential and stronger networks and network connections they may produce or be part of. Conversely, a lack of 'globalness' may be automatically interpreted as an expression of inward-looking localness which, in turn, suggests immediately marginality and thus 'weak' ties to other players. Yet

Figure 1: Composite Peripherality as Combination of Spatial Peripherality ('edgeness') and Network-shaped Peripherality ('in-between-ness')

		Spatial Peripherality ('edgeness')	
		High	Low
Network-shaped Peripherality ('in-between-ness')	High	**'Downward spiral':** Least connected, combines spatial and social peripherality, danger of downward spiral of marginalization	**'Passive':** Centrally located but not capable to connect well – excluded? Lethargic? Discouraged?
	Low	**'Held back':** Spatial 'on the edge' peripherality (externally perceived?) with good network-based connectivity. Suggests initiative and capacity within 'periphery'.	**'Advantaged':** Highly connected, 'strong' links, important node in network, sought after node and network

such direct causality is somewhat simplistic and has been questioned (Amin, 2002).

Nevertheless, irrespective of the particular nature of their relationship to each other, it is possible to distinguish two main dimensions of peripherality which intersect and interrelate (see Figure 1) and, in doing so, also shape each other:

Network-based 'in between' marginalisation refers to exclusions and thus marginalisations of actors, be they persons, institutions or places (as grouped local actors). Here, marginalisation is the result of being situated 'between' the main corridors of communication (Herrschel 2009), that is in the meshes of a network web. The reasons for this are diverse, including the impact of past experiences, personalities, established ways of doing things, local circumstances and, possibly, an exclusion or rejection by other actors for lack of 'attractiveness' and likely benefit from involvement. The result is a weaker engagement with policy-making actor networks, either because of limited capacity to 'link up', or because of defensive barriers around the network to protect its members from new entrants who may 'disturb' the existing balance of power.

'Conventional' spatial peripherality of places as the backdrop to actor engagement, shaping their ambitions, interests, priorities and expertise. This form of 'on-the-edge' peripherality also has a distinct external dimension to it. This is, because the degree to which localities or regions are perceived as 'peripheral' by those *outside* (that is in the core areas) and thus little 'advantageous' to engage with. This, in turn, may well curtail the scope of such 'remote' places or actors to step out of such peripheralisation. Nevertheless, even in such contextual spatial peripherality, some actors may be more astute than others in a similar situation to engage with other actors after all and manage to actively participate in policy-making networks. In effect, the networking skill of such actors counteracts (or overcomes) the barriers created by actual or perceived peripherality.

Differences in the responses by policy makers to their relative geographic centrality or peripherality – whether perceived or actual - lead to varying combinations of the two types of peripherality - 'on the edge' and 'in between', which result in com*posite peripherality*', as shown in Figure 1. In case of the two types of peripherality coinciding, the result a 'double peripherality' could well lead to a mutual reinforcement of marginality. Being on the spatial 'edge' and not well connected socially will make breaking out of such marginality very difficult, as there are unlikely to be many other actors willing to engage and 'team up' with such a peripheral case.

Governance of 'In between' and 'on the edge' peripheralities

Conventionally, regions have been part of a hierarchy of clearly bounded territories (Leitner, 1997, Leitner et al, 2002 ; Paasi, 2002). More recently, regions have increasingly become also associated with less formalised alliances around actor networks (Clegg, 1997) which were brought together by shared policy objectives at a particular time (Herrschel 2005, 2009). In this 'new', less territorially fixed understanding of sub-national regionalism, it is economic pressures which continue to be seen as the main drivers of these changes. They push for flexible responses through variable horizontal cooperation between localities, institutions, administrative departments and individual policy makers. Yet it still does not seem entirely clear whether, following actor network thinking (Lagendijk and Cornford, 2000), actors are not, in fact, also shaped by their very own actions in their ways of doing things, so that there is a behavioural loop. This could mean both a further (defensive) entrenchment in set ways by established actors and networks *vis-a-vis* emerging new players on the policy-making arena, in a bid to preserve the status quo and such existing influence. Alternatively, however, it could mean a positive engagement with such emergent new players in the search for new, even innovative, ways of defining and implementing specific policy agendas.

Some twenty years ago, Castells (1989) and, shortly afterwards, Sassen (1991) argued that cities and city regions had gained a 'new strategic role' in a globalisation and knowledge-driven 'new spatial logic', first and foremost revolving around economic development (Herrschel and Newman, 2002). This 'new logic' involves dynamic, continuous change, lesser importance of administrative spatial entities, variable collaborative arrangements as drivers of economic and political (and social) spatialities and a growing reliance on communicative social-political networks and connections. Castells (1996) implies this differentiation between 'cores' and 'the rest' when he refers to the contrast between the new concept of regions and city regions as dynamic 'spaces of flows'. They contrast with the conventional perception of territory as contiguous, static 'space of places'. There is thus a shift from understanding territory as a fixed localisation of places to the (new) idea of spaces being variably defined, also as 'in betweens' in a networked arrangement. Consequently, it is the linear spaces that matter, leaving 'the rest' in between behind. And Taylor (2004) demonstrates that the proclaimed World City Network as top level international network *per definitionem* focuses on a selected few big metropolitan nodes only, relegating the rest to *relatively* more peripheral 'also rans'. Communicative 'distance' – actual and/or perceived - between actors is thus not necessarily a direct function of geographic distance alone, but also of organisational arrangements, political affinities and personal and institutional cultures and practices. The resulting "geographies of centrality and marginality" (Paasi, 2006, p 194), be they spatial or social-cultural, will, by their very nature, create new, and reinforce old, inequalities and divisions, inclusions and exclusions in relation to identified centres and 'cores'.

The search for new forms of collaborative, flexible and network-based mechanisms of governance may well entrench old, and create new, exclusions and marginalisations. While on the one hand such a 'new regionalist' trend may help enhance economic competitiveness through improved international visibility of economic spaces through joint marketing and representation of a larger entity, it does not necessarily do so for all places and actors 'contained' within such larger co-operative entity. Nor will it grant all of them the same degree of influence on policy proceedings, thus raising questions about democratic representativeness and the legitimacy of policy.

Conventionally, peripherality has been understood in a spatial context, usually in the context core-periphery models and here variable (uneven) economic development. Peripheries have thus become associated with marginality, that is being on the edge of contiguous spaces, where 'edge' is understood as remoteness, distance from central nodes. This concept has underpinned established spatial development policies with their focus on managing perceived disadvantages of an area, especially distance as economic cost as expressed through transport cost and derived -peripherality indices (Combes and Lafourcade, 2005). Changes here, especially the rapidly growing role and reach of low cost flights, as well as the development of the Trans-European Network (TEN) of high-speed railway lines have altered the degree of peripherality in many instances. Yet both connectivities are strictly linear, linked into networks of varying mesh sizes, and highly selective in their localized de-peripheralising effect by their sparse setting of stations, for instance.

The now expansive trans-European route network of the airline Ryanair illustrates this change most drastically. Preferring for cost reasons to fly to little known second and third tier airports, often former military airstrips, it has connected many small provincial places to an international flight network. Yet many of these places serve as little more than transit points for the ultimate destination for passengers who are being ushered there by special transfer buses. And these just by-pass the localities that gave the respective airports their names. The impression of connectivity by those places featuring on the Ryanair route map, may be useful as a first step of raising awareness of a locality and its region, but that does not necessarily translate into a real step out of peripherality.

The notion of peripherality, and how to address it, may thus appear less clear cut than initially assumed. In most instances, it is associated with geographic distance from a presumed core/centre, 'Remoteness' and 'edgeness' become seen as two sides of the same coin. They are being assessed with the help of "peripherality indices' (Copus, 1999; Schürmann and Talaat, 2000) related to accessibility. By contrast, peripherality as 'in between-ness' reflects the notion of 'being left out', by-passed, or simply being 'excluded' or 'pushed aside', even if located in a *geographically* central position. Copus (2001) terms this 'aspatial peripherality', as this contrasts with the conventional geographic understanding of 'spatial peripherality'. The term 'in between peripherality', as suggested here, tries to reflect the patchy nature of the mesh defined by the network linkages and connections, and varying points of reference for defining 'peripheral' or 'marginal' as a relative quality.

Connectivity through physical infrastructure effectively manifests and perpetuates the status quo of who is 'in' and who is 'out' of the competition for achieving better economic opportunity and development for being perceived as too peripheral. And spatial peripherality also translates into functional political peripherality with its impact on the nature of local agendas, the composition and relevance of actors, the quality, reach and effectiveness of alliances, and the types and creativity of networks, including their ability to redefine and rejuvenate themselves in response to changing conditions and circumstances. The growing importance of such non-spatial factors requires, so Copus (2001), to revisit existing concepts and presumptions which were based on a spatial paradigm of 'remoteness' and 'centrality' as expressions of economic opportunity, or the lack of it.

Given their varying and complex nature, networks and their characteristics and functioning have attracted attention from both sociologists and economists, although the two approach the topic from quite different directions. While economists have focused on networks from a strategic, managerial business perspective, driven by an economic rationality, sociologists have focused more on the personality factor and the circumstances within which actors are situated and, subsequently, on the basis of which they make their decisions (see e.g. Burger and Buskens, 2009). As Couldry (2006) points out, it is the number of connections that produce influence, power and relevance. Networks depend in their 'impact' on the power, influence and effectiveness of those using it and, in return, circumscribe an actor's scope for 'being heard' and make effective policy. There has been some discussion on the essence of an actor network, focusing on its on the one hand integrated, systemic, 'active' organising as well as 'passive' organised nature (Silverstone 1994) and, on the other, its more open, *ad hoc* and personality-based so-ciological characteristics as an inter-personal 'network' (Law, 1999).

This reflects a difference in emphasis on the underlying *ad hoc* nature of networks, which changes with the characteristics, *modi operandi* and objectives of the participating members. Their agen-das, at a particular time, are thus expected to shape the network which, in turn, will circumscribe scope and likely agendas for the actors. The question then is, how responsive to changing conditions and circumstance a network is and can be, and what scope there is for actors to join or leave in response to their changing objectives, priorities and conditions. Will those shaping the network allow newcomers, be they places, individuals or institutions, to join and, potentially, 'upset' the established balance of power and ways of doing things within it?

By their very nature, actor networks are much more difficult to change and 'engineer' compared with 'geographic distance', where building a motorway or high speed rail link or opening a new airport, even if by simply converting former military airstrips, may provide an effective means of overcoming 'distance' and thus marginalisation from development and decision-making processes.

Such 'hard' infrastructure' is relatively easy to deliver and allows politically effective highly visible big physical projects and grand openings with ribbon cutting ceremonies. On that basis, peripherality indices have been constructed to measure peripherality across the EU, for instance, with reachability of places the main focus (see e.g. Copus, 1999). Other, so-called 'soft infrastructure', such as skills, expertise, attitudes, image and economic structure, is more difficult to manipulate and pinpoint to individual 'big projects'. Making people and institutions communicate, work together, trust each other and become part of functional networks is yet more difficult to 'facilitate'. There needs to be a shared perception of advantages for all concerned emanating from such an engagement. Only then, a 'new player' will be accepted to an existing network, or an individual actor will want to join a network. With growing competitive pressures, especially following the financial crash of 2008, there will be much less willingness to accept actors and places that are not seen as making a positive contribution to the whole network, benefiting all involved. There need to be clearly definable advantages resulting from such a move. The scale of such engagement varies, too, embracing national, international (e.g. EU, see e.g. Alonso, 1991) and global (Wanmali and Islam, 1997) definitions of 'periphery'.

Regions, peripherality and 'spaces *between* flows'

The in effect virtual nature of network-circumcribed spaces of governance (Herrschel, 2007, 2009; Allen et al 1998, Heeg et al 2003) permits, in principle, actors to join and leave without having to surrender powers or being tied in institutionally with high exit barriers. This is one of the main advantages of such arrangements as viewed from the individual participants concerned, as it allows to retain powers and thus about the legitimacy of subsequent policy decisions. The degree to which shared and agreed policy agendas can bundle otherwise diverse actor interests and formulate, coordinate and collaboratively implement them, is significantly shaped by macro-political (that is primarily national) contexts (Kantor 2008).

The Baltic Sea Region is one such network-based space, embracing different spatial scales from local to international, with the Baltic Sea providing the geographic focus and identification, while the regionalisation processes – cutting across spatial scales and involving differently sized countries (Jaakson R, 2000) – occur at the policy-specific level. They are increasingly focused on ecological initiatives next to (sustainable) economic development between differently sized groups of countries. A recent Nordregio Report (Baldersheim et al, 2009) argues for the growing emergence of a 'network regionalism' with a more collaborative *modus operandi*, increasingly to replace the much more competitiveness-driven and economy-focused 'new regionalism'. How far such developments can be interpreted as a shift to yet another type of regionalism remains, however, to be seen. The picture seems to be complex, even 'messy', with different *modi operandi* overlapping and being pursued simultaneously by individual actors who seek to follow perceived 'best effectiveness' of different policy approaches.

Conclusions: Network regions and peripheries through both 'edgeness' and 'in between-ness'

Concern about economic (global) competitiveness drives an increasingly localised urban-, especially city-region-, focused policy agenda at national and EU levels. This threatening to undermine cohesion agendas, as its highly selective nature dissects wider, geographically coherent policy spaces, such as regions, into more narrowly defined network constructs with their emphasis on linear connections between singular nodes. These nodes can sit at different scales, comprising individual actors, such as organisations, institutions or individuals, but also whole localities, especially cities and city regions. The nature of networks means that space gets effectively reduced to a number of narrow, avenues of communication and interaction between actors, rather than encompassing two-dimensional territories. The scope to belong to a *network* as a strategic objective is quite different from the so far much more spatially driven territorially-based approach (different source and nature of peripherality), where the location of an individual actor in an area also means automatically belonging to it. In contrast, by their very nature, `networks cannot cover a space contiguously. Instead, they 'leave out' – deliberately or unintentionally – some sections by subdividing a space into separate 'corridors of (preferred) connectivity', separated by the 'by-passed' areas – or institutional or individual actors - in between these 'corridors'. Size and number of these in-between spaces depend on the density of actor nodes (organisations, localities, personalities) and network connections, and reflect new, or reinforce old, divisions between the 'included' and 'excluded', that is the *de facto* marginalised. And this marginalisation is not solely a geographic phenomenon, but includes social relationships and communication. Geography, of course, continues to matter, as it circumscribes developmental prospects of spaces *per se,* whether economy or environment, for instance, based on actual or perceived reachability and thus likely relevance for decision makers. But there are further, more detailed, sharper differentiations that operate through socio-political relationships and linkages, and create variable and potentially volatile and unpredictable inclusions and exclusions. Individual actors may choose to engage with only a certain group of actors, not, however, others, although they would all be equally 'reachable'. While physical infrastructure in its varying presence immediately translates into a public perception of difference in accessibility -usually expressed as distance costs (Copus 2001) -, social-political connectivities are much less obvious to identify. They are thus more difficult to gauge and predict in their likely impact. They are also much less easy to alter or, indeed, utilise. While physical infrastructure can be modified through investment, thus altering perceptions of distance and thus marginality, connectivities between political and economic actors are much more difficult to influence, observe, let alone measure. In contrast to physical infrastructure, they may also seek to actively protect the status quo with all its inclusions and exclusions, as they may suit the incumbents' agendas. As a result, marginalised actors, in their varied forms, may find it difficult to join, so as not to upset the existing relationships and balances of power negotiated between those who are part of the system and thus 'included' in the process of shaping and implementing decisions and control, and those who are not.

Different strategies may thus be required for new entrants to join existing networks and thus overcome their exclusion from, and marginality to, them. These differences require further, detailed study to gain a better understanding of response strategies, mechanisms and roles, and the capabilities of different types of actors to move between, and join and/or establish new, networks to pursue their individual – also varying over time - goals. How are the various emerging new divisions getting noticed and responded to? How do they manifest themselves? And does the scale of operation and ambition matter? What are the respective roles of 'real' and 'imagined' qualities of marginality? In the European context, divisions between those actors and areas that are either 'included' or 'excluded', either entirely or only for selected agendas and policy processes, may well lead to a two-speed Europe, where, in the longer run, "a small number of metropolitan city regions and a patchworks of functional spaces in the regions in between and in the periphery will characterise the spatial pattern of Europe" (Kunzmann, 2010, p 612). And this pattern will be very different from the ideas of a spatially coherent and cohesive continent.

REFERENCES

Albrechts, L and Mandelbaum, S (eds, 2005): *The Network Society. A New Context for Planning.* London: Routledge

Allen, J., Massey, D. and Cochrane, A. (1998): *Rethinking the Region.* London: Routledge.

Alonso, A (1991): *Europe's Urban System and Its Peripheries.* In: Journal of the American Planning Association, Vol, no , pp 6 - 13

Amin, A and Thrift, N (1995): *Globalisation, Institutional Thickness' and The Local Economy.* Chichester: Wiley.

Amin, A (2002): *Spatialities of Globalisation.* In: Environment and Planning A, vol 34, no 3, pp 385 – 399

Baldersheim, H; Haug, A and Øgård, M (2009): *The Rise Of The Networking Region: The Challenges Of Regional Collaboration In A Globalized World.*

Nordic Research Programme 2005-2008. Report 10. Stockholm: Nordregio. ISSN 1654-2290.

Borgatti, S and Everett,M (2006): *A Graph-theoretic perspective on centrality.* In: Social Networks, vol 28, no 4, pp 466-484

Burger, M and Buskens, V (2009): *Social Context and Network Formation: An Experimental Study'*, In: Social Networks, 31(1), 63-75

Cappelen, A; Castellacci, F; Fagerberg, J and Verspagen, B (2003): *The Impact of EU Regional Support on Growth and Convergence in the European Union.* In: JCMS: Journal of Common Market Studies, Vol 41, no 4, pp 621–644.

Castells, M (2010): *The Rise of the Network Society,* Volume I: The Information Age: Economy, Society, and Culture. Oxford: Blackwell-Wiley, 2nd ed

Castells, M (1996): *The Space of Flows.* In: M Castells (ed): The Rise of he Network Society. Vol 1: The Information Age. Pp 376-482. Oxford: Blackwell

Clegg, S. (1997): *Frameworks of Power,* London: Sage.

Combes, P and Lafourcade, M (2005): *Transport costs: measures, determinants, and regional policy implications for France.* In: Journal of Economic Geography, vol 5, no 3, pp 319-349

Copus, A (1999): *A New Peripherality Index for the NUTS III Regions of the European Union.* ERDF/FEDER Study 98/00/27/130. A Report for the European Commission, Directorate General XVI.A.4 (Regional Policy and Cohesion). Aberdeen, Sep 1999. Unpublished. Available under (accessed 10 Dec 2009): http://citeseerx.ist.psu.edu/viewdoc/download?doi=10.1.1.131.4848&rep=rep1&type=pdf

Copus, A (2001): *From Core-periphery to Polycentric Development: Concepts of Spatial and Aspatial Peripherality.* In: European Planning Studies, Vol. 9, No. 4, 2001, pp

Couldry, N (2006): *Actor Network Theory and Media: Do they Connect and on What Terms?* In: Andreas Hepp, Friedrich Krotz, Shaun Moores, and Carsten Winter (eds): Konnektivität, Netzwerk und Fluss: Konzepte gegenwärtiger Medien-, Kommunikations- und Kulturtheorie, pp 101-117. Wiesbaden: Verlag für Sozialwissenschaften.

Cox, K (1997): *Spaces of Globalization: Reasserting the Power of the Local.* New York: Guilford Press

ESDP (1999): *European Spatial Development Perspective, Towards Balanced and Sustainable Development of the Territory of the EU.* Luxemburg: CEC.

Grabher, G (2006): *Trading Routes, Bypasses, And Risky Intersections:* Mapping The Travels Of `Networks' Between Economic Sociology And Economic Geography. In: Progress in Human Geography, vol 30, no 2, pp 163-189

Heeg, S., Klagge, B. and Ossenbrügge, J.(2003): *Metropolitan Cooperation in Europe:* Theoretical Issues and Perspectives for Urban Networking. In: European

Planning Studies, vol 11, no 2, pp. 139–153.

Herrschel, T and Newman, P (2002): Governance of Europe's City Regions. London: Routledge.

Herrschel, T (2009): *Regionalisation, 'virtual' spaces and 'real' territories.* A view from Europe and North America. In International Journal of Public Sector Management, vol 22, no 3, pp 261-272;

Herrschel, T (2005): *Creative Regionalisation. Making Regions for Upscale and Downscale Consumption* – Experiences from Post-socialist Eastern Germany. In: Geojournal, vol 62, no 1, pp 63-69,

Herrschel, T (2007): *Regions between imposed structure and internally developed response.* Experiences with twin track regionalisation in post-socialist eastern Germany. In: Geoforum, Volume 38, Issue 3, Pages 469-484.

Hospers, G (2003): *Beyond the Blue Banana?* In: Intereconomics, Vol 38, no 2, pp 76-85.

Jaakson R (2000): *Supra-national Spatial Planning of the Baltic Sea Region and Competing Narratives for Tourism.* In: European Planning Studies, Vol 8, No 5, pp. 565-579

Jones, C; Hesterly, W; Borgatti, S (1997): *General Theory of Network Governance*: Exchange Conditions and Social Mechanisms. In: Academy of Management Review, vol 22; no 4, pp 911-945.

Kantor, P (2008): *Varieties of city regionalism and the quest for political cooperation:* a comparative perspective. In: Urban Research & Practice Vol. 1, No. 2, July 2008, 111–129

Keating, M (1998): *The New Regionalism in Western Europe.* Cheltenham: Edward Elgar

Kunzmann, K (2010) *After the Global Economic Crisis*: Policy Implicatons for the Future of the European Territory. In Informationen zur Raumentwicklung, no 8/2010, pp 801-812. Bonn: Bundesinstitut für Bau-, Stadt- und Raumforschung.

Lagendijk, A and Cornford, J (2000): *Regional Institutions and Knowledge* – Tracking New Forms of Regional Development Policy. In: Geoforum, vol 31, pp 209-218.

Law, J (1999): *After ANT: Complexity, Naming and Typology.* In: Law, J and Hassard, J (eds): Actor Network Theory and After. Oxford: Blackwell, pp 1-14

Leitner, H (1997): *Reconfiguring the Spatiality of Power*: the Construction of a Supranational Migration Framework for the European Union. In Political Geography, vol 16, no 2, pp 123-143

Leitner, H; Pavlik, C and Sheppard, E (2002): *Networks, Governance and the Politics of Scale.* Inter-urban Networks and the European Union. In: Herod, E and Wright, M (eds): Geographies of Power: Placing Scale. Oxford: Wiley, pp 274-303

MacLeod, G (2001): *New Regionalism Reconsidered*: Globalization and the Remaking of Political Economic Space. In: International Journal of Urban and Regional Research, vol 25, no 4, pp 804 - 829

Paasi, A (2006): *Cities in a World Economy.* 3 ed., London: Pine Forge Press.

Paasi, A (2002): *Place and region: regional worlds and words.* In: Progress in Human Geography, Vol. 26, No. 6, pp 802-811

Radaelli, C (2000): *Policy Transfer in the European Union*: Institutional Isomorphism as a Source of Legitimacy. In: Governance, vol 13, no 1, pp 25–43,

Sassen, S (1991): *Global Cities and Global City Regions* – A Comparison. In: A J Scott (ed): The Global City. London: Princeton University Press

– Sauders, P (1994): *Welfare and Inequality: National and International Perspectives on the Australian Welfare State.* Cambriege: Cambridge University Press)

Schürmann, C and Talaat, A (2000): *Towards a European Peripherality Index User-Manual.* Report forGeneral Directorate XVI Regional Policy of the European Commission Dortmund, November 2000. Published as Berichte aus dem Institut für Raumplanung, no 52. Accessible through: https://eldorado. tu-dortmund.de/handle/2003/26579

Scott, J (1988): *Social Network Analysis.* In: Sociology, Vol. 22, No. 1, 109-127

Silverstone, R (1994): *Television and Everyday Life.* London: Routledge

Taylor, P.J. (2004): *The New Geography of Global Civil Society*: NGOs in the World City Network. In: Globalizations, vol. 1, no. 2, pp. 265–277

Wanmali, S and Islam, Y (1997): *Rural Infrastructure and Agricultural Development in Southern Africa*: A Centre-Periphery Perspective. In: The Geographical Journal, Vol. 163, No. 3, pp. 259-269

Whitehead, M (2003): *'In The Shadow of Hierarchy'*: Meta-Governance, Policy Reform and Urban Regeneration in The West Midlands', In: Area, vol 35, no1, pp. 6-14.

PETTER BOYE – LINNAEUS UNIVERSITY, SWEDEN

The Role of OECD Territorial Reviews in Policy Conception and (Contemporary) Regional Development

Introduction

In 2003 the OECD came out with the first in a series of territorial reviews on urban and metropolitan areas[1]. Until 2010 it has been almost 20 reports on metropolitan regions and in addition to these, also many reviews of OECD countries including metropolitan regions. The OECD territorial reviews are believed to be important and there are different kinds of indications on that. Firstly, *the processes of making these reports are engaging a lot of different actors and resources* from OECD and, especially the regions involved who are financing the reports.

Secondly, *policy-makers and other decision-makers frequently read these OECD reports*. In an international conference[2], held in Gothenburg in April 2010, where an estimated 70 policy-makers and researchers were present, more than 50 percent had read at least one OECD territorial report in the past twelve months.

Thirdly, *policy-makers often refer to OECD reports*. According to Alasuutari & Rasimus (2009), who studied documents from national policy debates in Finland between 1991 and 2008, about 3 percent of the total amount of documents referred to OECD. A similar study in Canada (Alasuutari & Pal, 2010), between 1997 and 2009 also shows a substantial amount of references to OECD in national policy documents.

During the international conference in Gothenburg 2010 the role of OECD territorial reviews on metropolitan areas was discussed among policy-makers involved in regional development. The discussion focused on a set of questions, which were believed to be exceedingly intriguing.

- What are the OECD conclusions and suggestions on regional governance?
- How do they correspond with contemporary practice?
- Is there a specific 'OECD policy' or does the perspective in the territorial reviews only reflect the opinions in each region? Does it matter?
- *How* has the OECD perspective on metropolitan policy developed and *why*?

This chapter will highlight these questions, by discussing: (1) the role of policy and concepts in regional development, beginning with what we know about regional policy transfer and policy learning; (2) the OECD influence on policy concepts and (3) how region (policy) concepts influence practice.

The questions above are relevant to the on-going strategic development process in the Öresund region and the Stockholm region. In 2010, Stockholm did a follow-up of the OECD territorial review from 2006 and in 2011 the OECD will present a territorial review of Skåne County; situated in the Swedish part of the Öresund region. In this chapter the experiences from the development in these and other regions are compared with the development of the framework used in the OECD territorial reviews.

The model used in this chapter to explain concept-driven processes was originally developed during comparative studies of transnational regionalization processes in the late 1990's (see Boye, 1997, 1999) and has then been further developed (e.g. Boye, 2008). It has, after this, been further developed during a series of longitudinal studies of strategic processes in the Öresund region. The model builds mainly on a theoretical framework of the social institutional theory

(Whitley, 1992) and the resource based theory (Wernerfelt, 1984; Barney, 1991; Grant, 1991; 1996). The general methodology used is case study (e.g. Yin, 1991; Merriam, 1998) and abductive approach, being a mix of deduction and induction (Alvesson & Sköldberg, 1994; Boye, 1999). The model of concept-driven processes is here related to the theories of policy transfer (e.g. Stone, 1999; Dolowitz & Marsh, 1996) and policy learning (Hall, 1990), partly using a similar theoretical framework. The main perspective used focus on social construction and the role of institutional agents.

The role of policy and concepts in regional development

From policy transfer to policy learning

As a starting point we will look at the purpose of the OECD territorial reviews of metropolitan areas as expressed by OECD in 2003[3]:

"The objectives of territorial reviews are:

a) identify the nature and scale of territorial challenges using a common analytical framework;

b) assist governments in the assessment and improvement of their territorial policy, using comparative policy analysis;

c) assess the distribution of competencies and resources among the different levels of governments; and

d) identify and disseminate information on best practices regarding territorial policy and governance."

Regarding the purpose of the OECD territorial reviews of metropolitan, this can be seen as a matter of "policy transfer" (see e.g. Stone, 1999; Dolowitz & Marsh, 1996). Stone (1999) refers to Dolowitz & Marsh (1996) and Evans (1999), arguing that the term policy transfer is related to other terms, emphasizing certain aspects of such transfer. Following this discussion, policy transfer can be seen as the result of four types of processes:

First, *lesson drawing* (Rose, 1993) is a voluntaristic process where a decision-making elite import policies developed in another country or region. Stone (1999) points out, by referring to Robertson (1991), that lesson-drawing is not politically neutral.

Second, *external inducement* (Ikenberry, 1990) is a coercive, not voluntaristic process where policy makers in one country or region have an impact on how policy is developed in another country or region.

Third, *policy convergence* or *policy diffusion* (e.g. Stone, 1999) is a process driven by structural forces where the policy-making elite has a more passive role. This kind of process tend to be more coercive and the regional policy becomes more reactive towards external forces, e.g. in the EU.

Fourth, *policy learning* (Hall, 1990) is a process characterized by cognition and redefinition of interest based on new knowledge. This kind of process influences the underlying beliefs and ideas upon which policies are made. This process, as pointed out by Stone (1999), does not necessarily end up with policy transfer. It may as well result in a new unique policy or termination of a certain policy. Compared to the three other processes, this kind of process seems to be characterized by being voluntaristic and driven by structural forces rather than by strong policy-making elites

Furthermore, OECD territorial reviews are tools for cross-national (or regional) policy comparisons and, in that way they can contribute to innovation. Schneider & Ingram (1991) argue that national governments tend to be introverted and unless examples from other countries (and regions) are brought forth through analysis, changes will be incremental.

Regional policy and context dependence – towards an idea- and concept-driven development process

Comparative studies can be used, not only to learn what can be transferred from one region to another, but also to learn about unique contexts in different regions. In order to learn about the strategic pre-conditions concerning the development of growth poles in cross-border regions a comparative study of three growth poles was conducted in the end of the 1990's (see Boye, 1997, 1999). The regions: the Hong Kong-Guangdong region (in China), The SIJORI-region, including Singapore-Johor (in Indonesia)-Riau (in Malaysia) and the Öresund region represented different geopolitical contexts.

At the same time they were all cross-border metropolitan regions with an internationally competitive industry. The comparative study focused on an industrial regionalization process and revealed three ideal types of transnational industrial regionalization processes: market-, policy-, and idea-driven processes.

The market-driven integration process, which seems to be the pre-dominant mode in Hong Kong, is based on resource-complementarities, such as a factor market with heterogeneity in demand and supply among actors in different sub-regions. If left to natural market forces, this will develop a high degree of economic connections linking the sub-regions. Such economic linkages between regions can take several forms, including: investment flows; flows of labour, skill, and technological know-how; commodity/service flows through vertical value chain linkages or general trades through market transactions; and flows of household and tourist consumptions spending. In an ideal situation, the establishment of these regional ties through free-market competitive forces would cause allocations of resources to be optimized, resulting in net welfare gains from the efficient exploitation of resource complementarities and agglomeration economies (Barney and Ouchi 1986). This exploitation, by actors trying to maximize their profit through rational calculation, will include vertical specialization across the border, resulting in economies of scale and scope[4] (Chandler 1990, Milgrom and Roberts 1992).

The policy-driven integration process, which to a high degree seems to characterize the SIJORI region, is based on government regulations and policy regimes. Consequently, inter-regional economic linkages may fail to develop fully or not at all. The process is initiated by or pursued according to a vision usually expressed in a written contract or document. Ordinarily a course or principle of action is adopted or proposed by the government, following a previous decision or agreement, committing it to participate in the process as a facilitator. This political intention or plan generally includes facilitating cross-border flows of investments, labour, finance, and goods; or the provision of adequate infrastructure for transport and communication, as well as promoting investments in the region, including reducing the political risk involved. Due to the critical role of the government, this aspect of regionalization processes can also be seen as a "top-down" government-driven integration process.

The idea-driven integration process, which is particularly visible in the Öresund region, is based on one or more abstract ideas or general notions held by the dominant coalitions in the region. Such images or regional definitions are utilized to give the region an identity or image in order to create a favourable position in the international arena and attract investors to the region. Popular regional concepts or identities usually have a functional approach to an international arena, such as seeing regions as: competence centres, infrastructure and communication hubs and gateways, potential home markets, etc. Concepts are commonly used to communicate an *idea* or *mental picture*, trying to justify the allocation of additional resources, feeding a further integration process. Often it seems as if the regionalization process in the Öresund region is driven by multiple competing ideas and concepts that, in turn, vary during the process.

These are all processes aimed at increased interaction. However, unlike the market-driven process, which is mainly based on the activities of companies, and the policy-driven process, which to a great extent depends on the government's intentions and actions, the idea-driven process involves a mix of significant institutional agents. Different organizational actors, such as local authorities, firms, labour market organizations, educational and research organizations, have their own intentions and activities, and this influences the formation of the region.

Over time, these three driving forces that are briefly described above may occur in one region as a mix or in sequence, even though one is more dominant than the others. In the Öresund region, for example the regional development process includes different phases. The agreement to build a bridge between Sweden and Denmark in 1991 is an example of a political decision followed by a period consisting mainly of idea-driven process in the mid and late 1990's. The bridge, which was opened in 2000 in combination with differences in cost regarding labour, living, commodities and services in Copenhagen (Denmark) and Skåne County (Sweden) stimulated cross-border market integration. This in turn has increased the demand for a second physical link between the countries and in 2010 political decision-makers in Skåne County started to lobby for a new tunnel. At the same time it was decided for an OECD territorial review of Skåne County.

The anatomy of region concepts and the role of institutional agents

In the end of the 1990's, there were over a hundred mission and vision documents dealing with the Öresund region. However, only a few of these visions have been able to attract people's attention and grow stronger, thus favouring further action in line with that particular vision.

Some of these visions are more elaborate, and outline a distinct role or function for the region in a particular business or industrial context. These "region concepts" span from notions developed to position the region in its geopolitical context (e.g. a Learning Region in Northern Europe[5], a Hub for the Baltic Sea, a Maritime Centre located at the gateway to the Baltic Sea[6], etc.), to concepts based on particular competencies (e.g. Öresund Food Network, Medicon Valley, etc).

However, of all the mission and vision statements and region concepts proposed, just a few tend to endure, while others fade away. Strong region concepts, on the other hand, seem to survive, and serve as a trigger for action. These powerful concepts or cognitive frames are crucial to the constitution of the Öresund region – the region, as a concept, becomes the soil of the region itself. At the same time, the Öresund region becomes a stage for new concepts that, in turn, will trigger off further action and developments in the region. There are many competing concepts in the arena. They are the key elements – the essence – of the platform for action. Some of these region concepts tend to become institutionalized. These institutionalized concepts incorporate values and norms as well as enforcement mechanisms, such as incentives and sanctions. They do not solely have a crucial role in terms of guiding the development of the Öresund region, but they also have a persuasive effect on industry-related activity within the area. Old concepts generate new ones, and as a consequence, this emerging region, based on regional industrial concepts, could encourage the creation of new concepts, thus giving new meaning to the region.

A closer analysis reveals that the concepts that survive seem to contain five elements. To begin with–as concepts–they are *metaphorically rich,* giving a vivid impression of the core ideas in the concept. This implies, for example, the use of picturesque language in outlining the meaning of the concept, as well as symbols and metaphors for the key idea behind the concept, for example, "hub," "gateway," "bridge," "valley," "nexus" or "link." It is interesting to note how many of these metaphors allude to different forms of spatial clustering. The key idea here is to *establish cognitive frames* that "logically" and persuasively lead one's thoughts in a certain direction. This is often supported by "theoretical" arguments, using concepts such as economies of scale and scope, the notion of industrial clusters and core competencies, learning regions, innovation systems, triple helix and so on.

Another element often contained in the concept is its *positioning in a geopolitical context,* such as; "Northern Europe," "Scandinavia," "The Baltic Sea Region," or even the positioning in a global context in terms of "international competencies" or "global competitiveness." Embedding the concepts in a wider competitive context of, for example, international regionalization (this is especially evident within the EU) also relates the region to potential "competitor" and "customer" markets.

A third element which characterizes many of the region concepts is that they are based on *existing local competencies,* in terms of industry (e.g. "food industry," "medico-tech industry" etc), trade (e.g. "transport hub," "maritime centre" etc.) or service ("digital university" etc.). This makes the concept trustworthy, and secures adequate support in the region. But it is not only the "hard" competencies that are counted, but also those related to values, norms, and regulative institutions. The choice of the "Human Capital" as the brand concept actually indicates that "soft" competencies are considered to be particularly important in the Öresund region.

The fourth element is the use of *legitimating analogies* in the description of the concepts. Frequently this takes the form of comparisons or analogies to existing prosperous regions or metropolitan areas (e.g., the San Francisco Bay Area, Silicon Valley, Hong Kong, Singapore, or the Boston-Cambridge region in Massachusetts) that, in a way, are expressions of collectively valued standards. Reference to OECD and different regions and countries within also relate to this element. This legitimacy aspect is also recognized by Alasuutari and Rasimus (2009), who point out that the regions within OECD, are believed to be the most sophisticated and dynamic market economies. Furthermore, regional policy-makers might try to follow OECD standards of best practice, as it will contribute to the regions image of being qualified.

Finally, region concepts also contain references to *supportive agents and agencies* in and outside the region. The inscription of firms, labour market organizations, universities, government agencies and international governmental organizations such as the OECD, act not only as supporters, but also as partners in the various concepts, strongly support the case that has been made. Alasuutari and Rasimus (2009) identified different reasons for referring to OECD. Together with those mentioned above they also found three that relate more to the OECD itself. Firstly, OECD is believed to be reliable as its recommendations are based on research and science. Secondly, OECD is believed to be neutral and following its recommendations will contribute to increased competitiveness. Thirdly, OECD is believed to stand for "modernity" and adopting its conceptual framework will give the regional policy a sense of development towards something better (See also Lodge, 2005). A similar point is made by Eklund (2007), who studied the policy process of adopting the innovation system concept in Sweden. He found that, the use of the innovation system concept transferred legitimacy from the OECD to the already existing strategy of making the universities a resource for the economic needs in society. "If other countries in the OECD had transformed their research policy into an innovation policy, Sweden risked falling behind if it did not do the same." (Ibid: 135). However, Eklund also points out that the adoption of this popular OECD concept was not a "passive fashion-following reception", but rather a process where "domestic actors actively pursuing their own agendas, picking up and using fashionable concepts if and when it benefitted them" (Ibid: 145). This process is similar to how strategic actors in the Öresund region used popular region concepts in order to influence the development in line with their own interests.

The OECD *influence* on policy concepts

A policymaker perspective

Several scholars have recognized the OECD as an important agent influencing national and regional policy processes, as mentioned before. For example: OECD playing the role as referent in a process of *policy learning* (Hall, 1990) or the transfer of policy from international organizations, such as the OECD to national policy debates, giving the OECD a role as a *transfer agent* (Stone, 2003).

There are some basically different ways in which the OECD can influence policy concepts in particular countries and regions. Firstly, policy-makers can *adopt the content* of OECD-policy, i.e. recommendations and views of development trends etc. Secondly, policy-makers can *bench mark* their region's development in comparison with other regions and countries. Thirdly, policy-makers can, by referring the OECD, bring *legitimacy* to an already existing policy.

Experiences from Finland and Canada regarding OECD as an international referent in national policy debates show that there are different kinds of references. In Finland, Alasuutari & Rasimus (2009) identified four categories of references to the OECD, which where also evident in Canada (Alasuutari & Pal, 2010):

- *Comparisons between OECD countries (ranking – 'lagging' or 'leading')*. This category can be seen as a matter of bench marking.
- *The OECD as a body of expertise (a neutral body)*. This is a matter of legitimacy.
- *OECD models and recommendations (a source of detailed models and public policy recommendations)*. This is a matter of adopting content.
- *Adaption to global development trends (countries' need to adapt*

to global trends). This can be seen as a matter of adopting content.

The references to OECD are based on some common assumptions. In the Finnish case Alasuutari & Rasimus (2009: pp. 99-102) identified five assumptions for references to the OECD:

- OECD's image and respectability from credibility of science-based recommendations.
- OECD represents the 'most dynamic and advanced market economies'.
- Seeking an image of competence by emulating OECD standards.
- Following OECD recommendations will contribute to developing competitiveness.
- The importance of being 'modern' – taking part in the evolutionary process.

These assumptions can also be seen in the Swedish case concerning the innovation system concept (Eklund, 2007), where reference to OECD was made in order to give legitimacy to an already existing project.

In addition to the assumptions listed above there is also one, saying that *uniqueness is not important* and that *standard models are unproblematic.* When it comes to adopting the content of the OECD policy, policy-makers in different countries tend to de-emphasize the uniqueness of their own region or country. In the study by Alasuutari & Pal (2010), Canadian ministers referred to "...the OECD as an objective source of basic international models..." "...to portray policy initiatives as simple routine, reflecting standards of models that existed throughout the OECD and hence were unremarkable." (p 22) "In most of the references, the objective seemed to be to minimize national uniqueness and emphasize the overwhelming force of global trends and the consequent need to adapt to them." (ibid. p 22).

The OECD perspective on how to influence policy
- What does the OECD say about the territorial reviews influence on policy?

In addition to the national/regional perspective given by the previous discussion concerning national policy-makers references to the OECD we can take OECD's perspective. One way to do this is by

(1) studying the purposes and objectives given in the OECD reports and (2) studying what the OECD say about their own conceptual framework. In order to better understand the content of the OECD policy framework and how has it changed we will compare some statements from territorial reports covering different metropolitan regions during the time between 2003 and 2009.

• The purpose of the OECD territorial reviews

In order to see the change over time we will look at three different reports, i.e. OECD territorial reviews of metropolitan areas. The first, OECD Territorial Reviews – Öresund, Denmark/Sweden (OECD, 2003), says the following:

"The objectives of territorial reviews are: a) identify the nature and scale of territorial challenges using a common analytical framework; b) assist governments in the assessment and improvement of their territorial policy, using comparative policy analysis; c) assess the distribution of competencies and resources among the different levels of governments; and d) identify and disseminate information on best practices regarding territorial policy and governance." (p 3).

The statement above is implying "a)" that it's possible to identify the challenges in each region using a common framework. This is in line with the policy-makers assumption, which was discussed earlier, saying that *uniqueness is not important* and that *standard models are unproblematic*. Concerning "b)", it's also saying that 'comparative policy analysis' is an important method when it comes to assess and improve territorial policy. This objective is in line with one of the reasons for the Finnish and Canadian policy-makers referring to the OECD. Regarding "c)", where the objective is to 'assess the distribution of competencies and resources among the different levels of government', particular regional interests might explain it. This concerned a cross-border region (i.e. the Öresund region) competing with Stockholm, the capital of Sweden. The last objective, "d)" says that the OECD reviews will identify 'best practices regarding territorial policy and governance'. This might contribute to regional policy concepts in two ways (1) bench marking and (2) legitimacy, as best practice will be found among those regions that have been reviewed.

In the second report: OECD Territorial Reviews – Stockholm, Sweden (OECD, 2006), the objectives statement has changed compared to 2003. It says the following:

"Responding to a need to study and spread innovative territorial development strategies and governance in a more systematic way, the OECD created in 1999 the Territorial Development Policy Committee (TDPC) and its Working Party on Urban Areas (WPUA) as a unique forum for international exchange and debate. The TDPC has developed a number of activities, among which a series of specific case studies on metropolitan regions. These studies follow a standard methodology and a common conceptual framework, allowing countries to share their experiences. This series is intended to produce a synthesis that will formulate and diffuse horizontal policy recommendations." (p 3).

Now OECD points out that the objective is to '...study and spread innovative territorial development strategies and governance in a more systematic way...' and '...allowing countries to share their experiences...'. This statement is a change towards a "policy learning" perspective rather than a "lesson drawing" perspective, which was the case in the objectives in 2003. Furthermore, the OECD is arguing that the series of reviews '...is intended to produce a synthesis that will formulate and diffuse horizontal policy recommendations.' This formulation, even if it's not as specific as in 2003, implies an instrumental view on causality between the common conceptual framework and the policy recommendations to a region.

In the third report: OECD Territorial Reviews – Copenhagen, Denmark (OECD, 2009), the two last sentences in the objectives formulation were changed.

"These studies following a standard methodology and a common conceptual framework, allow countries to share their experiences, and are intended to help formulate and diffuse horizontal policy recommendations." (p 3).

115

The formulation '...produce a synthesis that will...' was edited to '...help...' which is a less instrumental view.

• The OECD policy framework

In the OECD Territorial Reviews – Öresund, Denmark/Sweden (OECD, 2003) four focus areas were considered (see table 1 below). The same four were used in the case of Stockholm in 2006, but *Networking and knowledge development* was altered into *Innovation and knowledge (clusters)*. In 2009, in the case of Copenhagen – that is a part of the Öresund region, OECD added two new focus areas: *entrepreneurship* and *urban amenities*. The following change in the policy framework indicates a shift in perspectives, from manly economics to include also sociology, geography and business.

A framework for comparative studies with the ambition to consider areas, such as innovation and entrepreneurship stress the need for relevant indicators in addition to the more traditional economic parameters used in earlier OECD reviews. It can be noted that the new OECD framework and conclusions from 2009, compared to the 2003 review were more in line with the results from the studies in the end of the 1990's (Boye, 1997 and 1999), using a social construction perspective.

The recommendations given on *governance* are in line with the present challenges in the three regions respectively. In the Öresund region, there was a need for cross-border policy, which neither one of the two national governments have the necessary mandate to develop. The suggested solution was "light institutions". In the Stockholm report (2006), Stockholm was considered as the key region of Sweden. The main argument in the report is that Sweden needs Stockholm and that it is important to develop the city for the competitiveness of the whole nation. In the third case, concerning Copenhagen (2009) it was now realized that governments solely cannot come up with a fruitful strategy for competitiveness – they have to involve industry etc. "Partnerships" were the suggested solution. This was a different interpretation of the regional context compared to the Öresund region review in 2003.

Table 1: The OECD policy framework – focus areas, i.e. determinants of urban competitiveness.

Öresund, 2003	Stockholm, 2006	Copenhagen, 2009
Common labour market	Integrated labour market	Labour skills profile
Networking and knowledge development	Innovation and knowledge (clusters)	Innovation
		Entrepreneurship
Physical infrastructure	Physical infrastructure "the enabling environment"	Transport infrastructure
		Urban amenities
Governance: "Light institutions"	Governance: Need for a national strategy for Stockholm	Governance: "Partnerships"

Following the OECD conceptual framework urban competitiveness is assumed to be relevant on four different markets, i.e. metropolitan areas compete for: (1) product markets (exports), (2) inward investments, (3) desirable residents and (4) recognition and favours from higher levels of government. (OECD Copenhagen review, 2009). Furthermore, places are considered to have local, regional, national, continental and global rivals (especially for metropolitan areas) to compete with.

When it comes to what decides urban competitiveness, we can as discussed above see that the OECD in 2009 lists five different determinants: (1) Skills, (2) Innovation, (3) Entrepreneurship, (4) Infrastructure and (5) Urban amenities. However, at this time compared to earlier versions of the framework they express a greater awareness of limitations due to specific pre-conditions regarding geographic characteristics of the urban region as well as the particular firm sector structure. This becomes evident in OECD's conclusions concerning its own conceptual framework:

- "Many determinants are dependent on local context and circumstances.
- There is no universal model of urban development that can be applied to every urban area.
- There is a considerable amount of path dependency in urban economic trajectories.

• This means that the economic performance of every metropolitan area has to be studied, taking its peculiarities into account." (OECD territorial review, Copenhagen, 2009, p. 259).

How region (policy) concepts influence practice

The evolution of region concepts – a matter of policy learning

Region and policy concepts can be seen as elements in strategy processes and in the development of regional strategic platforms. In such perspective, region (policy) concepts embody *both process and structure*. Firstly, in a spatial or geographical dimension, concepts create centres and peripheries as well as territories and borders. Secondly, when it comes to knowledge and resource structures, region concepts are embedded in the cognitive structures of the strategic platform, where the same concepts elucidate the platform. As new region concepts develop and come into use, the regional strategic platform will undergo a change and embrace new meanings, thus fostering new ways of seeing, making sense and acting in slightly different ways than before. This can be described as a regional in-stitutionalization process.

Thus, region concepts play a major part in the regionalization process, as they are a way of seeing, thinking and making sense, and they trigger action (they are a way of acting). However, region concepts not only constitute the base for the process, but they are also a product of it, in that they keep undergoing change. When actors gain new experiences, new action patterns develop and new ideas evolve. For example, the region concepts that have come to life during the Öresund regionalization tend to originate from current theories, favourable archetypes and existing local structures in a way that they become *both the base and the product of the regional development process.*

These cognitive structures bring a certain degree of *isomorphism* to the regionalization process, which becomes visible in, for example, the use of archetypes (i.e., trying to copy successful regions without reflecting on conditional differences). There is a will among the participants in the Öresund regionalization to become like certain other–"ideal"–regions, for example, like a new Silicon Valley. Such "exemplary" regions seem to inspire regional activity. This aspect can also be argued to be a risk as these strong isomorphic tendencies might result in a regional development process imitating regions in other parts of the world, which have developed under completely different circumstances.

Over time, strong concepts become *institutionalized* and taken for granted. They become so convincing that they provide a common view of what the region is going to be like. Region concepts are also influenced by values and norms, for example, social expectations of what the region will look like in the future. These expectations, in addition to cognitive structures, influence the way in which people, participating in the regional development process, act. Region concepts also relate to the regulative structures, for example, as they tend to influence local means of control in the form of harmonization of national tax policies and labour market regulations, such as different rules for job certification and social security.

Region concepts support the formation of teams of resources and the development of *shared knowledge*. Region concepts therefore organize local activities. The capability of the strategic platform is the outcome of knowledge integration (see Grant 1996) through the social activities of local actors. These activities, in turn, are embedded and formed in a context of role-related social expectations (normative institutions), mental patterns and symbols (cognitive institutions) (see Tsoukas 1996), and constraints and regulations by current rules and laws (regulative institutions). These kind of social activities are possible within a local community (i.e., within spatial proximity), which enables the substantial interaction between individuals that is required.

The organizational competencies of the platform originate from the collective capability to use teams of resources in certain purposeful ways. In this way, it can be argued that region concepts become institutionalized competencies. Sometimes these *collective competencies develop into sources of sustainable competitive advantages* and become the core competencies of the region.

Conclusions

What reasonable expectations we can have on the OECD territorial reviews in the future depends on how we consider the following issues, which in turn can be derived from the questions in the outset of this chapter and the theoretical and empirical discussion above.

Firstly, the OECD policy framework seems to be the mixed outcome of:

- A traditional economist perspective focusing on nationally aggregated data
- Trends among countries and regions that have been studied
- 'New' additional perspectives from social sciences etc
- The specific context in the reviewed region
- The specific strategic agenda of the policy-makers in the reviewed region

The past ten years the OECD policy framework has become broader, incorporating more aspects and in that way coming closer to the complex reality of the policy-makers and is now showing more respect to regional uniqueness. As a consequence there seems to be a tendency towards viewing the OECD policy (i.e. on urban and metropolitan regions) as a mental framework for a fruitful strategy process, rather as a universal recipe for success. Furthermore, the OECD reviews become less a tool for benchmarking and more a way of profiling and positioning the metropolitan region on a national and, even more important, on an international arena. The latter is in line with the findings of Porter & Webb (2007), who points out the importance of the OECDs "identity-enhancing role".

How do we catch a 'target', which is not only moving but also changing? As, for example recognized in the 2010 follow-up of the OECD review of Stockholm in 2006 the strategic situation has changed, partly because of proceedings in the intended development and partly due to changes in the geopolitical context, i.e. increased globalization, financial crisis and increased international focus on energy and climate. Altogether, this makes the 2006 framework partly insufficient when it comes to dealing with future challenges.

How important is innovation? On one hand, the better the match between the OECD territorial review and the policy-makers agenda, the greater the chance that the policy recommendation will be used in the forthcoming strategic development of the region. On the other hand, letting an already established local agenda influence the territorial review may risk the development process to be incremental and miss the opportunity of innovation.

How important is timing? Strategic development processes of regions seems to have different phases (i.e. being mainly market-, policy- or idea-driven) and the OECD recommendations that are brought forth might have more or less impact on the forthcoming decisions and activities in the region depending on how the characteristics of the framework matches the current phase.

One major future challenge for the OECD is to find relevant indicators that, on the one hand, can cope with new global trends and major changes in the international geopolitical environment, and that, on the other hand, can cope with specific characteristics and contexts of individual regions.

NOTES

1. Helsinki, Finland (2003); Öresund Copenhagen/Malmö, Denmark/Sweden (2003); Vienna/Bratislava, Austria/Czech Republic (2003); Melbourne, Australia (2003); Athens, Greece (2004); Montreal, Canada (2004); Mexico City, Mexico (2004); Busan, Korea (2005); Seoul, Korea (2005); Milan, Italy (2006); Stockholm, Sweden (2006); Newcastle in the North East, United Kingdom (2006); Randstad Holland, Netherlands (2007); Madrid, Spain (2007); Cape Town, South Africa (2008); Istanbul, Turkey (2008); Toronto, Canada (2009); Venice, Italy (2010).

2. "The role of the regions" – Workshop in Gothenburg, Sweden, 28-29 April 2010.

3. OECD Territorial Reviews – Öresund, Denmark/Sweden, OECD, 2003, p 3.

4. Economies of scope can be achieved by locating different parts of a value chain, which often requires different mixes of factors, in different locations that have the appropriate factor endowments. Economies of scale can be achieved either in distribution, financial, and business services or in public infrastructure networks, such as telecommunications and transportation facilities.

5. See e.g. Maskell & Törnqvist, 1999.

6. See e.g. Ernst & Young, 1992.

REFERENCES

Alasuutari, P. & Pal, L. 2010. *The OECD as an International Referent in Natio-nal Policy Debates: Comparing Canada and Finland.* Paper presented in the 18th NISPAcee Annual Conference. Warsaw.

Alasuutari, P. & Rasimus, A. 2009. *Use of the OECD in justifying policy reforms: The case of Finland.* Journal of Power 2, (1): 89.

Alvesson, M. & Sköldberg, K. 1994. *Tolkning och Reflektion.* Lund: Studentlitteratur.

Barney, J & Ouchi, W., eds. 1986. *Organizational Economics – Towards a New Paradigm for Understanding and Studying Organizations.* San-Francisco: Jossey-Bass.

Barney, J. 1991. Firm Resources and Sustained Competitive Afdvantage. *Journal of Management* 17(1): 99-120.

Boye, P. 1997. Market- Policy- and Concept-driven Integration Processes: Three Transnational Regions Compared. In *The Öresund Region Building*, ed. Berg, P-O & Lyck, L. Copenhagen: Nyt fra Samfundsvidenskaberne.

Boye, P. 1999. *Developing Transnational Industrial Platforms – The Strate-gic Conception of the Öresund Region.* Lund and Copenhagen: School of Economics and Management, Lund University and Scandinavian Academy of Management Studies.

Boye, P. 2008. *The European integration and the growth of the Øresund Region – How an idea driven process creates powerful institutions supporting industrial competitiveness.* Paper prepared for the 10th annual conference on European integration, Swedish Network for European Studies in Economics (SNEE), Mölle, Sweden.

Chandler, A. 1990. *Scale and Scope – The Dynamics of Industrial Capitalism.* Cambridge: Harvard University Press.

Dolowitz, D. & Marsh, D. 1996. Who Learns from Whom: A Review of the Policy Transfer Literature. *Political Studies*, 44(2): 343-357.

Eklund, M. 2007. *Adopting the Innovation System Concept in Sweden.* Uppsala: Uppsala University.

Evans, M. 1999. Understanding Policy Transfer: A Multi-level, Multi-disciplinary Perspective. *Public Administration.*

Grant, R. 1991. The Resource-based Theory of Competitive Advantage – Im-plications for Strategy Formulation. *California Management Review*, Spring: 114-135.

Grant, R. 1996. Towards a Knowledge-based Theory of the Firm. *Strategic Mana-gement Journal* 17, Winter special issue: 109-122.

Hall, P. 1993. Policy Paradigms, Social Learning and the State: The Case of Eco-nomic Policy making in Britain, *Comparative Politics,* 25, pp. 275-297.

Ikenberry, G. J. 1990. The International Spread of Privatization Policies: Inducements, Learning and 'Policy Band wagoning', in E. Suleiman & J. Waterbury (eds) *The Political Economy of Public Sector Reform and Privatization*. Boulder: Westview Press.

Lodge, M. 2005. The importance of being modern: international benchmarking and national regulatory innovation. *Journal of European Public Policy* 12:4 August: 649-667.

Lyck, L. 2006. Öresundsregionalisering – *Medicon Valley*. Copenhagen: TCM-CBS.

Maskell, P. & Törnqvist, G. 1999. *Building a Cross-Border Learning Region – Emergence of the North European Öresund Region*. Copenhagen Business School Press.

Milgrom, P. & Roberts, J. 1992. *Economics, Organization, and Management*. Engelwood Cliffs: Prentice Hall.

Merriam, S.B. 1998. *Qualitative Research and Case Study Applications in Education*. San Francisco: Jossey-Bass.

OECD. 2006. *OECD Territorial Reviews – Competitive Cities in the Global Economy*. OECD Publications, Paris.

OECD. 2009. *OECD Territorial Reviews: Copenhagen, Denmark*. OECD Publications, Paris.

OECD. 2006. *OECD Territorial Reviews: Stockholm, Sweden*. OECD Publications, Paris.

OECD. 2005. *Building Competitive Regions – Strategies and Governance*. OECD Publications, Paris.

OECD. 2003. *OECD Territorial Reviews: Vienna-Bratislava, Austria/Slovak Republic*. OECD Publications, Paris.

OECD. 2003. *OECD Territorial Reviews: Öresund, Denmark/Sweden*. OECD Publications, Paris.

Porter, T. & Webb, M. 2007. *The Role of the OECD in the Orchestration of Global Knowledge Networks*. Paper presented at Canadian Political Science Association, May 30, Saskatoon, Saskatchewan, Canada.

Rose, R. 1993. *Lesson Drawing in Public Policy: A Guide to Learning Across Time and Space*. Chatham, N-J.: Chatham House.

Schneider, A. & Ingram, H. 1988. Systematically Pinching Ideas: A Comparative Approach to Policy design. *Journal of Public Policy*. Vol 8. No 1 Jan. – Mar.). pp. 61-80.

Stockholmsregionen i utveckling – Uppföljning av OECD Territorial Reviews: Stockholm. 2010. Regionplanekontoret vid Stockholms läns landsting, Stockholm.

Stone, D. 1999. Learning Lessons and Transferring Policy across Time, Space and Disciplines. *Politics* , 19(1) pp. 51-59. Oxford: Blackwell.

Stone, D. 2003. *Transnational Transfer Agents and Global Networks in the 'Internationalisation' of Policy.* Paper prepared for the "Internationalisation and Policy Transfer" workshop, Tulane University, New Orleans.

The Öresund Region – A Baltic Gateway. report on location factors in the Öresund Region. Malmö and Copenhagen: Ernst & Young, 1992.

Tsoukas, H. 1996. The Firm as Distributed Knowledge System – A Constructionist Approach. *Strategic Managemnt Journal,* 17 (winter special issue)): 11-25.

Wernerfelt, B. 1984. The Resource Based View of the Firm. *Strategic Management Journal,* 5: 171-180.

Whitley, R. ed. 1992. *European Business Systems – Firms and Markets in Their National Contexts.* London: Sage.

Yin, R.K. 1994. *Case Study Research. Design and Methods.* 2nd Edition. Thousand Oaks: Sage.

ANDERS LIDSTRÖM – UMEÅ UNIVERSITY, SWEDEN
JEFFEREY SELLERS – UNIVERSITY OF SOUTHERN CALIFORNIA, USA

Governance and Redistribution in Metropolitan Areas – *a Swed–US Comparison*

Introduction

Metropolitan areas in the western world are characterized by their inner diversity. Large cities and their surroundings harbour extensive numbers of specialized trades and businesses, are melting pots for different cultures and religions, and provide opportunities for various lifestyles and ideas to develop. Along with this, metropolitan areas are also places of extensive social and economic inequalities. These are typically territorially structured and consist of segregated communities of different social and economic status.

Strong underlying forces produce and reinforce these tendencies towards metropolitan diversity. Essentially, these forces are connected to the way capitalism and market mechanisms function. However, in most western countries there is also a broad awareness that too extensive segregation may be a disadvantage for the metropolis as a whole. Therefore, policies have been developed that aim to reducing metropolitan disparities in services and opportunities.

This chapter investigates to what extent national and metropolitan governments are successful in counteracting social inequalities. We have selected two countries with very different policies of redistribution – the social democratic state of Sweden and the market liberal homeland of the US. In each of these, we examine two metropolitan areas in order to assess the extent to which the system of governance and the policies to counteract inequalities are successful. We focus in particular on policies of education. Does national and/or metropolitan governance matter for counteracting inequalities in this sphere of policy?

The national contexts of the metropolis in the US and Sweden

Four different aspects may neatly summarize differences in national context. These are differences in citizens' values, welfare systems and development of metropolitanization and urbanization.

Citizens' values

As part of the contrast in the political culture of the two countries, it is well known that Swedish and U.S. citizens embrace different sets of social and political values. Respect for various forms of authority, levels of general social trust and beliefs about democracy and governmental institutions differ in significant ways between the two countries.

Opinions of U.S. and Swedish citizens toward a number of representative items in the World Values Survey exemplify these contrasts. (These results from the 1999–2004 or 2005–2007 waves of the survey.)

- 68 percent of Swedes, compared to just under 40 percent of Americans believe that "most people can be trusted".
- Perhaps partly as a result, belief in democracy is also somewhat stronger in Sweden. 76 percent of Swedes, compared to 46 percent of Americans, feel that having a democratic political system is "very good" for the political system. 50 percent of Swedes, compared with 40 percent of Americans, believe that democracy, despite its problems, is better than any other form of government.
- By comparison with Swedes, Americans are more likely to support greater respect for authority. 60 percent of U.S. respondents, compared with 24 percent of Swedes, found that this would be a "good thing".
- Levels of religiosity also differ greatly. 96 percent of Americans say they believe in God, and 57 percent say God is "very important"

in their lives. By contrast, 53 percent of Swedes say they believe in God, and only 8 per cent say God is "very important" in their lives.

Worlds of welfare and capitalism

A large literature on welfare states and related aspects of capitalism has brought out major differences between the institutional and economic systems of developed countries. Sweden and the United States have figured prominently in these analyses, often as models of distinct varieties of capitalism and welfare provision.

Because local and regional governments often provide a large portion of welfare states services in both countries, the contrasts in welfare sates have special importance for local and regional governance. In Esping-Andersen's (1990) typology of different types of welfare states, Sweden corresponds to a Social Democratic model. In this model, the state provides generous welfare services across a wide set of sectors. Provision is broadly egalitarian, offering the same benefits regardless of class or income.

By contrast, the U.S. welfare state has typically been taken as the most characteristic example of a liberal welfare state. This type of welfare state delivers the most limited welfare state services of any of Esping-Andersen's three types. Provision by the state is even more limited, as private or nonprofit organizations provide such services as education, health, and pensions for large potions of the population. Those services the state provides are usually subject to means testing rather universal provision.

Other comparative literature on the Swedish and U.S. political economies has highlighted other broad contrasts that accompany these. Corporatist interest intermediation, with participation by encompassing peak organizations representing labor and business, has been a regular feature of politics and policymaking in Sweden. In the United States the corresponding organizations are much more fragmented, limited in membership and less powerful.

Hall and Soskice (2001) have also taken Sweden and the United States as opposed types of governance at the level of the firm. Along with Germany, Sweden exemplifies the coordinated market economy in which firm governance, industrial relations, education and training systems are a product of mutual adjustment and organizational integration through formal representatives of business and labor. Capitalism in the United States, by contrast, depends on markets rather than coordination as the main influence on these domains of firm governance.

Local government systems

In particular the systems of central-local relations make for contrasting background conditions for metropolitan governance.

There are two tiers of directly elected local government in Sweden. 290 municipalities have extensive responsibility for primary and secondary education, social services, land use planning and local public infrastructure. The upper tier consists of 19 county councils and two regions. Their main task is the responsibility for health care but the two regions (Skåne and Västra Götaland) have additional powers in the field of regional development. Central government regulates local and regional government autonomy mainly through the local government act, but also through special regulation, particularly in the major welfare areas. However, local government also has a general competence and an unlimited right to levy a proportional local and regional income tax. Central government provides additional resources and equalizes economic preconditions between different local authorities. Local autonomy and the right to taxation are guaranteed by the constitution. Central-local government relations are also affected by the strong presence of basically the same political parties at all levels of government and by a strong joint interest organization for local government – The Swedish Association of Local Authorities and Regions.

In the United States, local government is a creature of the state governments rather than the national constitutional order. In effect, this means that each of the fifty federal states has its own system of local government. Despite greater institutional diversity among local government institutions than in most countries, local government in most states follows broadly similar patterns. Two tiers of local government common to nearly all the states are the municipal level and the county level. In addition, most states authorize a range of functionally specialized local governments, and local residents often have powers to create new local governments. Although local government powers were long limited to specific statutory authorizations, today most states authorize some form of general power in "home rule" legislation or state constitutional provisions. The largest single responsibility of local government is education. It also provides such functions as public safety, fire protection, planning and zoning and in many cases various utilities. Local governments have traditionally been self-financing, most often through locally raised property taxes. In recent decades, however, many localities have increasingly depended on other locally raised sources like sales taxes or user fees. In the sector of education, some state governments have stepped in to replace local governments as the main source of funding, often in ways designed to compensate for inequities in resources between school districts. Although state-level local government associations can sometimes play a significant role in shaping the conditions for local governance, their influence has remained considerably weaker than that of their Swedish counterparts. Due in part to nonpartisan local electoral rules in most states, but also to a more general disjuncture between national and local politics and policy, national parties play a remarkably limited role in the local politics of metropolitan regions.

Urbanization and metropolitanization

Beyond institutions and culture, the contrasts also extend to the settlement structure of metropolitan regions in the two countries. Partly as a result of differences in planning and policy, but also as consequences of other factors, common processes of urbanization and metropolitanization have followed different trajectories in the two countries.

- In both countries, over eighty percent of residents live in urbanized localities, defined as places with populations of 5,000 or more. However, metropolitanization has advanced much further in the United States. In 2000, nearly 80 percent of the U.S. population lived in metropolitan regions with 200,000 or more people. Only 32 percent of Swedes lived in the three metropolitan regions of this size (Stockholm, Göteborg and Malmö).

- In the US, the largest metropolitan areas are much larger than those in Sweden. Although the US also contains a host of metropolitan regions the same size as those in Sweden, regions the size of the largest Swedish metropolitan regions generally occupy lower places in urban hierarchies there.
- Planning regulations are stricter in Sweden than in the US, leading for example to more controlled growth in the city centers and less urban sprawl.
- Systems of public transport (trains, trams and busses) are typically more extensive and used more frequently in Sweden than in the US.
- As a consequence of these differences, the inner city is usually not a poor area in decay in Sweden. Among large metropolitan regions in the US, however, this is a typical pattern.

The social and spatial settings of metropolitan regions demonstrate legacies from previous decades and even centuries of these practices. For purposes of this comparison, the patterns of social inequality across these regions furnish different levels of challenge for efforts to alleviate spatial disparities.

Stockholm and especially Göteborg are much smaller in terms of area and population than the two U.S. metropolitan regions, and also more densely populated and more ethnically homogenous. The Stockholm metropolitan area is much denser than metropolitan Göteborg, with the population in an equivalent surface area. It contains approximately twice as large an immigrant population, and is much more segregated than the metropolitan area of Göteborg. In greater Stockholm, the wealthiest municipality has an average income that is almost twice (1.96) as big as that of the poorest. In greater Göteborg, the wealthier is only 27 percent richer than the poorest municipality. The differences in average wealth are larger between the city districts within Göteborg than between the municipalities in the Göteborg area. Hence, inequalities are primarily a within-city phenomenon. In Stockholm, segregation within the main city is approximately on the same level as between municipalities. Hence, tackling inequalities requires both within- and between-city measures.

Both LA and Minneapolis are larger in population and occupy much more territory than Stockholm. Los Angeles is a megacity with over eleven million residents. Although the urbanized area does not extend as far as the metropolitan boundary drawn by the census, even that area is several times the size of greater Stockholm. Minneapolis, however, approximates the size of Stockholm even though it does so within a much larger territory. Both LA and Minneapolis have a more stratified socioeconomic structure and greater ethnoracial diversity. Gini coefficients for income are .43 in greater Minneapolis and .49 for greater Los Angeles. By contrast, the municipal Gini coefficients in greater Gothenburg average only .31, and in greater Stockholm only .36. The U.S. regions are also much more segregated than either Swedish region. Unlike metropolitan LA, however, Minneapolis remains mostly a region of citizens with European ancestry and is ethnically and racially more homogenous. This has not prevented wide inequalities and spatial sorting, both within the central city and among localities throughout the region.

Institutions of metropolitan self-government in Stockholm and Göteborg

Metropolitan self-government in the *Stockholm metropolitan region* is organized mainly through a directly elected county council and cooperation between municipalities (and county councils).

The Stockholm county council (Stockholms läns landsting) has roughly the same territory as the commuting region. Originating in the late 1860s, the county only covered the area surrounding the city of Stockholm. However, in 1968 the area of the city itself was also included under its jurisdiction. The county level in Sweden was set up for functions that required self-government for larger populations than municipalities. From the early years, their main function has been the responsibility for public health care. In addition, they are also in charge of regional public transport, regional cultural institutions, regional planning and some economic development functions. The county council in Stockholm is different from the others in the country through its extensive responsibility for regional planning and public transport in the Greater Stockholm area.

The main decision-making body is a 149-member directly elected assembly, chosen by the citizens of the county every fourth year. There is also an executive board and a number of more specialized committees for different functions. The Stockholm county council is mainly funded by its own citizens. The main source is a proportional income tax which provides 84 % of its resources. The county councils set the level of the tax independently. No prior consultations with central government, the municipalities or the citizens are required.

The county council has a major city-regional function as the regional planning authority for the Greater Stockholm area, which it has been granted by Parliament thorough special legislation. The county council decides on the regional development plan which includes the general use of land in the area and the structure of the main systems of roads and other forms of transportation. This gives the county council an important role vis-à-vis the 25 municipalities in the county area by both coordinating and providing a basis for their development activities. Its decisions have consequences not only for the municipalities but also for the neighbouring county councils in the larger Mälar region (se below). For this reason, the decision about the development plan is preceded by an extensive consultation process.

As the county council is in charge of a major public welfare system this involves considerable redistribution from those in tax-paying ages to those in most need of health care and medical services. A system of intra-regional tax equalization between the wealthy and less advantageous municipalities within the Stockholm county council area existed between 1978 and 2003. This was abolished as it distorted the national system of tax equalization. Today, Sweden only has a national system of tax equalization that also contributes to redistribution within the Stockholm region. Almost half the municipalities in the Greater Stockholm area are net contributors to the system. The extremes are the municipality of Danderyd, that pays 12 800 SEK/citizen every year, and Botkyrka municipality, which receives 10 100 SEK per citizen and year.

There is also an indirectly elected unit addressing various metropolitan issues in the Stockholm area. *The Council for the Mälar*

Region (Mälardalsrådet) is formally a voluntary association with 56 municipalities and the five county councils in the area around Lake Mälaren as members. Although this is much larger than the daily commuting area, it is clearly functionally linked to Stockholm. A 300-member assembly, representing all member municipalities and county councils meets once per year. The assembly elects a board of politicians and four committees for the major functions of the council.

The purpose of the council is to promote regional development by providing a meeting-place for its members and for businesses and the civil society to discuss and coordinate issues like infrastructure, transportation, international benchmarking and higher education. It has no formal decision-making functions and very limited resources but provides an informal basis for policy coordination and common promotion of the area. It has no function as equalizer between different parts of the region.

In the current discussions about establishing larger directly elected regions in Sweden, the politicians in Greater Stockholm have been reluctant to commit themselves to any particular solution. Both a very large region, corresponding to the Mälar Region area, and a more limited expansion of the present county council area have been considered although none of them has gathered sufficient support among local and regional politicians. In addition, politicians from other parts of Sweden have been eager to emphasize that the Stockholm region must not be too dominant in a national context.

In the **Göteborg metropolitan region** the directly elected unit of regional self-government – *The region of Västra Götaland* (Västra Götalandsregionen) was established in 1999 as an amalgamation of four county councils. The region is still formally an experiment but it was expected to gain permanent status from the Parliament in 2010. Although half of its population lives outside the Göteborg commuting area, the region provides important functions with relevance for the metropolitan area.

Many of the functions of the region correspond to those of the previous county councils. These include the responsibility for public health care and public dental care but also for cultural institutions and regional public transport. In addition, the region has the main responsibility for regional development which in most other parts of the country is a task for central government units at county level. The region establishes a regional growth programme for Västra Götaland, and this includes a specific programme for the Göteborg metropolitan area (carried out through the Business Region Göteborg, se below)

The region of Västra Götaland is governed by an assembly of 149 directly elected councillors. The assembly appoints a regional executive board and specialized committees. The region derives most of its resources (80 %) from the regional income tax. In the same way as in Stockholm, the assembly has the full powers of deciding the level of its income tax.

Through the responsibility for health care, the region has a redistributive function between different citizens in the region, although the territorial effects of this are not clear. However, it seems likely that municipalities with a large share of elderly people, who usually consume more health care, gain from this redistribution whereas those with a large share in working ages contribute to it.

The major unit for municipal cooperation in the Greater Göteborg area is *The Göteborg Region Association of Local Authorities* (Göteborgsregionen, GR), which covers a territory that fairly well corresponds to the commuting area. The Göteborg Region has 13 member municipalities and has a more specific focus on common tasks and problems in the metropolitan area than the Västra Götaland region.

The Göteborg Region is an indirectly elected unit. The main decisions are taken by a 91 member council, appointed by the member authorities according to their population size. In order to safeguard that the region is not totally dominated by its centre, the statutes stipulate that the number of representatives from the city of Göteborg must not exceed 45. The council appoints a board and specialized coordinating committees. Most of the revenue are various forms of user fees but about a quarter of the resources are paid by the municipalities as membership fees.

The Göteborg Region has, in the same way as Stockholm county council, been given the task of setting up a regional development plan. However, this is not granted through special legislation but by a decision of the government. Compared to Stockholm county council, the Göteborg Region is more focused on negotiating agreements between the municipalities with regard to the use of land, rather than setting binding priorities. The Göteborg region owns a separate company – Business Region Göteborg – that is involved in various business development projects.

Apart from the role as regional planning authority, The Göteborg Region has a number of more specific functions that are carried out on behalf of the municipalities. The municipalities decide themselves which functions they want to coordinate through the region. For example, the Göteborg Region organizes joint admission to upper secondary education in the metropolitan area and joint purchasing between the municipalities. It also coordinates labour market measures and environmental protection activities and offers training programmes for municipal personnel and an arena for exchanges of ideas and experiences. The Göteborg Region has very limited redistributive functions within the area although the coordination of some functions may perhaps benefit smaller municipalities rather than the larger ones.

The national tax equalization system is a net provider of resources to all municipalities in Greater Göteborg, although there is a span within the commuting area between the coastal island municipality of Tjörn that only receives 74 SEK per citizen and year and Lilla Edet further inland that gets 5 700 SEK/citizen.

Institutions for Metropolitan Governance
in greater Los Angeles and greater Minneapolis

Arrangements for metropolitan governance in the two U.S. metropolitan regions demonstrate the range of variation in the United States in institutions for addressing the metropolitan scale. Some of the arrangements, such as counties and councils of representatives from municipalities, resemble arrangements in greater Stockholm and greater Gothenburg. The varying arrangements for different policy sectors and the pervasive use of special districts have served as the main institutional mechanisms for coordination beyond the local scale.

The five county governments of the *Los Angeles metropolitan area* have been the most powerful institutions for addressing issues beyond the level of municipalities. The counties were created by the state government in 1852 and have retained identical boundaries since that time. Counties are governed by five member Boards of Supervisors, who are elected every four years from separate districts. County authorities are especially strong in the sizeable "unincorporated" areas, those portions of each county without municipal governments. In these areas, which include much of the less densely inhabited areas but also a number of urbanized areas like parts of East Los Angeles, counties provide all services and exercise full authority over planning.

Revenues for the counties come from a mix of sources. Intergovernmental revenues in 2007 comprised 47 percent to 61 percent of the total. Nearly all of these funds are categorical or based on specific state or federal programs. There is no system for equalization of county revenues, but intergovernmental funding levels for programs like welfare correspond to proportions of eligible recipients within a county. Other general revenue sources include property and sales taxes, user fees and service charges. Some counties also maintain separate "enterprise funds" for operations like public hospitals or transit.

The only body with a purview that extends to all five counties is the Southern California Association of Local Governments. Established in the 1950s as a result of federal requirements to set up regional transportation authorities as a requirement to make states and localities eligible for federal transportation funds, this is now the largest metropolitan planning organization in the United States. It exercises a variety of mandated federal and state responsibilities, including development of regional transportation plans, demographic projections for the region, monitoring compliance with federal air pollution laws, environmental reviews, and preparation of regional housing needs assessments and hazardous waste management plans. This association is essentially an advisory body and lacks the authority to enforce planning or other decisions.

Much of the governance that takes place beyond individual municipalities occurs through the elaborate network of special districts. Some of these bodies exercise authority over large portions of the metropolitan population. The Los Angeles County Metropolitan Transportation authority, for instance, runs bus and light rail transportation systems that extend through most of the 88 localities within Los Angeles County. Metro is the result of a 1993 merger between two prior transit organizations. The thirteen member Board of Directors for this state-chartered organization includes representatives appointed by the City of Los Angeles, the County of Los Angeles and several other cities within the County.

In the *Minneapolis-St. Paul (or Twin Cities) metropolitan region*, the second tier of local government is somewhat more fragmented than its California counterpart. Counties in the Twin Cities Region within Minnesota were created between 1849, when Minnesota became a Territory, and 1857 when it became a state. Counties are smaller in Minnesota than in California. With one-fifth the population of greater Los Angeles, the census-defined metropolitan area of Minneapolis-St. Paul in 2000 included eleven county governments in the state of Minnesota and two in the state of Wisconsin to the south. Hennepin County, where the central city lies, contains 33.5 percent of the metropolitan population compared to 38.9 percent for Los Angeles County. Counties are governed by a board of five individuals (seven in counties with populations over 10,000) elected from districts to serve a four-year term. Counties also elect a variety of other offices, including auditors, recorders, treasurer, surveyors, clerks of court, judges of probate, assessors and attorneys. As a system of townships provides for local services even outside incorporated cities, no unincorporated areas exist in which counties provide the kind of services they do in metropolitan Los Angeles.

The largest source of revenues for county government in Minnesota is an "ad valorem" property tax, based on the value of an undivided piece of property or building. In 2007 this traditional mechanism for local government funding in the United States furnished 35 to 50 percent of county revenues among Minneapolis area counties. Although counties set their own tax rates, the state employs a system of "class rates" to prescribe the percentage of different properties subject to taxation. More of the revenues for counties in Mineaopolis (30 to 50 percent) come from the state or the federal government. "Categorical aids" aimed at providing for specific programs or services, or targeted federal grants make up most of this amount. Fees for services comprised from 9 to 22 percent of county revenues.

Minneapolis has also been home to one of the most robust U.S. experiments in metropolitan institution-building. The Twin Cities Metropolitan Council was created in 1994 to exercise a variety of functions in the seven-county region at the center of the metropolitan area, an area including St. Paul, Minneapolis and most of the most urbanized municipalities. The Council grew out of the Metropolitan Council of the Twin Cities, a planning agency created in 1967 to serve as a research and planning arm for the transportation, aviation, sewer and park systems of the region. The 1994 reorganization merged this agency with the Metropolitan Transit Commission, The Metropolitan Waste Control Commission and the Regional Transit Board. The resulting body has broad authority to develop policy plans for regional systems of transportation, aviation, parks, and water resources, assist communities in planning and coordinate plans for regional systems with local comprehensive land use plans.

As a proposal to make the seventeen-member governing board of the Council elective was defeated in the legislative process, members of the board are appointed by the governor of Minnesota and may be removed at will. Each member of the Board represents one of sixteen districts, with a chair appointed at large. In 2008–2009 forty percent of the Board's revenues came from state and federal sources. Forty-two percent came from user fees for wastewater treatment and transit services, and ten percent from a property tax. The Council also has authority to issue bonds.

A major complement to the Metropolitan Council has been the Fiscal Disparities Program. Enacted by the state legislature, this program redistributes revenues from municipal taxes on commercial and industrial property within the seven-county region of the Metropolitan Council. Proposed in 1969, the program was enacted in 1971 and went into effect in 1975 following delays due to legal challenges. The program reallocates forty percent of the revenue from taxation on commercial and industrial property from those municipalities with higher tax capacities to those with lower tax capacities. In 2008 the program redistributed up to $1041 per capita to area municipalities (in the town of Landfall, in Washington County). On the other side of the ledger, localities like the wealthy community of Wayzata paid up to $591 per person into the program. The redistributive effects of the program worked most to the benefit of the inner suburban areas, while rural growth centers paid the most per person into the program. The two central cities of St. Paul and Minneapolis were net contributors, at $77 per person and $12 per person.

The Metropolitan Council is the most prominent among a large number of special districts in the Twin Cities region. These are fewer in number than in metropolitan Los Angles, but occupy a similar place in local institutional arrangements. As in California, there is wide variety of these organizations, including library districts, hospital districts, family service districts, recreation and park districts, sanitation districts and soil and water conservation districts. Although these districts are self-financing, some rely on intergovernmental revenues as well as local taxation, fees or bonds. Many are governed by boards elected from citizens in general, service users or property owners. School districts are also governed by locally elected boards. Others, like the Metropolitan Council, are appointed, usually by participating local governments.

The local public education sector governed by these districts represents both the largest single sector of local government, employing the largest proportion of local public employees, and the principal focus of nationwide efforts to limit the extent of inequalities in the services local governments provide. 38 of 50 states, including both California and Minnesota, have instituted programs to reduce inequalities in spending among local education districts. In most instances these programs have necessitated intervention by state governments to reallocate and top up local revenues for education.

More limited efforts toward partial equalization may be found in a number of other specific sectors. County governments allocating state and federal funds from social welfare programs, for instance, have sought to equalize welfare access across much wider expanses of metropolitan territories than municipal governments could. County public transportation authorities in greater Los Angeles, and the Metro government in greater Minneapolis, have pursued transit networks throughout wide swaths of the metropolitan regions. In recent years, Metro has also extended regional planning to encompass allocations of new housing among the local governments within its jurisdiction.

Redistributive capacity

To ascertain the differences and similarities in metropolitan governance and its effects on social and spatial inequality, it is necessary to take into account several dimensions of metropolitan inequality. Our four-way comparison highlights national differences, but also the considerable variation in institutions, governance and regional structure within both Sweden and the United States.

Main territorial units and territorial equalization policies

In both countries, jurisdictional centralization and territorial redistribution among localities have been employed to reduce or alleviate disparities in local services between richer and poorer metropolitan communities. In Sweden these policies have been most extensive, and in Los Angeles the least extensive.

The main unit covering the territory of the metropolitan area (i.e. commuting region) is a directly elected county council in Stockholm and an indirectly elected unit of municipal cooperation in Göteborg. In the U.S. regions the hierarchically appointed Metropolitan Council in Minneapolis-St. Paul approximates the arrangement in Göteborg. Although it possesses regional authorities, its relationship with localities is largely one of coordination and assistance. It is also confined to the inner counties comprising only 38 percent of the metropolitan population. For greater Los Angeles, only advisory bodies exist at this scale.

The Swedish county councils and regional authorities have extensive resources and full political authority to set their revenues. In U.S. states like California and Minnesota, counties also possess the most encompassing territorial jurisdictions and arguably the greatest concentrations of fiscal and political resources to address disparities in services. Counties in California have somewhat more authority of this kind than counterparts in Minnesota. However, U.S. counties in greater Minneapolis and greater Los Angeles are more fragmented relative to the entire metropolitan region than counterparts in greater Stockholm and greater Los Angeles, and depend more for resources on categorical and specific intergovernmental grants.

Intra-metropolitan equalization (between municipalities) is mainly achieved in Sweden through the national system of tax equalization. The effects of this are extensive in the Greater Stockholm area and less dramatic in the Göteborg region. In the seven central counties of metropolitan Minneapolis, the Fiscal Disparities Program provides for an analogous reequilibration. However, this program is not only exceptional among U.S. metropolitan regions in its scope, but also remains limited by comparison with the Swedish national program. Fiscal Disparities applies only to the seven central Minneapolis counties with 38 percent of the population, and is based solely on tax capacities linked to commercial and industrial properties. No such program exists in California.

There and elsewhere within the United States, sector specific policies for equalization have provided the main means to equalize local services. Efforts to limit disparities in education expenditures in California and Minnesota provide the most notable example of these policies. Similarly, the county council/regional responsibility for health care in Sweden is also likely to contribute to intra-metropolitan equalization. In the U.S. metropolitan regions, where public health facilities comprise only a fraction of the total industry, any such effect is limited. The role of Stockholm county council and the Göteborg region as planning authorities offers considerable opportunities to set priorities for the whole metropolitan area. This role seems to be slightly more powerful in the Stockholm area than in Göteborg, where it seems to be carried out mainly through voluntary agreements and negotiations. The Twin Cities Metropolitan Council exercises analogous authorities of this kind, but the South Coast Association of Governments has few authoritative powers and less influence.

Public policy spending and outcomes: overall patterns

In metropolitan Sweden, municipal tax rates differ more narrowly among municipalities than does their mean income: between 17 percent and 22 percent in greater Stockholm, and between 20 percent and 22 percent in greater Goteborg. The system of fiscal equalization compensates for much of the differences in local revenues. The role of the two metropolitan regions in the equalization system differs considerably. Eleven of the twenty-two municipalities in greater Stockholm are net contributors to the system. All municipalities in the Göteborg metropolitan area are net receivers.

In greater Los Angeles, as in most U.S. metropolitan regions, limited fiscal equalization has permitted great diversity in local finances. Spatial sorting among residents and businesses has led to remarkable clustering across the region, largely on the basis of living and housing costs but also on the basis of racial and ethnic communities and lifestyle choices. Competition among communities for tax revenues, especially for the sales tax, has driven some expenditures higher and others lower. In some poor communities residents have pressed for more public services. In other municipalities, especially conservative ones, local residents have pressed to limit taxation and public expenditures. Overall and in a variety of specific areas, revenues and spending generally correlated with higher income.

In the inner counties of greater Minneapolis, the Fiscal Disparities program has been effective in limiting competition for tax revenues as well as fiscal disadvantages for some communities. However, expenditures statistics still show great diversity in local spending in most areas. A further consequence of the lower competition may be less downward pressure on revenues and expenditures than in greater Los Angeles. In 2002, revenues averaged $7 321 per resident in greater Minneapolis compared to $6471 per resident in greater Los Angeles. Spending levels in most specific categories still varied widely, often more than in greater Los Angeles. But the correlations with higher income are generally weaker.

Outcomes and Performance: The Example of Education

Despite the extensive system of redistribution in Sweden, fundamental societal and spatial inequalities remain. This can be seen through a comparison of the performance of local schools across the two Swedish metropolitan regions. The wealthy municipalities spend less on education but perform better. In the United States metropolitan regions, sectorally specific policies in the domain of public education have greatly limited the disparities in spending evident in other domains of municipal outputs. Funding equalization in the U.S. has constrained the advantages of higher income areas, but not eliminated it. Despite these measures, U.S. school systems in wealthy communities continue to perform significantly better, and their counterparts in poorer communities much worse.

In the Swedish metropolitan areas here is a negative relationship between resources in the equalization system and educational performance, i.e. those that receive most resources perform worse. In both, the correlation of education expenditures for compulsory education with mean income is significant and negative (-.32 in Stockholm, -.61 in Goteborg), while the correlations with unemployment and immigrants are positive and mostly significant (.26 to .39 in Stockholm, .266 and .009 in Goteborg). In Stockholm a similar relationship holds for secondary education. In Göteborg, upper secondary expenditures actually concentrate away from concentrations of unemployment and immigrants.

Education performance, as measured by compulsory education pupils qualified for upper secondary studies or by the percent of upper secondary pupils graduating within four years of studies, shows that the overall redistribution has failed to equalize outcomes. The positive correlations of compulsory education performance with mean income in both metropolitan areas (.835 in Stockholm, .653 in Goteborg) are somewhat stronger than the negative correlations with compulsory education spending. Despite the differences in redistribution evident from the spending patterns in the two regions, secondary school performance demonstrates similar patterns of greater success in higher income communities (.47 in Stockholm, .66 in Goteborg) and lower success rates in concentrations of immigrants

(-.60 in Stockholm, -.51 in Goteborg) and the unemployed (-.56 in Stockholm, -.54 in Goteborg). Except for a negative relationship between spending on upper secondary education and performance in the Stockholm region, there is no relationship between spending on education and educational performance.

Correlations in the U.S. metropolitan regions show the effects of the more limited, more varied approaches to funding equalization there. In California, figures for 2002 and 2007 indicate a shift as formulas for redistribution among education districts were contested and readjusted. In 2002, education spending correlated with higher income and poverty, but not with indicators of ethnic and racial minority concentrations. In 2007, this correlation had shifted in favour of immigrant communities but away from poverty concentrations or higher income areas. None of these correlations (generally under .30) ranged as high as in Sweden. The correlations in greater Minneapolis showed consistently higher education spending in both immigrant and minority concentrations (.39 to .59) but also significantly higher rates (.22) in higher income areas.

Against this pattern of more mixed, more limited redistribution, educational outcome data show remarkably consistent correlations to those in the Swedish regions. In Los Angeles, the correlations are in some respects lower than in Stockholm and Goteborg. Secondary school graduation rates correlate at .37 (2002) to .38 (2007) with per capita income, at -.37 to -.54 with unemployment, poverty, and minority concentrations, and at -.17 to -.20 with the foreign born population. In greater Minneapolis, graduation rates correlate somewhat more weakly with income (.16 (2002) to .20 (2007)) and with economic disadvantage (-.24 to -.31), but about as strongly with minority concentrations (-.39 to -.56) and more strongly with foreign born populations (-.25 in 2002, -.37 in 2007).

Systematic, place-based advantages and disadvantages in the educational system, then, have persisted despite comprehensive redistributive policies in Sweden and much more limited, sector-specific funding equalization in the United States. In the Swedish metropolitan areas, to be sure, the range of variation between levels of performance is significantly narrower. Standard deviations in educational performance there range from 2.1 percent to 4.6 percent, compared to standard deviations from 7.2 percent to 11.3 percent in the U.S. regions. But within this narrower range, the socioeconomic status of communities bears a relationship to educational performance that is in some respects more systematic than in the U.S. metropolitan regions.

Conclusions

Our four-way comparison has demonstrated wide diversity in arrangements for metropolitan governance at both the national and the metropolitan levels. National policies and institutions in Sweden, and arrangements in the United States at the state and metropolitan levels, have redistributed significant portions of revenues and resources between the richer and poorer communities of metropolitan regions. These efforts are generally greater and more effective in Sweden than in the United States, and stronger in greater Minneapolis than in greater Los Angeles.

Comparison of metropolitan outcomes, however, reveals shortcomings to even the most ambitious policies and institutions for redistribution. Surprisingly, patterns of metropolitan inequality in educational outcomes under the highly egalitarian Swedish system largely parallel those in the highly inegalitarian national system of the United States. Although the levels of disparities among outcomes are greater in the U.S. metropolitan regions, this contrast may be due as much to the greater diversity and heterogeneity of U.S. society as to differences in policies and institutions.

Neither large scale differences between national systems, nor institutions and policies within metropolitan regions have eliminated the social and economic forces that produce disparities in opportunities for the citizens of metropolitan communities. The resulting patterns of privilege and disadvantage pose parallel dilemmas for policymakers across the developed world.

JØRGEN AMDAM –VOLDA UNIVERSITY COLLEGE, NORWAY

Flexibility In Regional Planning

Introduction

Why flexibility in regional planning? The traditional means of spatial regional planning in Scandinavia have been to reduce possibilities and flexibility and, by land use planning and other law-based planning activities, to try to control development. Regional and local planning is a public activity, politically controlled by municipalities, counties and state, and connected to political and administrative borders and legislation. As Zeote and Spit (2002) have found in the Netherlands, paradigms and practice of regional (physical) planning have changed from a publicly controlled, comprehensive activity, to project-based changes controlled by private interests or public-private partnerships, see table 1. We have seen comparable changes also in Norway (Amdam 1998).

Table 1. Types of planning – the shift from physical to project planning.
Zeote and Spit (2002)

TYPE OF PLAN CRITERION		PROJECT PLANNING	PHYSICAL PLANNING
1.	Initiative	public and private partners	exclusively public
2.	Goals and objectives	redevelopment	co-ordination and safeguard material interests
3.	Positive or negative planning	positive	negative
4.	Societal impact	large (change)	small (defensive)
5.	Position of stockholders	central	'hidden' or lacking
6.	Arguments for the boundaries of the plan	derived from the project	from the planning system
7.	Creative vision	with strategic purposes	...
8.	Law on Physical Planning (WRO/Bro)	marginal position	determents the procedures
9.	Finance secured?	central	no essential element in the plan
10.	Product	contract	physical plan

The reasons Zeote and Spit (2002, p13) give for this change in the Netherlands are as follows:

The first is an old acquaintance in physical planning, namely the collision between the wish for more flexibility on the one hand, and the desire to assure material rights for actors within the territory, on the other. ..

The second reason concerns the absence of knowledge of other projects running more or less parallel, as well as other developments within the same region presents a problem. In project planning, most projects are either seen as isolated components in a larger program, or as islands within a region. ..

The third problem is closely related to the other two. It has to do with physical planning itself. As mentioned before, municipalities are reluctant to spend much money on physical plans. As a result, many plans in urban areas are too outdated (or very much outdated) to be used as functional framework for project planning.

Zeote and Spit (2002) focus on land-use planning and the change from proactive to a reactive public planning and development that is focusing on individual projects. Similar arguments have been forwarded based on studies in Great Britain by Haughton et al. (2010) and Healey (2007) and in Scandinavia (Amdam 1998, 2001). Typical recommendations vis-a-vis these challenges are to change public regional planning from a regulatory activity to a flexible, collaborative, proactive activity based on dialog between stakeholders and with a strong focus on power relations, complexity and partnerships, a new collaborative spatial planning (Allmendinger 2009, Amdam and Amdam 2000, Amdam R. 2005, Healey 2006, 2007, Innes and Booher 2010).

My project here is to examine some of the challenges related to regional planning in our complex society and to present and discuss a model developed by Amdam and Amdam (2000) and Amdam (2005) that try to cope with some of these challenges.

Challenges and complexity
What is a Region?

Regional and spatial planning is traditionally bounded by political and administrative borders. Legislation such as the Norwegian planning and building act, gives authority to municipalities and counties to produce and decide on spatial plans. These plans will usually cover only the specific area of the planning authority. This is because the purpose of planning is to control growth, and it does so through restrictions (see figure 1). But increasingly, local and regional challenges are not connected to the control of growth, but how to stimulate development and positive changes in industries, communications, urban, rural and natural environments.

Regional challenges and planning problems are not limited to public structures, and borders, as networks of regional systems are dynamic, compared to static administrative structures. New and better roads, railways etc change transport structures, settlement patterns, demand on services etc both in urban and rural areas. In industry there is a strong focus on clusters and industrial districts

(Porter 1990, Storper 1995), whose geographic pattern rarely corresponds to public structures.

While a region in legislative terms is a clearly defined political-administrative unit, like a county or a municipality, with equally clearly defined responsibilities and borders, in reality a region associated with flexible planning is based on economic, cultural, communicational etc networks, stakeholders and challenges, and these are dynamic over time. Even in the public sector, in Norway, due to new public management ideologies, state authorities and state-owned activities have been organised geographically in more than 30 different ways, with corresponding challenges of territorial coordination.

While traditional regional planning is territorial and tries to coordinate functions inside a specific territory, flexible regional planning need, to coordinate activities in terms of both function and territory, and to be dynamic regarding regional structure, challenges, stakeholders, processes etc, as well as initiatives, actions and responses.

Planning substance

Traditionally, the content of regional plans was defined by law and with a strong focus on land use. The challenge today is to maintain that role and continue to produce this form of land use plans, for which there is a high demand so as to coordinate individual projects (Zeote and Spit 2002). Yet if land-use planning is not sifficiently taking account of ongoing regional processes of change inside and outside of its boundaries, it will be overtaken by developments and become irrelevant. In a regulatory regime local and regional land-use planning tries to control other activities in the community. Today, this will only function, if there is clear agreement on content and purpose of land-use plans, illustrate, so that each individual decision maker accepts, and builds, on these plans. In a closed and stable system it might be possible to realise "command-style land-use plans". Today and in future, our communities and regions are and will need to be, dynamic vis-a-vis stakeholders, values, needs, challenges, activities etc. They are open systems that need a more flexible and dynamic approach to strategic planning.

Planning processes must focus on challenges as they evolve and try to develop strategies and actions that cope with specific challenges. Since regions are different and changes dynamically, regional planning must focus on the specific situation and challenges of the actual planning region.

Planning processes

Traditional regional planning is organised around the ideal instrumental and linear planning model, with its focus on objectives, alternatives, consequences, decisions and implementation (Amdam and Veggeland 2000, Allmendinger 2009, Friedmann 1987). Comprehensive instrumental regional planning must be controllable by actors with authority to maintain legitimacy. Typically, this is done by controlling participation and activity in stages. Formulation of objectives is seen as a political responsibility, formulation of alternatives and analyses of consequences, a professional activity, just as it is to prepare proposal for decision by the politically responsible authority. To function as a proper comprehensive process all challenges must be "equally mature". We must have proper knowledge regarding individual challenges and their interrelationships, so as to formulate comprehensive alternatives and actions, evaluate consequences and make decisions. Also, the deciding authority must have responsibility and possess power to implement planning decisions.

In a complex and dynamic society this kind of comprehensive instrumental planning will rarely work. The instrumental model may still be applicable for concrete and bounded projects, but the communicative changes in our society make it difficult, even dangerous, to follow this static model in a dynamic and unbounded, open reality. Fragmentation means that challenges and actions are related to a complex set of stakeholders. Knowledge can rarely be fully assessed and/or strategically controlled by stakeholders. Challenges and actions are continuously evolving and must be reconciled at different stages, often associated with problems of coordination with other projects. Plans and planning processes are competing for publicity, power, participation, resources, decisions and implementation and "problem solved" are often coming back in "new clouts".

Flexible regional planning is not one comprehensive, linear process of coordination, coordinated linear process, but combines a number of competing processes related to different but interwoven challenges, stakeholders, arenas etc, that need a way of coordination to function properly.

Stakeholders

Stakeholders are bearers of individual values, norms, intentions, knowledge, resources etc that are important in planning processes (Healey 2006). Legislation often defines stakeholders as people and organisations which hold direct economic or other interests, or upon whom the planning process and its decisions and outcomes may have a bearing on them. (Amdam and Veggeland 2000). Participation can be controllable in formal and traditional planning processes, but is a lot more difficult to do in complex and flexible planning processes.

One problem is that flexible regional planning must handle several interwoven processes related to a broad scope of challenges. Stakeholders' main interests are usually connected to only a few of these. Often it is difficult for stakeholders to establish connections between "cases and processes", and answer questions like "why must decisions regarding my plan be coordinated with something totally different?" Other problems are related to the relative power of stakeholders and their ability or inability, to influence other stakeholders, political processes, knowledge, mobilisation, alliance building etc. Stakeholders are also interconnected through multiple formal and informal networks and arenas.

In communicative planning even professional planners are viewed as stakeholders with their own specific values, norms, knowledge, standard solutions and actions, influenced by professional standards and experiences, competing with other stakeholders for influence (Healey 2006). No-one is really neutral and as Flyvbjerg (1993) put it, knowledge can give power, but power also control knowledge.

Flexible processes can and must bring together stakeholders that have common interests, and promote the building of power, while also functioning and as arenas for conflict negotiations and management. Organising planning processes regarding the participation and mobilisation of stakeholders is one of the most potent instruments in flexible regional planning.

Complexity

Table 2. Features of complex adaptive systems. Innes and Booher (2010 p. 32)

Features	Summary descriptions
Agents	The system comprises large numbers of individual agents connected through multiple networks.
Interactions	The agents interact dynamically, exchanging information and energy based upon heuristics that organize the interactions locally. Even if specific agents only interact with a few others, the effects propagate through the system. As a result the system has a memory that is not located at a specific place, but is distributed throughout the system.
Nonlinearity	The interactions are nonlinear, interactive, recursive, and selfreferential. There are many direct and indirect feedback loops.
System behavior	The system is open, the behaviour of the system is determined by the interactions, not the components, and the behaviour of the system cannot be understood by looking at the components. It can only be understood by looking at the interactions. Coherent and novel patterns of order emerge.
Robustness and adaptation	The system displays both the capacity to maintain its viability and the capacity to evolve. With sufficient diversity the heuristics will evolve, the agents will adapt to each other, and the system can reorganize its internal structure without the intervention of an outside agent.

On table 2 Innes and Booher (2010) have formulated some of the features of complex adaptive systems that are typical for the situations that regional planning has to handle today. As John Friedmann formulated in 1973 in his book "Retracking America, A Theory of Transactive Planning", regional planning is and must be, part of the continuous processes of change in our open societies. One way or another, we are all planners albeit with varying influence on processes, decisions, actions and responses.

Flexible regional planning as a system of processes must integrate with the dynamic processes of regional systems, promoting processes of learning and evaluation that stimulate cooperation and collaboration between actors, even if they prusue differing interests.

Flexible strategic and mobilising regional planning

In their book "Planning with Complexity" Innes and Booher (2010, p5) comment on the changes of focus in regional planning, and identify the following trends and characteristics:
- Traditional linear methods are replaced by nonlinear socially constructed processes engaging both experts and stakeholders.
- Traditional "scientific" expert knowledge is competes with lay knowledge, and such knowledge is seen as socially constructed and dependent of stakeholder values, norms and interests.
- New forms of reasoning are beginning to play a larger role and gain scholarly recognition and legitimacy. There is a shift from instrumental to communicative planning where storytelling and experience is important.

Typically, authors that study these changes, such as Patsy Healey (2006, 2007), John Forester (1993, 1999) or Innes and Booher (2010), recommend general principles that communicative planning must follow connected to Habermas' theory of communicative rationality. Principles are formulated, but rarely as "models for good planning". In a collaborative context "models" can be an obstacle to communication, understanding and promoting an "instrumental" thinking of process. Collaborative planning must be organised according to the specific conditions surrounding the process of planning. Using a "general model" in an unqualified way can increase problems, rather than solve them. As a teacher of regional planning I understand these arguments, but still see the need for some kind of "flexible regional planning model" that can be used as a basis for adapt general planning models to specific regional situations. With respect to the theoretical and practical challenges, Amdam (1995, 2000, 2001. 2003, Amdam and Amdam 2000, Amdam R. 1997, 2000, 2001, 2005) have tried to develop a general model for "flexible strategic and mobilising regional planning".

Flexible regional planning must include both communicative and instrumental perspectives and processes must be organised according to the characteristics of a specific region. Decisions on a new communication system or a new hospital structure with conflicting interests must be organised as communicative decision processes that try to coordinate complex realities, but must also be instrumental in implementing decisions once these have been taken by agreement between all concerned, following political decision processes as required. In a Scandinavian context, flexible regional planning must include also public formal regional planning due to the strong formal and de facto power held by municipalities and counties over service provision in the country's welfare society. Flexible regional planning can theoretically be organised without participation by the local and regional public sector, public planning tries to tackle challenges that require some form of involvement by the public need some kind. Can public regional planning be reorganised such that it functions as flexible regional planning, including all stakeholders and their challenges and actions? Can these processes build on and be coordinated with formal planning processes and and political–administrative processes of decision making?

Typically, we found in experiments and case studies that a flexible regional planning system need to be organised according to regarding five variables (see figure 1). But just as important is the participation of stakeholders in the relevant processes, and the kind of communication, collaboration, learning and understanding that develops from there. (Amdam R. 2005). This model will be presented next, followed by two recent case studies using this very model of dynamic regional planning.

Figure 1. Model for flexible and communicative regional planning system. Amdam 2005.

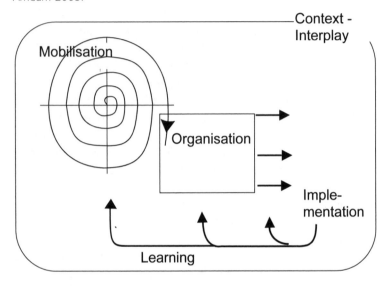

Strategic planning – mobilisation of stakeholders

Typical for open, dynamic regional systems is that many planning and decision-making processes occur in an continuously and uncoordinated way. Is it possible to agree on what constitutes a reasonable planning region, and to organise some mild form of a coordination as a mobilisation process, focusing on what are the most important challenges for the region and develop response strategies? Such mobilisation should ideally be continuous, but that is often difficult due to its inherent complexity. Is it possible to arrange specific meetings, processes, or arenas that focus on these challenges and that involve as many of the key stakeholders as possible? This is the central set of questions for strategic planning in our model for flexible regional planning. To develop an understanding and new knowledge of the challenges and tasks ahead, stakeholders need arenas, where their own norms, values, interests, challenges and actions are "confronting" those of others in an active learning dialogue. In the private sector, strategic planning usually is a very secret process that involves only a small elite of business owners and leaders. In the public sector a key challenge stems from the fact that wide range of actors needs to be involved in facilitating and accompanying regional change. And this needs to be negotiated. Instead of a secret process, a strategic regional planning process in our experience must involve all stakeholders within the public sector and outside that can and will have influence on the dynamic development of the region.

To formulate commonly accepted visions and strategies, one therefore needs a moral discourse which involves and mobilises stakeholders as part of a consensus-building processes (Amdam 2000, Amdam R. 1997, 2001) which tries to involve as many as possible. This can be facilitated in the form of workshops etc, but, most importantly, needs to use platforms for debate between stakeholders to develop a mutual understanding, strategies and actions. Successful mobilisation and collaboration usually leads to the development of a better understanding of the dynamics underpinning a current situation, and to the formulation of goals and strategies, for some of which specific actors (partnerships) will take responsibility in the form of developing more detailed operative plans and actions. This will then be the background for tactical and operational planning and its implementation.

To motivate, teach, and engage supporting groups, new social entrepreneurs etc. are an extremely important part of the mobilization and development process. In addition, it is important to draft detailed plans of processes with clearly defined, activity packages, time schedules, descriptions of the range of participants in the various planning phases, responsibility for reports, drafting documents, informal and formal decisions etc, and also clearly establish that the leaders themselves are responsible for this work. There is, of course, a danger that this can lead them to having too much control and influence, but this has not been a problem so far.

In most cases politicians have experienced mobilization processes as far less threatening than we expected in the beginning (Amdam and Amdam 1990, 2000). On the contrary, they have often expressed very positive attitudes to the experience and particular method of working, including the clear political element in the approach. We have even experienced that politicians and civil servants have adopted these methods in their own work with the planning of e.g. health and social welfare activities, compulsory education, planning in sports associations, voluntary organizations etc.

Tactical planning – organisation – partnerships

While the mobilisation process can develop agreement on visions, strategies and some tasks, further development of concrete strategies and organisation of the implementation of strategies, programs and projects must also be done. This process is dominated by an ethic-political discourse related to conflict solving which mainly involves stakeholders, politicians and administrators as representatives of common interests (Amdam R. 2001, 2005). Our experience shows that organising specific and concrete processes of communication that include major stakeholders with specific interests, have been successful in facilitating of concrete action programs and tasks. In most cases, groups involved in the strategic process took the responsibility for both planning and implementation of actions that they can do themselves. We give clear advice that during the tactical planning process "owners" of tasks need be identified and motivated and that stakeholders with conflicting interests must try to develop compromises. This includes seeking to motivate participants to identify what they can and cannot do themselves 'on the ground', and who ought to be responsible for what. Other questions revolve around motivation, identifying collaborative partners, establishing partnerships, and organising common activities (Amdam and Amdam 2000).

Some of the challenges regarding tactical regional planning and organisation of activities are connected to the Norwegian system of public administration and governance. Communes and counties are important actors in providing welfare both on behalf of the state and for local communities. In the Norwegian public planning system, strategic planning is closely linked to to the 4-year implementation programme (handlingsprogram) that every municipality and county must develop and which is revised every year. These days, they are dominated by the local authorities' responsibilities for welfare provision. In practice this operative planning is very difficult, since public activities are extremely dominated by state policy, and the state itself has no 4-year tactical planning. Since political compromises dominate state budgets, communes and counties have to change their plans each year according to new signals and resources coming from the state budget. This also means that, in practice, there are small differences between tactical and operative planning. It also means that tasks have to wait in a priority list which may easily change in response to central political actions.

This situation has also influenced on private-public partnerships which are crucial for regional planning and development. Local or regional public policy priorities are often based on area-based knowledge and understanding that is developed during processes of communication, but that has no influence on national planning. New and important private and/or public initiatives can be dependent on changes in priority in public investment and on contract partnerships that have a longer horizon than has public budget planning.

Operative planning, implementation of plans

If strategic and tactical planning has functioned according to its formal role in the system and followed procedure, most conflicts related to individual projects should have been solved at this stage, so that there are clear strategies for implementation. In some cases, there can still be differences in opinion of how "things should be done in practice", which can be solved by a pragmatic discourse involving only those responsible for the particular contested tasks and with a verified direct interest (Amdam R. 2001, 2005).

Challenges may arise from local communities, seeking to influence actions by external and, in some cases, internal actors and stakeholders. A truly flexible and dynamic regional planning must also be open to accommodate changing agendas and priorities. Yet a continuing the "plan must be followed" syndrome is a tremendous challenge for flexibilising regional planning.

Evaluation and learning

A fundamental part of communicative planning is learning as illustrated in figure 1 as "feedback process". Evaluation for learning is a continuous process.

Learning is also an important bottleneck in communicative development processes. If learning is monopolised, those at the centre of the process will develop a more important, powerful and "professional" position that can easily translate into a domination of the whole process. As Stöhr (1990) and Friedmann (1987, 1992) have shown this "monopolisation of power" is one of the most problematic challenges of development processes, from below, this kind of "power centralisation" can also easily develop in organisations like the commune (political elite group), county, in local NGOs, cooperatives etc. By mobilising a broad range of stakeholders, it is possible to empower new groups and the general public.

Institutional planning – context – cultural and institutional differences

Ideally communicative and collaborative planning processes should create common agreement on strategies, tasks etc, so that "formal decisions" would not be necessary. In practice reality, taking into account the complexity described above, this is impossible. There are always stakeholders inside or outside the planning community who do not involve themselves in consensus-building processes, taking into account control over resources, processes or other stakeholders. Implementing strategies, tasks and actions that are against their interests, lead to considerable compensation claims. Therefore it is important to make formal decisions according to formal procedures.

Another factor is the local and regional culture. Some regional communities enjoy a long and positive tradition of voluntary projects and mobilization and of doing things themselves. In these regions this method of working is stimulating and results in a more systematic and effective approach, because the development work is better coordinated and the purpose becomes more apparent. Here, it is natural for communities to ask what they themselves can do and what they can achieve in cooperation with other stakeholders. On the other hand there are those communities and regions where the initiative has to come "from above". Instead of their own activity and their own projects, they concentrate on making demands to the state, enterprises etc. It is an attitude which often leads to conflicts instead of cooperation and development.

The mobilization strategy presented here, not surprisingly, is most successful in the first type of communities and regions. Yet it is unlikely to succeed, and even can be counterproductive, if a community is of the "demanding variety", unless simultaneously great emphasis is placed on "cultural and institutional change" and, especially, on public mobilization. In such a case the role of the planner will not only be that of the leader of the process, but also that of the agent of change, which makes new demands and raises new problems, not least on the question of whose values are followed (Forester 1993, Sager 1994). But as shown by Healey et al (1999), such processes are necessary to develop higher institutional capital and the capacity and capability for change. In our experience communicative planning processes are often important arenas both for decision making and learning – learning to cooperate, to organize, to motivate etc. and also to learn how to learn and to develop relations and new friendships that can reduce fragmentation and division.

Norwegian examples
The Vennesla Case

Norway, and Scandinavia in general, have a long and strong tradition of combined action research regarding industrial democracy, with its strong focus on flexibility, learning and communication. Is it possible to transplant these models to regional planning? This was the idea of the Vennesla Case (Fosse 2009) as a part of a national programme. In his Ph.D. thesis, Jens Kristian Fosse, presents and evaluate a case study based on learning and planning theories. The planning process model used at the start of the project covered only part of the variables formulated in figure 1. They focused on mobilisation, organisation and implementation and using other terms. Using his thesis as base for my own evaluation. It follows that the industrial democracy model had to be changed regarding:

- *Context.* Compared to regional development and planning, action research on how to increase industrial democracy operates in rather closed systems, where participants know each other and usually have long-time relations and some mutual trust, at least in a Scandinavian context. Fosse found that, under such conditions, municipal and regional planning was a lot more open in terms of stakeholders involvement, commitment, networks, processes etc, so that the model and process plan used had to be reformulated and extended.

- *Strategy and mobilisation.* Dialog conferencing, modelled on industrial democracy, was used, but functioned differently. At enterprise level, this method usually leads to the formulation of concrete actions that were implemented in the next stage. This did not function at the broader level of 'regions', owing to, as Fosse concludes, the weak relations and degree of trust between stakeholders. On that basis, the outcome was an agreement on broader strategies and their implementation. This confirms out iowm experience (Amdam and Amdam 2000).

- *Organisation.* The concept of the Development Coalition was part of the original project, but functioned more as an arena for organising concrete actions and plans and establishing of public-private partnerships. Fosse found that compared to processes in businesses, coalition building was a lot more complicated, dependent on external authorities, other competing processes etc, plans were continuously reformulated in response to changes in context, stakeholders, economics etc.

- *Implementation.* The implementation of policies and projects was also more complicated in regional, open systems, owing to conflicting responsibilities etc.
- *Evaluation and learning.* In the models for industrial democracy, evaluation and common learning usually was an integrated part of activities, but not at the regional level. Fosse had to introduce a special dialogue conference with the focus on evaluating processes of negotiation and tasks. He concluded from that that the process must be reorganised in such a way that learning-focused evaluation is an integral part of all activities.

Fosse ends up with a model for learning in the planning process that is comparable to our model on figure 1, see figure 2.

Figure 2. Learning Processes in the Vennesla project (Fosse 2009).

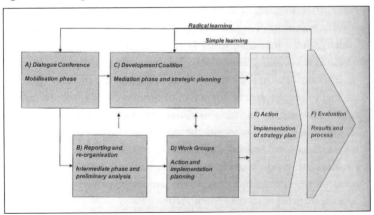

Regional partnerships

Ulla Higdem's (2007) PhD thesis studies "Regional Partnerships and their Constructions and Implementations" related to the counties of Oppland, Hedmark and Østfold. Her focus was private-public partnerships, but also looked at partnerships in regional planning and development processes. She found that the Norwegian regional planning system statutorily as formulated and institutionalised at county level did not function properly as such, and had to be "saved" by using informal and flexible programmes and projects. Partnerships are introduced nationally as "moderators" in response to EU regulation and policy, although they operate "in the shadow" of government.

- *Context.* Higdem (2007) shows that context and challenges vary from county to county. Their political-administrative traditions regarding planning and partnerships differ, as do their experiences. The flexibility available when organising specific programmes and partnerships "rescues" and gives content to, regional planning processes and facilitates the formulation of regional policy.
- *Mobilisation.* The formal system is "saved" by the direct involvement of stakeholders in project and programme groups, and by regional development planning processes, which, in some counties, are organised for sub-county level territories.
- *Organisation and action.* Partnership building and close coupling of stakeholders make possible the organisation of activities and strategies, whereas the formal planning system achieves only a rather low degree of organisational ability outside the formalised, technocratic responsibilities associated with the organisation of local government responsibilities between county and municipality.
- *Evaluation.* Evaluation and learning have no part in the formal regional planning system and have to be organised separately as specific processes in their own right.

Higdem (2007) shows that to have a proper flexible, dynamic and collaborative regional planning system is not necessarily all that is needed. Informal activates are needed too, such as programmes, projects, partnerships etc. They need to be, and are, organised according to the collaborative tradition in each region. This must be developed from below, as standardised, centrally defined models are too unresponsive to provide the needed region-specific framework.

Conclusions

The two cases above show that flexible and dynamic collaborative planning and development models have to be developed by stakeholders themselves, according to prevailing regional context, traditions etc. They also illustrate that the model for flexibly mobilising regional planning, such as discussed here, can be a sound basis for the organisation of flexible and dynamic regional planning.

REFERENCES

Allmendinger P. 2009 (2002): *Planning Theory*. Palgrave. Macmillan. Basingstoke.

Amdam, J. 1992: Local Planning and Mobilization: Experiences from the Norwegian Fringe, in M. Tykkyläinen (Ed): *Development Issues and Strategies in the New Europe*, pp. 21-40. Aldershot: Avebury.

Amdam, J. 1995: Mobilization, Participation and Partnership Building in Local Development Planning: Experience from Local Planning on Women's Conditions in Six Norwegian Communes. *European Planning Studies*, Vol. 3, No. 3, pp. 305-332.

Amdam J. 1997: Planning for rural and local development in Ireland and Norway. I Byron R., J. Walsh and P. Breathnach (eds.) *Sustainable Development on the North Atlantic Margin*. Ashgate. Aldershot.

Amdam J. 1998: *Fungerer (heller ikkje) den fysiske planlegginga?* Arbeidsrapport nr. 58. Møreforsking og MRDH. Volda.

Amdam. J. 2000: Confidence Building in Local Planning and Development. Some experience from Norway. *European Planning Studies*, Vol. 8, No. 5.

Amdam J. 2001: The Politics of Local Land – Use Planning in Norway. In Byron R. and J. Hutson (eds.): *Community Development on the North Atlantic Margin*. Ashgate. Aldershot.

Amdam J. 2003: Structure and strategy for regional learning and innovation – challenges for regional planning. *European Planning Studies*, Vol.11, No. 6.

Amdam, J. og R. Amdam 2000: *Kommunikativ planlegging*. Samlaget. Oslo.

Amdam, J. og N. Veggeland 1998: *Teorier om samfunnsplanlegging. Lokalt, regionalt, nasjonalt, internasjonalt.* Universitetsforlaget. Oslo.

Amdam R. 1997: Empowerment Planning in Local Communities: Some Experiences from Combines Communicative and Instrumental Rationality in Local Planning in Norway. *International Planning Studies.* Vol 2. No 3.

Amdam R. 2001: Empowering New Regional Political Institutions: A Norwegian Case. *Planning Theory & Practice.* Vol 2. No 2.

Amdam R. 2004: Sectorial Versus Territorial Regional Planning and Development in Norway. *European Planning Studies.* Vol 10 No 1.

Amdam R. 2005: *Planlegging som handling.* Universitetsforlaget. Oslo.

Flyvbjerg B. 1993: *Rationalitet og Magt. Bind 1 og 2.* Odense: Akademisk forlag.

Forester, J. 1993: *Critical theory, public policy and planning practice: toward a critical pragmatism.* Albany NY: University of New York Press.

Forester J. 1999: *The deliberative practitioner: encouraging participatory planning processes.* Cambridge, Mass. MIT Press

Fosse, J. K. 2009: *Learning in Planning. An Action Research Approach to Municipal Economic Development.* PhD thesis. Dept of Geography. NTNU Trondheim.

Friedmann J. 1973: *Retracking America. A Theory of Transactive Planning.* New York: Anchor press/Doubleday.

Friedmann J. 1987: *Planning in the Public Domain.* Princeton. New Jersey.

Friedmann, J. 1992: *Empowerment. The Politics of Alternative Development.* Cambridge MA & Oxford UK: Blackwell Publishers.

Haughton, G.P. Allmendinger, D. Counsell and G. Vigar 2010: *The New Spatial Planning. Territorial management with soft spaces and fuzzy boundaries.* Routledge. London.

Healey, P., A. Khakee, A. Motte and B. Needham (eds) 1997: *Making Strategic Spatial Plans. Innovation in Europe.* UCL Press. London.

Healey P. 2006 (1997): *Collaborative Planning. Shaping Places in Fragmented Societies.* Palgrave. Macmillan. Basingstoke.

Healey, P. 2007: *Urban Complexity and Spatial Strategies. Toward a relational planning for our times.* The RTPI Library series. Routledge. London.

Higdem, U. 2007: *Regional Partnerships and their Constructions and Implementations.* PhD thesis. Dept. Of Landscape Arcitecture and Spatial Planning. UMB. Ås.

Innes J. E. and D. E. Booher 2010: *Planning with Complexity. An introduction to collaborative rationality for public policy.* Routledge. London and New York.

Porter M. 1990: *The Competitive Advantage of Nations.* London: Macmillan.

Sager, T. 1994. *Communicative Planning Theory.* Aldershot, Hants: Avebury.

Storper M. 1995: *The Regional World. Territorial development in a global economy*. New York: Guilford.

Stöhr W. (red.) 1990: *Global Challange and Local Response. Initiatives for Economic Regeneration in Contemporary Europe*. The United Nations University. Mansell. London og New York.

Zoete, Paul R. and Tejo Spit. 2002. *Project Planning and Regional Planning: Linking as a Vital Challenge*. Paper to AESOP conference July 18–23, 2002 at Volos, Greece.

Vigar, G., P. Healey, A. Hull and S. Davoudi 2000: *Planning, Governance and Spatial Strategy in Britain. An Institutionalists Analysis*. Macmillan Press LTD, Hampshire and London.

ELVIRA UYARRA – MANCHESTER INSTITUTE OF INNOVATION RESEARCH, ENGLAND

Regional Innovation Systems Revisited:
Networks, Institutions, Policy and Complexity

... In that Empire, the Art of Cartography attained such Perfection that the map of a single Province occupied the entirety of a City, and the map of the Empire, the entirety of a Province. In time, those Unconscionable Maps no longer satisfied, and the Cartographers Guilds struck a Map of the Empire whose size was that of the Empire, and which coincided point for point with it. The following Generations, who were not so fond of the Study of Cartography as their Forebears had been, saw that that vast Map was Useless, and not without some Pitilessness was it, that they delivered it up to the Inclemencies of Sun and Winters.[1]

Introduction

Since the 1980's the region has been central to discussions about innovation and competitiveness and understanding the dynamics of innovation at regional level a concern for scholarly research and for practitioners seeking to improve regional economic prosperity. Concepts such as regional innovation systems have been coined to convey the idea that firms interacting locally and adequately supported institutionally are able to achieve higher rates of innovation, and ultimately generate quality jobs and growth in the region. The presence, characteristics and performance of such regional configurations have been of key interest for academics and policy makers,

169

in parallel with the emergence of an agenda for regionalisation of industrial policy and economic development policy in many countries in Europe since the 1990s.

Despite the popularity of the concept 'regional innovation system' (RIS) in the academic literature and in policy practice, multiple interpretations and uses of the term coexist. For instance while some scholars view RIS as subsystems of national or sector-based systems presenting particular spatial features, other portray them as smaller-scale versions of national systems (Lagendijk, 1999; Howells, 1999; Iammarino, 2005, Uyarra, 2010). Doloreux & Parto (2005) identify three dimensions of regional innovation systems, namely: the interactions between different actors in the innovation process, the role of institutions, and the use of regional innovation systems analysis to inform policy decisions. More generally, Werker & Athreye (2004) differentiate between micro and meso approaches explaining regional innovation; while the former concentrate on the entrepreneurial behaviour of innovative firms, the latter focus on the structural elements manifested in the institutional set-up of regional and industrial systems. Related literature on national innovation systems (NIS) is no less heterogeneous, with numerous usages and interpretations (Miettinen, 2002; Balzat & Hanusch, 2004; Sharif, 2006; Lundvall, 2007). Despite the popularity of the concept 'innovation system' in the academic literature and in policy practice, the term itself remains ambiguous (Doloreux & Parto 2005; Uyarra, 2010). This fuzziness (Markusen, 2003), even 'black boxing' of the term, may have obscured certain aspects influencing regional development while overstating others (Uyarra & Flanagan, 2010).

This chapter draws from contemporary literature on the region and from innovation studies in order to critically examine different interpretations that have over time been associated with the use of the term 'regional system of innovation'. The chapter attempts to critically discuss these changing views, while at the same time connecting the literatures on RIS and NIS. The chapter therefore commences with a glance at firm network approaches to regional innovation systems, which put the emphasis on dense and closely collaborating communities of firms that are found to be characteristic of successful agglomerations. The chapter then continues with an examination of scholarly accounts that use the term 'system' as a metaphor to reflect the key role played by institutional and governance structures in economic development. The third section critically considers how recent literature views innovation systems as an *artefact* and as a target for policy action. The chapter suggests that this use of the concept has led to an instrumental view of innovation and regions at odds with the ideas that originally inspired the concept. Recent contributions from evolutionary and complexity economics are reviewed in the fourth section as alternatives to understanding evolutionary, diverse, and multi-level dimensions of regional systems. However, questions remain in relation to methodology, ontology and policy. Finally, some conclusions are drawn in the last section.

Systems as networks: local interactive learning

A key feature of innovation system approaches is an understanding of innovation as an interactive and dynamic process that relies on learning and networking. It recognises that firms rarely innovate in isolation but rather in networks of related actors. Networks act as coordinating devices enabling inter-firm learning and diffusion of know-how, facilitating access to complementary assets and providing an organisational platform to combine different competences required for innovation (Oerlemans et al, 2007). Pressured by increasing global competition, rapid technological change and shortening product life-cycles, firms – particularly small or medium sized ones (SMEs) – increasingly rely on innovation-related cooperation with a variety of partners such as customers, competitors, suppliers and universities. Stressing the importance of interactive learning and knowledge sharing for innovation, particularly in relation to user-producer interactions, Lundvall (1992) thus defined innovation systems as "the elements and relationships which interact in the production, diffusion and use of new, and economically useful, knowledge". These micro-foundations place interactive learning and knowledge at the centre of analysis and are the starting point of discussions on the bottom-up dynamics of regional innovation systems (Cooke et al, 1997; Howells, 1999). Relationships and networks among regional components are a key defining feature of RIS, and localized processes of learning and knowledge accumulation an explanatory factor of higher levels of regional competitiveness (Cooke, 1998; Koschatzky & Sternberg, 2000).

The localised nature of innovation networks has been the focus of 'knowledge spillovers' studies, which demonstrate that firms benefit from the proximity of private and public R&D activities, the more so the more knowledge intensive firms are (Audretsch & Feldman, 1996). With the assumption that knowledge is either codified (and thus readily transferred) or tacit, such studies suggest a 'typical distance decay function in communication' (Howells, 1999). Other accounts have stressed to a greater extent the relational and cultural underpinning, or embeddedness, of such networks. Post-Marshallian accounts of industrial districts in Italy and elsewhere (see e.g. Pyke et al., 1990), depict geographically localized productive systems, characterized by a large number of SMEs specialized in different phases of the production and distribution processes of an industrial sector. Related literature on the 'innovative milieu' (Aydalot, 1986) and 'new industrial spaces' (Scott, 1986) reiterated the symbiotic relationship between innovation, networks, and proximity.

Such accounts, mainly based on case studies of successful agglomerations, emphasise localized processes of learning and knowledge accumulation as sources of regional competitiveness. Regional economies displaying dense networks of inter-firm and public-private interactions are associated with better than average growth performance (Cooke & Morgan, 1993). Linked together by reciprocity, trust, cultural and social ties, these local networks are seen to generate a coordination system that outperforms other coordination mechanisms such as the market (Oerlemans et al, 2007), creating an environment that facilitates the sharing of tacit knowledge. However straightforward explanations based on attributing geographical dimensions to degrees of knowledge tacitness have recently been challenged (Cowan et al, 2000). It has also been argued that other types of proximity (cognitive, social, institutional, organizational) are able to act as partial substitutes for physical proximity (Boschma, 2005). Furthermore, and despite the interest in social interaction in networks, network concepts and methods have rarely been applied to understand such mechanisms (Cantner et al, 2010). While social and culturally embedded networks are considered a key property of successful agglomerations, the structural properties of such localised networks and their impact on innovation outcomes are given less attention in the literature (Grabher, 2006; Oerlemans et al, 2007), an issue to which we will return in the final section of this chapter. From a policy design view, there is a risk of uncritically adopting a 'networks are good, more networks are better' approach, potentially overstating external factors of innovation vis-à-vis internal capabilities (Freel, 2002) and underplaying variety in the drivers, structure and impact of collaboration.

Discussions on inter-firm relationships have generally focused on the institutional context in which actors are embedded, rather than on networks per se. The so-called 'institutional turn' within economic geography has emphasized the role of institutions in influencing firms' behaviour, particularly in relation to inter-firm networking and industrial relations (Martin, 2000). Cooke & Morgan (1993, p. 555) note that local innovation networks are enabled by a "number of institutions of a private, semipublic, and public nature which act as a 'life-support' system, especially for SMEs". Notions such as the 'network paradigm', 'institutional thickness' and 'learning regions' are used to refer to such "microregulatory networks of institutions which give spatial definition to interfirm networking" and serve to connect firm-network innovation approaches and social capital to the problem of regional development (Cooke and Morgan, 1993; see also Florida, 1995; Amin & Thrift, 1995; Asheim, 1996; Morgan, 1997). Connecting these contributions to the general literature on systems of innovation, the concept of 'regional systems of innovation' takes the learning region further by focusing on the governance of systemic institutional interrelations characteristic of successful regions. The next section explores this issue further.

Systems of innovation as an heuristic concept

Institutions are considered in the innovation systems literature to be key determinants of the rate and direction of technological change. For Freeman (1995: p.20), institutional differences in the mode of "importing, improving, developing and diffusing new technologies, products and processes" are instrumental to understanding the variation in technological capabilities across countries and regions. Pioneered by Freeman's (1987) study of Japan, a number of scholars (notably the contributions to the edited volume by Nelson, 1993) sought to examine the extent to which the presence (or absence) of macro-level institutions mattered for innovation in different countries. These studies provided a comparative-historical narrative to explain the influence on innovation of various kinds of interactions and interdependencies between organisations and institutions. National innovation systems were perceived as a "historically grown subsystem of the national economy" in which institutions would interact and influence the carrying out of innovative activity (Balzat & Hanusch, 2004; p.197).

The motivation of comparative analyses of national and regional systems of innovation was to contrast diverse settings (and therefore learn from diversity and differences) rather than to provide any form of general explanation of how systems function. It did not provide a "sharp guide to what exactly should be included in a system of innovation" (Edquist 1997; 27). Systems of innovation thus conceived become a useful metaphor for empirical research rather than a clearly articulated term. And, although aimed to inform policy, these analyses made no presumption of what constituted a 'right' or 'efficient' configuration of systems (Miettinen, 2002). While a national domain was early on adopted on the basis that many institutions influencing innovation have a national character, other appropriate levels (local, sectoral) at which to study the innovation system were also suggested (Lundvall, 1992). To some, the regional level was viewed as the natural level from which to develop innovation policies and institutions to support innovation and the development of industrial clusters. Cooke et al (1997; p. 479) considered the region as an appropriate unit for the analysis of innovation systems, for some of the "basic characteristics which distinguish a state can sometimes be distinctive in certain regions". It is not surprising that early uses of the notion of RIS were associated with dynamic regions with strong autonomous governments such as Baden Wurttemberg or the Basque Country, or with regions with ambitions to achieve similar levels of autonomy. Such regions were seen to feature strong institutional density, or 'thickness' (Amin & Thrift, 1995) and a strong social and cultural embeddedness of interrelations. The regional institutional infrastructure supporting innovation is therefore a key defining feature of regional innovation systems.

These top-down views stress the presence of institutions that deliberately promote innovation and knowledge, as well as the wider socio-economic system in which political and cultural influences and specific modes of governance determine innovation structures and performances (Howells, 1999). For Cooke (2001), an ideal institutional configuration includes issues such as autonomous taxing and spending, influence on infrastructure, and university-industry strategy; a cooperative culture and consensus, and organizational aspects such as harmonious labor relations at the firm level and inclusivity, networking and consultation at the policy level. Based on this characterisation, the existence of a RIS would be a special case, a rare event, characteristic only of a small number of regions (Cooke, 2001). Elsewhere, the national system of innovation would be dominant, as it is generally at the national level where scientific priorities are set, and where basic research and university training are funded (Cooke, 2005).

Fløysand & Jakobsen (2010) and Lundvall (2007) criticise what they perceive as a narrow definition of innovation systems, biased towards science based innovations and towards formal knowledge vis-à-vis contextual and informal knowledge. This bias "rules out most rural contexts where certainly innovation can also be observed" (Fløysand & Jakobsen, 2010,p.2). It could also be argued that this characterization of regional systems suffers from a 'structuralist' bias whereby the configuration of actors and institutions becomes the key explanatory factor of innovation performance and economic development, underplaying the dynamics of actors' routines and interactions (Uyarra & Flanagan, 2010). RIS thus are interpreted as smaller-scale versions of national systems, or as national systems 'writ small'. According to Iammarino (2005), such a 'shift' of NIS features down to the regional scale, although providing the necessary conditions to distinguish RIS, it is not by itself sufficient. Finally, while regional institutional structures are important for understanding differential patterns of economic activity, they tell us relatively little about the nature of institutional change and about the dynamics of system evolution: How are institutional structures created? How do they change? Can successful regional innovation systems be sustained over time?

Systems as artefacts: RIS as policy tool

The interest in systems of innovation has over time led to a more instrumental view that suggests ways to create well-functioning innovation systems. Indeed the idea of an 'innovation system' has morphed into a policy tool, a trend that can be observed not just in the national systems of innovation literature but also in some regional policy approaches. 'Systems of innovation' have shifted from a heuristic device or metaphor to understand variations across different institutional settings to a 'model' that regions or countries should aspire to build if they want to succeed in the knowledge economy. This use of the innovation system concept implies a structure or mechanism that can be nurtured and supported. Systems are considered as a tool, a target, and often an outcome of policies, a machine or artefact performing certain 'functions', whose performance can be improved or fine-tuned through the right policy levers. Similarly, performance comparisons or benchmarking *across* systems have taken centre stage, while less attention has been placed on systemic dissimilarities and context, country and history-specific structures and elements of particular systems (Balzat & Hanusch, 2004). Contrary to the institutional interpretation of systems, the existence of systems is here presupposed, even if they are weak or underperforming. Fløysand

& Jakobsen (2010, p.2) thus note that "with the development of strong linkages between research and policy, the [system] approach has been reconstructed as a standardized model for best innovation practice and used instrumentally for adjusting system failures within national, regional and even local innovation systems".

Some Innovation systems approaches have thus moved away from detailed empirical studies of 'real' systems, trying instead to identify all the general determinants of innovation—namely the factors (actors, functions, relationships) that have an impact on innovation. In this sense, Hekkert et al (2006; p.414, my emphasis) define innovation systems as a "heuristic attempt, developed to analyse *all* societal subsystems, actors and institutions contributing in one way or the other, directly or indirectly, intentionally or not, to the emergence or production of innovation". If we can understand all the determinants of innovation, system approaches automatically become a useful "conceptual framework for government policy making" (Edquist, 1997; 16). In other words, understanding the activities that foster or hamper innovation, i.e. how innovation systems 'function', allows us to "intentionally shape innovation processes" (Hekkert et al, 2006). The question that concerns scholars is therefore the identification of the set of functions[2] that are (or should be) fulfilled by the different actors or components. The performance of the system depends on "how well the functions are served within the system" (Hekkert et al, 2006). Thus the performance of the 'system' becomes a causal explanation of innovative activity and the identification of its determinants makes its management and improvement feasible (Miettinen, 2002; 46).

A tendency towards a normative use of systems can equally be perceived in policy oriented regional development studies. Christopherson & Clark (2007) consider the shift from firm-network innovation systems to an effort to make the learning region 'real' through policy initiatives to be a critical turning point. The shift from networks to learning regions and regional innovation systems has moved the discussion into the arena of policy-making, focusing on the rationale for investing collective monies in nurturing innovation systems. In order to favour development, it is argued that investment is needed in the institutional infrastructure supporting innovation in regional systems. As Freel (2002; p.633) notes, such policies are "premised on the belief that there exist, or may exist with sufficient encouragement or facilitation, distinct regional innovation systems within Europe".

I have argued elsewhere (Uyarra & Flanagan, 2010) that the influence of RIS as a normative concept favours the diffusion and adoption of a simplistic view in relation not only to the presence of a 'regional innovation system' in all regions but also to the implicit assumption that such systems are unproblematically amenable to regional policy intervention. Furthermore, the reverse causality is often implied: that RIS are the result of regional innovation policy and therefore that we can evaluate or assess regional policies by measuring the performance of the RIS. Besides the obvious problems of attributing cause and effect, it is important to remember that systems approaches tend to draw inspiration from `best practice' regions whose development has often had little or nothing to do with regional innovation policy (Hospers et al, 2008).

These policy-oriented considerations also raise important questions about legitimacy and governance. For instance about how regional governance structures are shaped, about accountability, decision-making and monitoring, inclusion and exclusion. In essence it raises questions about "whose interests are represented in processes of institutionalisation, in strategy development, in policy design and implementation" (Lagendijk, 1999). According to Christopherson & Clark (2007; p.11) "new regionalism is an effort to manufacture a scale – the region – in which local actors believe they can act effectively regardless of the political and economic realities operating on them" (See also Bristow, 2005; Lovering, 1999). The region is conceived as an 'actor' interacting with and competing in the world economy, rather than the firms themselves, somehow providing a blurred and misleading distinction between regions and firms. Agency and power seem to be absent in regional innovation systems in relation to the role of firms. Christopherson & Clark (2007; p.6) state that firms, particularly large ones, "actively shape the conditions in which they make choices through political as well as economic action at all geographical scales". This means that firms' capacities are embedded in political territories, but they are also shaped by firms' strategies across scales as they attempt to construct markets. We have argued elsewhere (Flanagan et al, 2011) that by reducing actors to the 'functions' they perform in the system, they are seen as passive targets of public policy to be transformed by policy-induced learning into exhibiting behavioural changes, and are therefore denied agency in relation to public policy and the shaping of the system.

Finally, a fixation with the regional scale as the natural unit of analysis for innovation has led to a view of regions as 'islands of innovation', underestimating the importance of non-local relationships and overstating the incidence and benefits of lasting proximate relationships. Cooperative, trust-based relations in local inter-firm networks may be the exception rather than the rule, and where they are strong they may even lead to cognitive lock-ins and reduce adaptability of regions (Grabher, 1993, Oinas, 2002). A closed view of the region presupposes that not only are innovation networks largely local, but also that the innovation in products & services and the benefits they generate are also local. The presumption is therefore that invention and innovation take place in the same region, which justifies policy efforts to couple the supply of and demand for innovation in the region, in a sort of input-output model of regionally bounded knowledge transmission.

Ultimately, instrumental approaches to systems of innovation sit uncomfortably with the idea of innovation as a complex, uncertain, contingent and heterogeneous phenomenon, which prevents a complete identification of the factors influencing technological change. According to Rosemberg (1992, p.186), *"the essential feature of technological innovation is that is fraught with many uncertainties. This uncertainty [...] has a very important implication: the activity cannot be planned. No person, or group of persons, is clever enough to plan the outcome of the search process, in the sense of identifying a particular innovation target and moving in a predetermined way to its realization."* All-inclusive attempts to understand systems run the risk of confusing the map with the territory (Nelson, 1977), the system with 'real regions', and 'operational' with 'conceptual' innovation systems (Cooke, 1998). The behaviour of the 'system' cannot be explained by the individual attributes or 'functions' of the actors, no more than decoding the 3 billion 'letters' of the human genome has helped us understand the behaviour of living systems.

Evolutionary and complexity views of innovation systems

Recent scholarly contributions, mainly from evolutionary economic geographers, have sought a dynamic explanation of the evolution of regional systems (Boschma & Frenken, 2006; Journal of Economic Geography, 2007; Economic Geography, 2009; Boschma & Martin, 2010). Such approaches are distinguished from the institutional views that attribute spatial variations in economic activities to institutional differences among territories (Boshma & Frenken, 2009). Centred on a consideration of the economy as a dynamic, irreversible and self-transformational system, evolutionary approaches are less concerned with how systems should look than with the *adaptation*, *resilience* and *change* of system configurations. Discussions have shifted from the economic growth and performance of regions to a broader focus on the adaptation and resilience of places against endogenous and exogenous shocks (Pike et al, 2010, Hassink, 2010, Pendall et al, 2007). To do so, they employ concepts and metaphors such as variety, selection, adaptation, emergence and self-organisation derived from evolutionary biology (Frenken & Boschma, 2007, Essletzbichler & Rigby 2007;), complexity theory (Martin & Sunley 2007), and network science (Glückler 2007).

Despite the use of different concepts and methodologies, these approaches share the common feature of trying to link the micro-economic behaviour of agents (firms, individuals) that operate in territorial contexts with the spatial evolution of industries and networks at the meso-level of the economy (Boschma & Frenken, 2006; Boschma & Martin, 2007). They therefore provide an integrative, micro to macro, view of regional innovation systems (Dopfer et al, 2004; Werker & Athreye, 2004; Iammarino 2005; Boschma & Frenken 2006).

Characteristic features of evolutionary approaches include a consideration of boundedly rational actors and their routines as the unit of analysis; the role of diversity in development processes; the non-linear, dynamic and path-dependent nature of economic development; and the dynamics of adaptation and coevolution of economic, technological and institutional environments. Evolutionary economic geographers have sought to demonstrate how place matters in such evolutionary processes, in other words "how the spatial organization of economic production, distribution and consumption is transformed over time" (Boschma & Martin (1997, p.3). There is clearly a link between geography and evolutionary processes such as path-dependency, as evidenced by the quasi-fixity of geographical patterns of industrial activities and their evolution over time (David 1985). As Martin & Sunley (2006; p. 427) note, economic history shows that "there are some areas and regions that have repeatedly been the site of path-forming innovations or new industrial sectors".

However, the use of metaphors such as variety, selection and retention derived from evolutionary biology poses questions in relation to their interpretation. For instance: what is it that evolves? (what is the ontological unit of enquiry?) At what spatial level does selection operate? How does co-evolution of spatial structures, institutions and micro-economic behaviours take place and how does it vary spatially? How do path-dependence and lock-in manifest and at what spatial levels? (Boschma & Martin, 2007; see also Martin & Sunley, 2006; Essletzbichler & Rigby, 2007; Hassink, 2010).

Some scholars have explicitly defined systems of innovation as complex systems (e.g. Katz, 2006; Metcalfe & Ramlogan, 2008). The characteristics of complex systems include a dynamic structure with interdependent constituents that interact in complex and non-linear ways. 'Limited functional decomposability' implies that macro-level functioning of systems cannot be deduced from knowledge about the system components. Complex systems are open, with boundaries that are difficult to identify, and structures that span many scales. Such openness contrasts with the 'operational closeness' implicit in many system approaches (Martin & Sunley, 2007). They also exhibit emergent properties or behaviour, arising out of micro-level behaviour and interactions and which cannot be predicted by the properties of the system constituents or the system itself. Finally, complex systems are able to self-organize, and emergent properties may change structures or create new ones. This has implications in terms of trying to predict innovation outcomes in conditions of uncertainty and complexity. Change is non-linear, discontinuous and probabilistic rather than deterministic. As a result, cause-and-effect relations are "distributed, intermingled [...] and not directly controllable, so policymakers need to become more comfortable with strategies that aim to influence rather than control" (OECD, 2009: p.13).

These systemic characteristics would preclude any attempt to manipulate, let alone create, systems. There is therefore no clearly identifiable 'system' with clear boundaries, that systems are linked to a problem or purpose, and that they are therefore not stable but transient. Rather than a holistic explanatory framework for understanding all determinants of innovation, innovation systems are more useful to understand specific (or "local") innovation problems (Metcalfe & Ramlogan, 2008). Problem oriented accounts of systems introduce a dynamic dimension, as opposed to the static orientation of most case studies of regional innovation networks, as they are underpinned by a theory of firm path dependency and of industry evolution (Christopherson & Clark, 2007).

The role of geography in underpinning complex adaptive systems is not clearly understood. However a point of connexion between relational economic geography, evolutionary and complexity theory can be found in the study of knowledge and connectivity in networks (Martin & Sunley, 2007). While networks have been a common feature in the analysis of regional innovation, and are considered key determinants of economic development (Metcalfe & Ramlogan, 2008), their use to explain the spatiality of relations has been rather selective (Bunnel & Coe, 2001; Lagendijk, 2002; Grabher, 2006). Grabher (2006; p.165) argues that economic geography, while recognising the importance of networks, has not taken a "systematic interest in the behavioural consequences of network configuration". This selective view of networks, associated with the embeddedness-network paradigm, emphasizes strong, locally embedded, cohesive networks, while neglecting weak, extra-local networks and links based on uneven power relations (Grabher, 2006). It therefore tends to neglect dominant positions of certain actors within networks. New theoretical perspectives in graph theory and statistical physics, Grabher (2006) argues, justify a re-examination of the properties of complex networks and their link with geography. Such developments have revealed properties associated with certain network configurations, with important implications for the creation and diffusion of knowledge as well as for the vulnerability or robustness of networks.

For instance, research by Albert & Barabási (2002) revealed that many networks have scale-free properties, with significant implications for network dynamics. The distribution of links in such networks follows a power law, which implies that the majority of nodes are relatively poorly connected, while a few exhibit extremely high connectivity. This is due to a particular pattern of growth of the network, which is not random or strictly proportional to the time of entry as previously assumed. It is likely that relationships with new nodes are based instead on 'preferential attachment', whereby new nodes would choose to connect with the nodes in the network that have greater connectivity. This generates a scale-free network characterised by the coexistence of a small number of hubs capturing most links and a majority of nodes having few links. Such configurations are found to be common in the internet, in citation networks among scientists, and in some innovation networks (Barabási, 2001). Scale-free networks influence performance in terms of knowledge diffusion, generating small world effects (Watts & Strogatz, 1998). The properties of high connectivity with the short average path length (small world effect) make them well suited for the evolutionary articulation of complex knowledge and the high speed of knowledge diffusion (Pyka, 2007).

Geography influences such network trajectories and, in turn, localized network evolution would influence regional innovation. According to Glückler (2007), the combination of preferential attachment, local embedding and multi-connectivity constitute cumulative retention mechanisms that induce path-dependence in networks, mechanisms that are themselves often mediated by geography. Frenken (2006) stresses the role of geography in the emergence of small worlds network effects. Since geography often acts as a constraint on search behaviour, he argues, its effect may to some extent counteract the effect of preferential attachment. Co-location, or 'being there', may also constitute a strategy to increase the propensity of contact due to spatial proximity (Glückler, 2007). Firms (particularly SMEs) may find it advantageous to locate in "information rich' and contact intensive innovation agglomerations (Howells 1999). It may be such local processes of search and scanning, and not just the effect of 'local' institutional embeddedness, what explains the localised nature of networks (Freel 2002). The degree of local connectivity, and the benefits of those connections, differ among local firms in clusters and along the life cycles of clusters (Menzel & Fornahl, 2009). The interplay between network topologies and geography leads to a diverse landscape of spatial network typologies, rather than to a dichotomous one of local clusters vs global links. Glückler (2007) suggests a fourfold typology of global bridging networks (between densely local networks and extra regional clusters), local bridging networks (between different but co-located clusters), local brokering (whereby only the weak ties are co-located), and mobile brokering (interconnected but geographically distributed actors who meet repeatedly in temporary clusters).

Certain properties of networks also make them more resilient and robust. In network theory, a scale free topology implies that a significant fraction of nodes can be randomly removed from any scale-free network without them breaking apart. Barabási (2000) thus notes that "most systems displaying a high degree of tolerance against failures share a common feature: their functionality is guaranteed by a highly interconnected complex network". However, despite such apparent robustness, they also present vulnerability around key positions, as external shocks affecting key hubs, i.e. highly connected actors, can lead to cascading failures due to their high degree of interconnectivity. Mainly employed in the study of communication infrastructure and disaster studies, the idea of *resilience* is increasingly used in relation to the adaptability of regions to external shocks. Although its contribution to our understanding of regional economic adaptability has been questioned (Hassink, 2010), it is clear that relations between agents are integral to the concept of regional resilience (Pike et al, 2010). Grabher & Stark (1997) frame this debate in terms of *legacies*, *linkages* and *localities*. They emphasize the presence of a rich diversity of organizational forms, and of strong and weak ties between social actors within social networks. Loose couplings that indirectly connect social agents, often bridging structural holes (Burt, 1992) between relatively isolated groups of actors, are crucial for the adaptability of networks. Research on 'related variety' (Frenken et al, 2007) also suggests that diversified regions, presenting a variety of generic competences and open to extra local links would be more likely to adapt to changing conditions and would be less susceptible to lock-in effects. As Pike et al note (2010, p.65), "diversified economies are more adaptable because they act as a 'shock absorber', dissipating negative effects across and array of economic activities and places rather than concentrating and reinforcing them."

Recent departures in evolutionary economic geography are helpful to understand the evolutionary, diverse, and multi-level dimensions of regional systems. Concerns have however been raised in terms of the limitations of selectively importing theoretical frameworks and concepts from physical sciences (Grabher, 2006). Indeed, Martin & Sunley (2007) question the extent to which a single, unified, 'meta-theory' of complexity can be equally applicable to diverse phenomena. Also problematic in Martin & Sunley's view is the strong reliance of complexity theory on formal modelling vis-à-vis ontological foundations, which leads them to suggest a social-ontological approach that analyses how complexity is spatially distributed, spatially embedded and spatially emergent. Coe (2010; p.2) in turn laments that certain methodological tools used in evolutionary and complexity theory remain, for many economic geographers, "alien and largely impenetrable, and the inbuilt assumptions and conceptualizations of space in EEG models will continue to be troubling".

Other authors have questioned the usefulness of distinguishing between institutional and evolutionary economic geography, and critique the treatment of institutions, social agency, and power relations by evolutionary economic geographers (McKinnon et al, 2009; Essletzbichler, 2009). McKinnon et al (2009) consider that evolutionary approaches downplay the influence of the spatial context on firms routines and suggest the need to reassert place-specific institutional environments and arrangements within and beyond the firm (albeit not restating the primacy of territorial institutions in influencing economic geographies). They argue that the analytical lens should go beyond organizational routines and situate evolutionary concepts within the broader conception of geographical political economy. Boschma & Frenken (2009) justify the distinction between institutional and evolutionary economic geography since the latter considers that the influence on firms' routines of territory-specific institutions is less significant. They suggest that "territorial institutions are [. . .] orthogonal to organizational routines" (p.152). Institutions may explain some interregional variety of routines, however they are more likely to be the outcome of processes of routine replication among firms through spinoffs and labor mobility. In their view, variance in innovative patterns of firms may be explained by sectoral, rather than regional, specificities (see also Malerba, 2002).

Linked to the treatment of institutions, Uyarra (2010) and Flanagan et al (2011) perceive a gap in evolutionary approaches and in general in innovation studies, in relation to the understanding of policy processes. Attention to policy is at best restricted to suggesting what policy makers ought to do (normative analysis), while being less concerned with what policy makers actually do (Wohlgemuth 2002) and how that conditions the dynamics of innovation. Assumptions in relation to policy are based on an evolutionary understanding of the economy, but not of the political process, which tends to be treated as a 'given' (Kay 2006)[3]. The impact of a policy is influenced not only by a changing economic landscape (the objective of innovation policy is always a moving target) or on the processes of co-evolution or mutual learning between the policies and the socio-economic system, but also on when it is implemented and on the path previously followed. Public policies, just like innovations, are complex and uncertain and display irreversibility and path-dependency effects: they are adopted not on a tabula rasa but in a context of pre-existing policy mixes and institutional frameworks which have been shaped through successive policy changes (Uyarra, 2010). Past policy decisions clearly constrain the range of options available for current decision makers (Kay, 2006). Successful policies (or actors) become institutionalised and thereafter form part of the foundation for the beliefs of actors. They are 'legacies' that gradually institutionalise, and as institutions they restrict or enable options for future policy makers (Kay, 2006). Thus, when formulating policies, regions should not only take the knowledge and institutional base of the region as starting point, but should also consider existing policy mixes and past policy history, for they will enable or constrain new policy goals (Uyarra, 2010).

When acknowledged, discussions of policy complexity are generally accompanied with recommendations for more and better coherence and more effective coordination. Such attempts are however assumed to be unproblematic. Indeed co-ordination problems can never be completely solved by new co-ordination mechanisms as those new mechanisms inevitably contribute further to the complexity they seek to manage, a problem exacerbated by the fact that it is rather easier to create new mechanisms than it is to remove existing ones. The absurd but logical outcome is that additional coordinating mechanisms will periodically have to be created to coordinate the older ones, and so on and so forth in an infinite regress[4] which is, again, predicted by the 'map and the territory' metaphor[5].

Conclusion

The discussion about the use and interpretation of the regional innovation system concept provides us with an opportunity to review different approaches to the spatial embedding of innovation and the different views that, over time, have stressed different factors influencing prosperity and resilience of places, as well as different conceptualisations and methodological approaches. Discussions of regional innovation and competitiveness have shifted from privileging locally and culturally embedded networks towards highlighting other explanatory dimensions such as the strength of institutional support for innovation, the presence or absence of specific functions in systems, and degrees of connectivity enabling adaptation and resilience of places.

The concept of systems of innovation has emerged out of the interplay of academic discussions and policy efforts to drive and co-ordinate economic development policies (particularly in supranational organisations such as the OECD). However, the instrumental view of systems that tends to dominate in the sphere of innovation policy analysis has devalued its relevance to inform policy. It privileges a closed view of systems and a simplistic view of the policy process. Regions as 'spaces' are clearly subject to the effects of policies made and implemented at multiple levels and at different times, they are not closed systems governed solely by their own regional innovation policies. Recent contributions from evolutionary and complexity economics that advocate a more open and dynamic view of regional systems, complemented by a more nuanced interpretation of the role of institutions and policy in regions open a promising avenue of research.

Acknowledgements. Many ideas in this paper are a result of the author's participation in the peer review group 'Developing and testing a conceptual framework for a systemic regional innovation policy in Skåne'. The author wishes to thank the group coordinator Arne Eriksson and the funding organisations Region Skåne and VINNOVA. The author also acknowledges the financial support of the Autonomous Province of Trento, sponsor of the OPENLOC research project.

NOTES

1 Jorge Luis Borges, Collected Fictions, Penguin 1999.

2 Broad functions are for instance knowledge producing, knowledge using, intermediating or policy-making functions.

3 However a few evolutionary economists have explored the dynamics of policy processes (e.g. see Slembeck, 1997; Witt, 2003; Pelikán and Wegner, 2003).

4 The author wishes to thank Kieron Flanagan for this comment.

5 Any map of a territory would, to be truly accurate, have to contain a representation of itself representing the territory, including a map representing the territory, and so on, in infinite regress.

REFERENCES

Albert, R. & Barabási A.L. (2002) *Statistical mechanics of complex networks.* Reviews of Modern Physics, 74, 67–97.

Amin A. & Thrift N (1995) *Globalisation, institutional 'thickness' and the local economy'.* In: Healey P, Cameron S, Davoudi S, Graham S, Madani-Pour A (eds) Managing cities: the new urban context. Wiley, New York, pp 91–108

Asheim B (1996) *Industrial districts as 'learning regions':* a condition of prosperity? Eur Plan Stud 1(4):379

Audretsch, D.B. & Feldman, M. (1996) *"knowledge spillovers and the geography of innovation and production"* American Economic Review, 86 (3), pp.630-40.

Aydalot P (1986) *Milieux Innovateurs en Europe.* Economica, Paris

Balzat, M. & Hanusch, H. (2004) *Recent trends in the research on national innovation systems.* Journal of Evolutionary Economics, 14: 197–210.

Barabási, A-L. (2000) *Linked: How Everything Is Connected to Everything Else and What it Means for Business, Science, and Everyday Life,* New York: Penguin.

Boschma R (2004) *Competitiveness of regions from an evolutionary perspective.* Reg Stud 38(9): 1001–1014

Boschma R (2005) *Proximity and innovation:* a critical assessment. Reg Stud 39(1):61–74

Boschma R. & Frenken K (2006) *Why is economic geography not an evolutionary science?* Towards an evolutionary economic geography. J Econ Geogr 6(3):273

Boschma, R. & Martin, R. (2007). Editorial: *Constructing an evolutionary economic geography Journal of Economic Geography.* Vol. 7, Iss. 5; p. 537–549

Boschma, R. & Martin, R. (2010) *The Handbook of Evolutionary Economic Geography.* Edward Elgar Publishing Ltd, Cheltenham.

Boschma, R.A. & K. Frenken (2009), *Some Notes on Institutions in Evolutionary Economic Geography.* Economic Geography 85 (2), pp. 151-158

Bristow G, 2005, *Everyone's a 'winner':* problematising the discourse of regional competitiveness Journal of Economic Geography 5 285–304

Bunnell, T.& Coe N. (2001) *Spaces and scales of innovation.* Prog Hum Geogr 25(4):569–589 Camagni R (ed) (1991) Innovation networks. Belhaven, London

Burt, R. (1992) *Structural holes.* Cambridge, MA: Harvard University Press.

Cantner, U., Meder, A. & terWal, A.J. *Innovator networks and regional knowledge base,* Technovation 30(2010)496–507

Christopherson, S., & Clark, J. 2007. *Remaking regional economies:* Power, labor, and firm strategies in the knowledge economy. New York: Routledge.

Coe, N.M. (2010) *Geographies of production* I: An evolutionary revolution? Prog Hum Geogr published online 21 June 2010,

Cooke P (1998) *Introduction: origin of the concept.* Chap. 1. In: BraczykH-J,

Cooke P, Heinderich M (eds) Regional innovation systems. UCL, London, pp 2–25

Cooke P (2001) *Regional innovation systems, clusters, and the knowledge economy.* Ind Corp Change 10(4):945–974

Cooke P (2005) *Regionally asymmetric knowledge capabilities and open innovation:* exploring 'Globalisation 2'–A new model of industry organization. Res Policy 34(8):1128–1149

Cooke P, Gomez Uranga M. & Etxebarria G (1997) *Regional innovation systems:* institutional and organisational dimensions. Res Policy 26:475–491

Cooke P. & Morgan K (1993) *"The network paradigm: new departures in corporate and regional development"* Environment and Planning D: Society and Space 11(5) 543–564

Cowan, R., David. P. &Foray, D. (2000), *"The explicit economics of knowledge codification and tacitness"* Industrial and Corporate Change, Vol. 9, No. 2. pp. 211–254.

David P (1985) *Clio and the economics of QWERTY.* Am Econ Rev 75(2):332

Doloreux, D. & Parto, .S (2005) *Regional innovation systems:* current discourse and unresolved issues. Technol Soc 27(2):133

Dopfer, K., Foster, J.& Potts, J. (2004) *Micro-meso-macro.* J Evol Econ 14(3):263

Edquist C (ed) (1997) *Systems of innovation: technologies, institutions and organisations.* Pinter, London

Essletzbichler, J & Rigby, DL (2007) *Exploring evolutionary economic geographies.* Journal of Economic Geography, 7 (5), 549–571

Essletzbichler, J. 2009: *Evolutionary economic geography, institutions, and political economy.* Economic Geography 85, 151–58.

Flanagan, K, Uyarra, E. &Laranja, M (2011) *Reconceptualising the 'policy mix' for innovation.* Forthcoming in Research Policy

Florida, R (1995) *"Toward the learning region"* . Futures, 27(5). pp. 527–536

Fløysand, A. & Jakobsen, S. (2010) *The complexity of innovation:* A relational turn. Prog Hum Geogr. Published online August 20, 2010.

Freel M S, 2002, *"On regional systems of innovation:* illustrations from the West Midlands" Environment and Planning C: Government and Policy 20(5) 633 – 654

Freeman C (1995) *The 'National System of Innovation' in historical perspective.* Camb J Econ 19:5–24

Freeman, C. (1987) *Technology policy and economic performance;* lessons from Japan. Frances Printer Publishers, London, New York.

Frenken K, Van Oort F.& Verburg T (2007) *Related variety, unrelated variety and regional economic growth.* Reg Stud 41:685–697

Frenken, K. (2006) *'Technological innovation and complexity theory'*, Economics of Innovation and New Technology, 15: 2, 137–155

Frenken,K. & Boschma, R. (2007) *A theoretical framework for evolutionary economic geography*: industrial dynamics and urban growth as a branching process, Journal of Economic Geography. Oxford: Sep 2007. Vol. 7, Iss. 5; p. 635–650

Glückler, J. (2007) *Economic geography and the evolution of networks, Journal of Economic Geography,* 7 (5), 619-634

Grabher, G. (Ed.) (1993) *The Embedded firm*: on the Socio-Economics of Industrial Networks. Routledge, London.

Grabher, G. & Stark, D. (1997) *Organizing diversity:* evolutionary theory, network analysis and postsocialism, Reg. Studies 31, 533–544.

Grabher, G. (2006). *Trading routes, bypasses, and risky intersections*: Mapping the travels of "networks" between economic sociology and economic geography. Progress in Human Geography 30:163–89.

Hassink, R. (2010) *Regional resilience*: theoretical and empirical perspectives Cambridge J Regions Econ Soc (2010) 3(1): 3–10

Hekkert, M.P., Suurs, R.A.A. Negro, S.O. Kuhlmann, S. & Smits, R.E.H.M. (2006) *Functions of innovation systems*: A new approach for analysing technological change. Technological Forecasting and Social Change, Volume 74, Issue 4, May 2007, Pages 413-432

Hospers, G., Sautet, F. & Desrochers, P. (2008) *Silicon somewhere*: is there a need for cluster policy? In Karlsson, C. (ed.) Handbook of research on innovation and clusters: cases and policies. Cheltenham: Edward Elgar Publishing. Pp.430-446.

Howells, J. (1999) *Regional systems of innovation?* In: Archibugi D, Howells J, Michie J (eds) Innovation policy in a global economy. Cambridge University Press, Cambridge, pp 67–93

Iammarino, S. (2005) *An evolutionary integrated view of regional systems of innovation:* concepts, measures and historical perspectives. Eur Plan Stud 13(4):497

Katz, J.S. (2006) *Indicators for complex innovation systems* Research Policy Vol. 35 (7) 893–909

Kay, A (2006) *The dynamics of public policy.* Edward Elgar, Cheltenham

Koschatzky K. & Sternberg, R. (2000) *R&D Cooperation in Innovation Systems –* Some Lessons from the European Regional Innovation Survey (ERIS), European Planning Studies, 8 (4), pp. 487–501

Lagendijk, A. (1999) *Good practices in SMECluster initiatives.* Lessons from the 'Core' regions and beyond. Research Report. Centre for Urban and Regional Development Studies, University of Newcastle Upon Tyne.

Lagendijk, A. (2002), *'Beyond the regional life world against the global system world*: towards a relational-scalar perspective on spatialeconomic development', Geografiska Annaler, Vol. 84B, p. 2.

Lovering J (1999) *Theory led by policy*: the inadequacies of the 'New Regionalism' (Illustrated from the Case of Wales). Int J Urban Reg Res 23(2):379–395

Lundvall, B. A., (2007), *'National Innovations Systems:* Analytical Concept and Development Tool', Industry- and Innovation, 14(1), pp. 95-119.

Lundvall, B.A. (1992) (ed.) *National Systems of Innovation*: Towards a Theory of Innovation and Interactive Learning. London: Pinter.

MacKinnon, D., Cumbers, A., Pike, A. Birch, K. & McMaster, R. (2009) *Evolution in Economic Geography: Institutions, Political Economy, and Adaptation.* Economic Geography 85(2):129–150.

Malerba, F. (2002), *"Sectoral systems of innovation and production"*, Research Policy, 2002, 31, p.247–264

Markusen A (2003) *Fuzzy concepts, scanty evidence, policy distance*: the case for Rigour and policy relevance in critical regional studies. Reg Stud 37(6):701

Martin R, Sunley P (2006) *Path dependence and regional economic evolution.* J Econ Geogr 6(4):395–437

Martin, R. (2000) *"Institutional Approaches in Economic Geography"* Handbook of Economic Geography. Ed. Eric Sheppard and Trevor J. Barnes. Blackwell Publishers.Peck, 2005

Martin, R. & Sunley, P. (2007) *Complexity Thinking and Evolutionary Economic Geography*, Journal of Economic Geography. Oxford: Sep 2007. Vol. 7, Iss. 5; p. 573

Menzel & Fornahl (2009) *Cluster life cycles* – dimensions and rationales of cluster evolution. Industrial and Corporate Change, Volume 19, Number 1, pp. 205–238

Metcalfe, S. & Ramlogan, R. 2008, *'Innovation Systems and the Competitive Process in Developing Economies'*, The Quarterly Review of Economics and Finance, Vol.48,(in press).

Miettinen, R. (2002) *National Innovation System*: Scientific concept or Political Rhetoric, Edita Prima Ltd., Helsinki.

Morgan K (1997) *The learning region*: institutions, innovation and regional renewal. Reg Stud, 31(5):491–503

Nelson R (ed) (1993) *National innovation systems*: a comparative analysis. Oxford University Press, New York

Nelson, R. R. (1977). *The moon and the ghetto*, WW Norton & Company.

OECD (2009) *Report on Applications of Complexity Science for Public Policy*: New Tools for Finding Unanticipated Consequences and Unrealized Opportunities. September 2009

Oerlemans L, Meeus M, Kenis P (2007) *Regional innovation networks*. In: Rutten

RPJH, Boekema FWM (eds) The learning region: foundations, state of the art, future. Edward Elgar,Cheltenham, pp 160–183

Oinas, P. (2002), '*Competition and Collaboration in interconnected places*: towards a research agenda' Geografiska Annaler, Vol. 84, No. 2, pp. 6576.

Pelikán, P. & Wegner, G. (2003). *The Evolutionary Analysis of Economic Policy.* Edward Elgar.

Pendall, R., Foster, K. A. & Cowell, M. (2007) *Resilience and Regions: Building Understanding of the Metaphor,* Working Paper 2007–12. Berkeley, CA:Macarthur Foundation Research Network on Building Resilient Regions, Institute for Urban and Regional Development, University of California

Pike, A. Dawley, S. & Tomaney, J. (2010) *Resilience, adaptation and adaptability* Cambridge Journal of Regions, Economy and Society 2010, 3, 59–70

Pyka, A. (2007) Innovation networks, in Hanusch, H. and Pyka, A. (2007) *Elgar Companion to Neo-Schumpeterian Economics.* Cheltenham: Edward Elgar.

Pyke F, Becattini G. & Sengenberger W (eds) (1990) *Industrial districts and interfirm cooperation in Italy.* International Institute for Labour Studies, Geneva

Rosenberg, N. (1992) *"Economic Experiments."* Industrial and Corporate Change, 1: 181–203.

Scott, (1986) "*Industrial organisation and location*: division of labour, the firm and spatial process" Economic Geography, vol. 62, no. 3 215–231

Sharif N (2006) Emergence and development of the national innovation systems approach. Res Policy 35(5):745–766

Slembeck, T. (1997). '*The Formation of Economic Policy:* A Cognitive-Evolutionary Approach to Policy-Making' Constitutional Political Economy 8(3): 225–254.

Uyarra, E. & Flanagan, K. (2010) *From regional systems of innovation to regions as innovation policy spaces.* Environment and Planning C: Government and Policy 2010, volume 28, pages 681–695

Uyarra, E., (2010), "*What is evolutionary about regional systems of innovation?*", Journal of Evolutionary Economics 20(1): 115–137.

Watts, D.J. & Strogatz, S. (1998) *Collective dynamics of small-world networks,* Nature, 393, 440–442.

Werker C & Athreye S (2004) *Marshalls disciples*: knowledge and innovation driving regional economic development and growth. J Evol Econ 14(5):505–523

Witt, U. (2003). '*Economic policy making in evolutionary perspective*' Journal of Evolutionary Economics 13(2): 77-94.

Wohlgemuth M (2002) *Evolutionary approaches to politics.* Kyklos 55(2):223–246

JOERG KNIELING – HAFENCITY UNIVERSITY HAMBURG, GERMANY

Metropolitan Networking in the Western Baltic Sea Region: *Metropolitan Region of Hamburg between Multilevel Governance and Soft Spatial Development*

Introduction

The paper discusses the emergence of new governance arrangements in the Western Baltic Sea Region, and explores their contribution to regional development as well as to territorial cohesion. A supra-regional co-operation of the Metropolitan Region of Hamburg brings together the core city of Hamburg and its farther away located rural hinterland in an alliance of joint responsibility; additionally, a meta-region reaching from Hamburg via Copenhagen to Oslo and Stockholm is intended to bind together the Western Baltic Sea Region's main agglomerations and hinterlands as a strategic alliance. In this transnational meta-region, spatial development mainly refers to informal ways of visioning and strategy making, as well as project implementation involving a wide range of different public and private stakeholders.

The reasons for these arrangements can be seen in two different developments influencing regional strategic efforts; economic competition and territorial cohesion. Since the Maastricht Treaty, the progress of European integration, as well as the accompanied increase of disparities in Europe, has increased the importance of approaches concerning economic, social and territorial cohesion within the EU territory. To balance disparities through modernising and compensating deprived areas, the EU has introduced a regional policy that includes 39% of the EU budget (Schön 2006: 385). These cohesion policies seem to be quite successful: "Evidence suggests that economic prosperity in the EU is becoming less geographically concentrated: the traditional economic core of Europe contributed a substantially smaller share of EU-27 GDP in 2004 than 1995, while its share of the population remained stable" (European Commission 2006: xii; BBR 2006a).

Currently, the growth rates of the old EU Member States are rather low, and therefore new member states are able to bridge the gap faster. Alternatively, economic activities have become more concentrated in major cities and metropolitan regions within the Member States (European Commission 2007; Schön 2006). These trends towards greater concentration trends comprise new regional disparities because the metropolitan regions are often encircled by poorer deprived and economically stressed regions. An example of this is the GDP growth rates of capital cities in the Czech Republic, Poland, Hungary or Slovakia between 1995 and 2001. The growth rates have been more than 50% above the national average, which points out that the positive growth rates in the new Member States are highly driven by the growth within the capital city (Schön 2006: 389). Now, not only new EU Member States have to deal with the challenges of different growth rates between central and peripheral regions. The issue of handling urban-rural relations is on the agenda of spatial development in several European states.

Against this background, innovative solutions are under consideration and formal planning is contextualized in new ways. The emergence of 'soft' forms of networking and co-operation, promoting regional development at different spatial levels, initiates a discussion about soft spaces and spheres with fuzzy boundaries (see Allmendinger and Haughton 2009, Waterhout 2010). According to the concept of fuzzy boundaries, cross-regional and cross-national co-operation and networking forms initiated by common features or challenges, are expanding. Therefore, the configuration of meta-, mega- or macro-regions, as well as metropolitan networking and the reflection of these processes with regard to existing formal structures and competencies, have become elements of the current debate on regional development and territorial cohesion in Europe, and in the western Baltic Sea Region (see Florida et al 2007, Schymik 2009).

Changing framework conditions for metropolitan regions

Economic framework

In recent decades a change from an industrial to a knowledge-based society has taken place. In the course of a structural change within the social and economic regulation the production, utilization and organization of knowledge has become the central source of productivity and growth. This change refers to the three dimensions of economy and policies, as well as knowledge and education (Knieling and Matern 2008):

- Economic structural change fosters the trend from the production of goods to service-based economies. The impact of "FIRE" (finance, insurance, and real estate), corporate headquarters, and business services increases, while industrial production becomes less important, in particular in agglomerations or metropolitan regions. In order to remain competitive, urban regions face the challenge to cope with this change from an industrial to a service and knowledge orientated location. At the same time, this process is accompanied by a change from a vertically integrated, fordist production, to a postfordistic flexible network organization (Blotevogel 2005a; Castell 2001; Taylor 2001).

- Economic globalization has intensified the world-wide exchange of people, goods, capital and investment, knowledge and ideas to a great extent. National economies have developed into a world economy in the production of goods, as well as in sharing services and markets for selling and buying. Due to these developments the character of large enterprises is changing as well: they act on an increasingly trans- and multinational level;, they are characterized by growing mobility, and they are losing their bond to their home regions. As a consequence, urban regions have had to intensify their efforts for remaining competitive locations. They face an intensified competition for capital, knowledge, labor and inhabitants (OECD 2001; Sassen 1991; Short, Kim 1999).

In a globalized economy physical distances and territories lose their importance while streams of people, goods, capital, ideas and information as well as relationships and interaction become more important (Castells 2001; Lash and Urry 1994). Thereby it seems that the thesis of metropolitan cities, respectively regions, as "nodes in the global net" where the linkages of the network economies meet, gets new relevance. Economic and political management concentrates in metropolitan regions; cultural as well as most product and process innovations find their starting point there (Taylor 2001; Sassen 1994).

Demographic framework

Not only business environments have changed within the last years. In many European states, demographic change has growing influence on regional and economic welfare. A stagnating and aging population stimulates the competition between regions for people, especially the skilled workforces' respectively "high potentials", and results in re-distribution processes of population on the regional level. In this context, location decisions by such 'high potentials' become increasingly important for regions. Their creative capital is seen as the leading power in the regional economic development. "Creatives" become an influential source for economic growth and regional development because of their impact on the regional in-novation capacity. The creative class is widely defined and can be found in all sectors of the working environment. Its creative output and innovations are specific criteria of a distinction. The creative class includes, in particular, scientists, artists, designer, architects or journalists. Additionally there is a group of "creative professionals" working in the knowledge-based information and communication sector (Florida 2003: 8).

To better understand the effects of the creative class for economic growth, Florida defines the "3Ts of economic growth": tolerance, talent and technology (Florida 2003: 10). Larger cities gain increasing importance, because of their ability to offer the 3Ts for economic growth in a higher extent, than rural regions or small towns. The agglomeration advantage s of larger cities generate creative and innovative milieux as determinants for economic growth.

Soft planning and fuzzy boundaries

Metropolitan regions have developed mainly along functional networks, cutting across institutionally defined territorial boundaries. As a result, a growing divergence between functional urban territories and institutional urban areas, i.e. administrative borders, can be noticed (Kübler and Heinelt 2005; Allmendinger and Haughton 2009). Subsequently, local, regional and national administrative borders are becoming less relevant. This indicates that private and public actors involved in building metropolitan regions are developing a diffuse form of governance, which relies on a looser, more negotiable, set of political arrangements taking their shape from a network of relations that stretch across and beyond given regional boundaries (Sohn et al. 2009, 923). Following this line of argumentation, regional development has to learn to work within complex multi-layered, fluid, and sometimes fuzzy, scales of policy and governance arrangements (Allmendinger and Haughton 2009, 618).

In the case of cross-border co-operation, the presence of state borders represents a specific geographic configuration that becomes even more complicated when the borders' function is as both interface and barrier (Sohn et al. 2009, 923). What becomes important here are the heterogeneous forms of trans-boundary governance (e.g. Schmitt-Egner 1998, Newrly 2002), including the multi-actor constellations from different political-administrative levels and sectors, who are often organised in networks. Spatial development in (cross-border) metropolitan regions can then be understood as not being based on formal procedures and instruments, but rather on the informal ways of acting , joint visioning and strategy making ('soft' side of spatial planning) (Waterhout 2010, 1). Metropolitan regions, generally speaking, are oriented towards their global integration (as nodes within the global 'space of flows'), as well as their local functionality concerning economy, housing, living, environment etc. As such, they represent various 'soft spaces' and spheres with 'fuzzy boundaries' (Haughton et al. 2010). Such spaces are not stable in time or space but for a certain period of time respond to and emerge from changes and initiatives in society. In other terms, they are not bound or related to any regulation, administrative system or policy framework (Waterhout 2010, 7).

In metropolitan areas, it becomes obvious that private actors, particularly economic players and civil organisations, attend to the concept of 'soft spaces' by focusing on selected issues in a specific area. This is not a new phenomenon. Economic actors, for example, have always been one of the driving forces behind urban development, and spatial planning has always tried to control these developments so as to reduce the negative impacts of market-oriented allocation (pollution, agglomeration etc.). But the involvement of private actors in spatial planning has taken a new dimension, extending 'traditional' public private partnerships (e.g. Heinz 2006) and putting a different emphasis on privatisation and deregulation (e.g. Häußermann et al. 2008, 280pp). Private actors start to reflect strategically about territories, either public or private. They form spatially and temporally limited networks, develop their own as well as independent spatial concepts or plans, and influence spatial development organisations via public events, announcements or consultations. In these situations, spatial development often seems to comply with the demands or proposals of private initiatives, without having a general pattern of spatial development in mind (Schneider-Sliwa 2003, 115).

To conclude, the multiplicity of actors involved in metropolitan development, the different sectoral approaches towards space and territories, the institutional fragmentation as well as the increasing number of private initiatives 'thinking spatially', all show that the 'traditional' planning system and approaches are challenged to adapt to new spatial complexities (Waterhout 2010, 1). Planning, of course, remains part of the formal regulatory apparatus, but at the same time it needs to operate within new associational networks (Allmendinger and Haughton 2009, 621).

Metropolitan Region of Hamburg

Starting point for describing new forms of territorial co-operation is the Metropolitan Region of Hamburg (MRH). Before explaining the new arrangements a short description of the MRH may give an impression of its tasks and organization.

With about 4.3 million inhabitants, the MRH is situated in Northern Germany, and specified by its cross-border and multi-level characteristic. The MRH includes 14 counties in the three German federal states of Hamburg, Lower Saxony and Schleswig-Holstein (see fig. 1). At this scale, a co-operation has been arranged on the basis of a formal inter-governmental contract, however, the co-operation lacks any formal steering competencies for the Metropolitan Region. Additionally, there are two counties in the Eastern German federal state of Mecklenburg-West Pomerania that have the status of associated members.

The current co-operation in the metropolitan area has been the result of a ninety year long process of regional development. Starting with joint spatial planning in the 1920s and the establishment of bilateral development funds on the federal state level in the 1960s, co-operation has been fostered by the resolution of a Regional Development Concept in 1994 and 2000. The Regional Development Concept addresses a wide range of territorial and development aspects. With the improvement of its organization and a thematic adjustment in 2006, the governance concept of the Metropolitan Region has significantly been changed.

Today, in addition to the Regional Development Concept, an Internationalization Strategy determines the guiding principles of the Metropolitan Region, addressing economic and marketing issues, in addition to the complex and comprehensive dimension of the Regional Development Concept. The reinforcement of international competitiveness, especially in areas like business, science, transport and culture, was constituted as a main objective of the co-operation. Deduced from the strategy documents an action program, the Operative Program formulates approaches and projects concerning implementation.

Territorially, the Metropolitan Region follows the concept of a variable geometry, enlarging the scale of co-operation flexibly in response to specific requirements as they arise. Besides this, a formal extension of the scale of co-operation has been under discussion as neighboring municipalities, such as the city of Lübeck or counties in the Eastern German federal state of Mecklenburg-West Pomerania, have applied to join the Metropolitan Region formally.

Apart from spatial reference and strategic orientation, the organizational structure of the MRH has changed considerably over the years. Today, an annual Regional Conference serves as a co-operation platform and brings together various public and private actors. The operational work is done in standing working groups, each chaired by one of the partners. This structure of informal co-operation is coordinated by a joint secretariat. The MRH is based on informal instruments like the regional conference, workshops, agreements and different kinds of networking processes, but lacks any formal competencies. The scope of activities reaches from mono-thematic to integrative cooperation, and from small-scale consolidation between neighbouring municipalities, to interregional and international partnerships (see Matern and Löwis 2010). Regional projects, such as investment in infrastructure and management structures, are fostered by the MRH development funds with about 3 Mio EUR annually.

Fig. 1:
Hamburg
Metropolitan Region

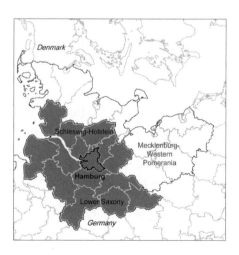

Supra-Regional Partnership Metropolitan Region of Hamburg / Northern Germany

In 2007, the Metropolitan Region of Hamburg initiated a wider area of co-operation, based on the federal government's 'good practice' project of "Supra-regional partnerships – Innovative projects for city-regional cooperation, networking and common responsibility" (BBR 2009). This project aims at fostering development through the building of partnerships between prospering and lagging sub-regions, respectively metropolitan regions and peripheral, mostly rural regions. The partnerships were meant to be characterized by bottom-up processes, volunteerism and equality of participants. The idea behind the partnership is the perception of a common responsibility for the territory (BBR, BMVBS 2008).

According to the "Guidelines for Spatial Development in Germany" (MKRO 2006) the metropolitan regions are intended to take over two functions: The metropolitan regions are growth coalitions which improve their performance and competitiveness at the international level by combining their regional potentials. These same metropolitan regions also become part of a supra-regional partnership, and contribute to a sustainable growth, not only within their areas but also in neighbouring, declining and lagging areas. Thereby, the guidelines take into account the territorial incorporation of metropolitan regions and the importance of networking between these different regions (Matern 2008).

Economic issues are the main content of supra-regional partnerships; which refers to the growth and development goals that have been privileged in spatial policies recently (see EU Lisbon Strategy 2000). Potentials for cooperation seem to offer common strengths, like a joint cluster management, as well as profiling complementary strengths (Keim 2006; Blotevogel 2006; Hahne and Glatthaar 2005). The basis for co-operation are existing relations, e.g. commuter relations or supply-chains.

The objectives of supra-regional partnerships can be concluded as the following (BBR, BMVBS 2008):
• rise of awareness for mutual dependencies,

- avoiding unfavourable re-distribution processes between regions,
- strengthening functional relations between urban and rural regions, and
- bringing together supra-regional stakeholders for a more balanced development.

MORO North, the supra-regional partnership-project in Northern Germany, includes an area of about 8 million inhabitants, with actors coming from the federal states of Hamburg, Lower Saxony, Schleswig-Holstein and Mecklenburg-West Pomerania; thus reaching far beyond the Metropolitan Region of Hamburg's boundaries (see fig. 2).

The network aims at boosting urban-rural partnerships and promoting sustainable growth in the northern parts of Germany, without requiring the generation of a new bureaucratic organization. To profile the supra-region and to increase the economical collaboration, the project is supposed to use the numerous existing cooperation forms within and between the MRH and the surrounded areas, and improve them.

Within the partnership, a number of projects have been developed in different fields. As an initial field of action, the cooperative organisation announced the expansion of meta-regional connections between the Metropolitan Region of Hamburg and the region of South-Denmark, and farther on towards the Øresund-Region. The following thematic fields have been investigated in MORO North:
- Economic clusters: Logistics, maritime economy and life sciences have been identified as economic activities, for which existing cluster-structures have been explored, to establish likely potential for extending these into the wider area of the supra-regional partnership. In all these fields, joint activities have started, and have been included into the agenda of further co-operation.
- Job market and qualification: In the supra-regional partnership, different institutions are in charge of qualification offers. The project achieved joint activities and a better coordination.
- Transportation: The main challenge in transportation is the accessibility of rural regions by public transportation. Although com-

muter linkages represent a strong relation – e.g. between Western Mecklenburg and Hamburg – accessibility especially regarding railway connections, is not satisfactory in terms of extent and quality of services. An improvement of services would facilitate commuting between rural areas and the metropolitan region – for urban opportunities and, inthe opposite direction, for leisure and recreation. It may also help tilt the modal split in favour of more public transport, and thereby contribute to better (and more sustainable) quality of life.

- Economic regional circuit: Within the rural sub-regions, agriculture is still an important sector of production, land use and employment. This potential can be used for the establishment of rural-urban-partnerships, especially since the value of fresh food and organic farming has become an important factor for the quality of city-life. Within the project the agenda is to explore concepts like regional sales counter, regional catering for events, regional farmed school lunch and networking between farming and gastronomy.
- Cultural heritage potentials: Within the partnership, it is intended to establish joint brand and excursion routes for leisure and recreation activities including cultural heritage sites, in urban and rural areas. The main target groups for this linkage between the architectural and landscape heritage sites are inhabitants of the Metropolitan Region of Hamburg and of neighbouring regions, e.g. Berlin, the Øresund or Hannover, as well as cruise tourists who stay for some days in the larger cities.
- Regional marketing: The result of this project was a new brand for the area of the supra-regional partnership: Northern Germany. It took some efforts to bring the decisive stakeholders together and convince them of the idea that a joint brand offers benefit for all participants.

In 2010, the supra-regional partnership agreed on a joint resolution that the co-operation will continue after the end of the pilot project phase in 2011. For the newly created 'Project Partnership North' (PP North) the partners made up a new organizational structure including a steering committee and projects. The committee's office will rotate between the responsible ministries.

Fig.2: Supra-regional partnership
Hamburg Metropolitan Region /Northern Germany

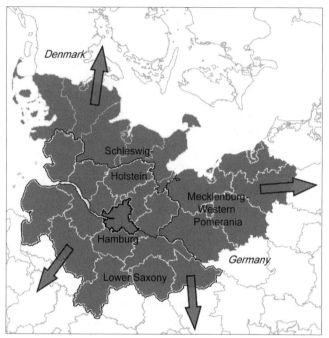

Compared with the MRH, MORO Nord is more complex in terms of scope, multi actor-structure and space. Its fourteen projects also integrate issues of spatial planning, e.g. the handling of diverse dynamics of regional development, relations between regions and territorial impacts, and aspects of regional growth by using and stimulating endogenous development trends (see Matern and Löwis 2010).

Meta-region Hamburg–Øresund–Oslo–Stockholm

Exclusive projects of MORO North relate to an even farther-reaching cross-national perspective of regional development creating a new meta-region. The MORO North-project 'Brückenschla–Fehmarnbelt', a networking project between the German, Danish and Swedish actors, gives 'food for thought' about the development of a meta-region ranging from the Metropolitan Region of Hamburg and MORO North, via Fehmarnbelt Fixed Link and Øresund Region to the areas of Gotenborg, Oslo and Stockholm (see fig. 3). With the discussions about high-speed-trains between Malmö and Oslo and respectively Stockholm, the improvement of traffic links between Hamburg, Copenhagen and Malmö gains in importance. Likewise, the purpose of upgrading the university network between Northern Germany and Øresund Region approves the development of a meta-region.

A wide experience of various INTERREG-projects and the strategic partnership 'Southwestern Baltic Sea TransRegional Area – Implementing New Geography (STRING)' benefit the building of the meta-regional cooperation area. The STRING-partnership between the German federal states of Hamburg and Schleswig–Holstein, Skåne (South Sweden) and the two Danish regions, Zealand and the Capital Region Denmark (Hovedstaden), introduced new bodies of cooperation (Fehmarnbelt Business Councils and Fehmarnbelt-Comittee) with the aim of working on joint development strategies in terms of research and science, biotechnology, regional policy, maritime economy, climate protection and renewable energies. An advancement of these structures of co-operation is intended to help constitute the Meta-region Hamburg–Øresund–Oslo–Stockholm. In addition, from an institutional point of view, the initiation of a European grouping of territorial cooperation (EGTC, see EU 2006) was discussed regarding facilitating and promoting the transnational cooperation in the meta-region (see Foth 2010). The EGTC is intended to serve as legal entity. Its competencies are defined in a binding co-operation convention established on the initiative of the members. The range of purposes is restricted by the prohibition of profit-oriented activities, but apart from these a wide number of subjects may be included in a poly-thematic approach of the meta-region.

Fig.3: Meta-region Hamburg-Øresund-Oslo-Stockholm

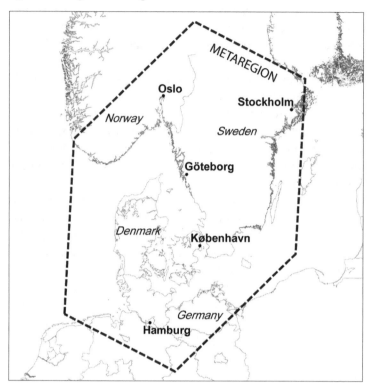

Conclusion

This chapters has shown that the Western Baltic Sea Region is a showcase for different kinds of networking lines. They refer to existing and prospective co-operations with different scale, scope, stakeholders and organizational structures. When discussing these examples against the background of the theoretical framework of soft development approaches and fuzzy boundaries, some potential as well as restrictions can be identified.

Meta-region: striking co-operation between metropolitan and macro-regional scale?

With regard to international competition regions are forced to reflect their current positioning and development strategies. Some metropolitan regions opt for strengthening their competitiveness by developing their internal potential through cluster-strategies in the field of regional economics, or by quality of life factors with regard to social, cultural or ecological standards. Other regions tend to improve their external relationships. These internationalization efforts may include para-diplomatic forms of networking, or building up formal relationships with selected partner-regions all over the world. Another approach is widening the regional scale by creating a farther-reaching co-operation area, a supra-regional partnership, or a meta-region. Those regions have to be coherent enough to join similar interests. Looking at the described meta-region, Hamburg–Øresund–Oslo–Stockholm, the common goals could simply be a common positioning as a north-western European metropolitan area. On a global scale, not all metropolitan regions included are big enough to gain attention sufficiently, thus co-operation might become a win-win-situation for all of them.

But why think about a regional level in between the metropolitan and the macro-regional scale? Is the Baltic Sea macro-region not adequate for positioning on the global scale? In fact, from the Hamburg point of view, this seems not to be the case. The macro-region offers excellent options for lobbying at EU-level and for co-operative solutions in a number of important policy fields concerning the Baltic Sea as the connecting element. But the interests of the western metropolises in the field of international profiling are seen to be specific. This may explain why a meta-region, as an additional scale of co-operation level, makes sense. Nevertheless this type of partnership leaves a lot of questions to answer concerning the effectiveness of the different, but parallel, co-operations, multi-level co-ordination or available resources.

Supra-regional partnership: instrument for territorial cohesion?

Whereas the meta-region is mainly concentrated on economic growth, the supra-regional partnership-approach aims at intra-regional cohesion. It allows a renewed definition of territorial cohesion that also deals with European policies. Core cities are supposed to take over responsibility for their farther hinterland, while rural areas are intended to intensify their relationship with the agglomeration, e.g. by exploiting their market function. Those decentralized forms of territorial cohesion could be seen as an additional instrument on both the European and the national scale. They could contribute to solving the conflict between agglomerations and rural areas over resources, by creating a partnership in solidarity. But those idealistic concepts have to be reflected against the background of competition at both the local and regional scale. Even after initiating a partnership, many conflicts of interests stay alive and restrict co-operation. Despite the partnership's opportunity for taking on a new role for conflict resolution and the exploration of joint interests. Despite the opportunity for the partnership to take on a new role, caution must be taken in knowing that the actors are still fighting for their individual interests. Therefore, achieving a new culture of co-operation would already be an important success and should not be underestimated.

Furthermore, the supra-regional partnership offers for both sides the possibility of widening their political options. Both are often restricted by focusing on their internal tasks and problems. By reflecting regional development from the point of view of the supra-region they may become aware of new dimensions as well as potential projects for local and regional development. In the case of some model projects from the German government's initiative of supra-regional partnerships, the rural areas have drafted position papers that outline their expectations of, and their intended contributions to the partnership with the core cities. These efforts show possible effects of cooperation at this new spatial scale.

Variability and flexibility: characteristics for successful territorial development?

Supra-regional partnerships are characterized by a variable geometry which provides flexibility in bringing together specific partner constellations depending on each project. But variable geometries can also lead to "cherry-picking," with major actors concentrating on promising projects, and neglecting aspects that might be of importance from the point of view of supra-regional cohesion. Therefore, it is suggested that partners from peripheral areas make sure that they include specific tasks, e.g. compensation or recreation. For a balanced and durable supra-regional partnership, a solid package of solutions, including demands of all included areas, seems to be necessary.

However, the emergence of soft forms of co-operation as well as of soft spaces offers a range of advantages. The geometry of the examined co-operation forms is mostly variably adapted to the treated subjects. This allows gathering main stakeholders with a core interest. Nevertheless this evolvement of fuzzy boundaries poses great demands on existing institutions and actors concerning openness, flexibility and consensus building of regional governance. It challenges the regional institutions to broaden the stakeholder integration vertically as well as horizontally. Soft development approaches are often determined by economic interests. But in terms of sustainability, a comprehensive approach is supposed to be wiser than a mono-thematic and selective one. A combination of economical, ecological and social regional strategies seems to better provide attractive living and working conditions.

NOTE

The article was prepared with assistance of Judith Bornhorst, who I thank for her commitment.

LITERATURE

Allmendinger, P. and G. Haughton (2009): *Soft spaces, fuzzy boundaries, and metagovernance: The new spatial planning in the Thames Gateway*. Environment and Planning A, vol. 41, 617-633.

BBR (ed.) 2006: *Espon Atlas – Mapping the Structure of European Territory*. Bonn.

BMVBS, BBR (eds.) 2008: *Überregionale Partnerschaften*, MORO-Informationen, vol. 3/1, Bonn.

European Union, Regional Policy 2006a: *Growing Regions, Growing Europe – Fourth report on economic and social cohesion*, Communications from the Commission, Brussels (online: http://ec.europa.eu/regional_policy/sources/docoffic/official/reports/cohesion4/pdf/4cr_en.pdf).

EU (European Union) 2006b: *Regulation (EC) No 1082/2006 of the European Parliament and of the Council of 5 July 2006 on a European grouping of territorial cooperation (EGTC)*, Official Journal of the European Union, No. L 210, p. 19-24.

Florida, R.; Gulden, T.; Mellander, C. 2007: *The Rise of the Mega Region*. Download: http://creativeclass.typepad.com/thecreativityexchange/files/florida_gulden_mellander_megaregions.pdf [19.04.2010].

Foth, R.B. 2010: *Großräumige Partnerschaft Norddeutschland / Metropolregion Hamburg, Grenzüberschreitende Kooperationen*. Paper presented at MORO-Workshop in Bonn, 25-26 March 2010, Bonn.

Haughton, G.; Allmendinger, P.; Counsell, D. and Vigar, G. (2010) *The New Spatial Planning*. Territorial Management with Soft Spaces and Fuzzy Boundaries, London and New York, Routledge.

Häußermann, H.; Läpple, D. and Siebel, W. (2008) *Stadtpolitik*, Frankfurt, Suhrkamp.

Heinz, W. (2006) '*Öffentlich-Private Kooperationsansätze (Public Private Partnerships) – Eine Strategie mit wiederkehrender Relevanz*', in: Selle, K. (2006) Zur räumlichen Entwicklung beitragen: Konzepte, Theorien, Impulse (Planung neu denken, Vol. 1), Dortmund, Rohn-Verlag, 146-162.

Knieling, J.; Matern, A. 2008: *Good Governance on European Metropolitan Regions*, Hamburg, Hafencity University Hamburg, neopolis working papers, urban and regional studies, no. 1, Hamburg.

Kübler, D. and Heinelt, H. (2005) '*Metropolitan governance, democracy and the dynamics of place*', in Heinelt, H. and Kübler, D. (eds.): Metropolitan governance: Capacity, democracy and the dynamics of place, London and New York, Routledge, 8-28.

Matern, A. and von Löwis, S. 2010: *In the Search of Soft Spatial Planning in the Metropolitan Region Hamburg*. Paper presented at the International Workshop '*Soft Spatial Planning – Territorial governance in a borderless Europe*', HafenCity University Hamburg, 21-22 January 2010, Hamburg.

MKRO (Standing Conference of Ministers responsible for Spatial Planning) (2006): *Concepts and Strategies for Spatial Development in Germany*, Berlin.

Schön, K.P. (2006): *Territoriale Kohäsion auf europäischer Ebene – Ziele und Wege*. Information zur Raumentwicklung, no. 6/7, p. 383-392.

Schymik, C. 2009: *Blueprint of a Macro-Region*. The EU Strategy for the Baltic Sea, SWP Research Paper, September 2009, Berlin.

Schymik, C.; Krumrey, P. 2009: *EU Strategy for the Baltic Sea Region – Core Europe in the Northern Periphery?* SWP Research Paper, Berlin. Download: http://swp-berlin.org/common/get_document.php?asset_id=5908 [17.11.2009]

Schmitt-Egner,P. (1998) *'Grenzüberschreitende Zusammenarbeit in Europa als Gegenstand wissenschaftlicher Forschung und Strategie transnationaler Praxis.* Anmerkungen zur Theorie, Empirie und Praxis des Transnationalen Regionalismus', in: Brunn, G.; Schmitt-Egner, P. (eds.), Grenzüberschreitende Zusammenarbeit in Europa. Theorie – Empirie – Praxis, Baden-Baden, Nomos, 27-77.

Schneider-Sliwa, R. (2003) *'Städte im Zeichen von Auflösung und Nachhaltigkeit'*, REGIO BASILIENSIS, 44/2 (special issue on 'Planungen im trinationalen Raum'), 111-124.

Sohn, C., Reitel, B. and O. Walther (2009) *'Cross-border metropolitan integration in Europe: The case of Luxembourg, Basel, and Geneva'*, Environment and Planning C: Government and Policy, 27, 922-939.

Waterhout, B. 2010: *Soft Spatial Planning – What, why and how?* Paper presented at the International Workshop 'Soft Spatial Planning – Territorial governance in a borderless Europe', HafenCity University Hamburg, 21-22 January 2010, Hamburg.

LISE LYCK – COPENHAGEN BUSINESS SCHOOL, DENMARK

Regionalization Experiences from Overcoming the Missing Links of Europe

Introduction

In 1984, the European Round Table of Industrialists published the book: "The Missing Links of Europe". This publication included a map showing for the first time a connection between the Danish islands, Funen and Zealand, a connection between Copenhagen and Malmø, and a connection between Denmark and Germany across the Fehmarn Belt.

The original policies in the then EEC (the later EU) were agricultural, competition, transportation and regional policy. The instruments included in these policies were envisaged to lead to an ever still closer and more coherent cooperation among the member states. From this perspective, the missing links caused considerable attention, and efforts began were initiated to address the missing links by having the ferry connections replaced by fixed links.

As a result of this political initiative, the Danish Parliament give the go ahead for constructing a bridge connection between Funen and Zealand over the Great Belt. The connection was to include both a link for trains and cars. It was decided that the best solution for the trains would be a combination of tunnel and bridge while the car connection should be a bridge. The bridge over the Great Belt was opened for crossing trains in 1997 and for cars in 1998. The connections were financed by the Danish State and it was decided that a user-fee for passing the bridge should cover the costs of the investment over time.

The next phase was to establish a fixed link between Denmark and Sweden across Øresund. both for trains and vehicles. The agreement between the Danish and Swedish governments, following intense lobbying by the two regions immediately affected, was concluded in March 1991. The connection should be a bridge and a Swedish-Danish corporation financed equally between Sweden and Denmark was established, with most of the necessary capital raised on the markets. Concerning the Øresund Bridge it was also decided that the users should finance the investment over time by paying a fee for passing the bridge. In July 2000, the Øresund-bridge was opened.

The Fehmarn Belt connection was agreed by the Danish and German State in 2007. The bridge will be financed by the Danish State and it is decided that there shall be a user fee for passing the bridge over time. It is decided that the connection shall be opened in 2018, but it is still not decided if it will be a bridge or a tunnel.

The text in the following section is based on *Lyck (2008)*. This chapter highlights the main experiences on regionalization based on the two already established connections, Great Belt and Øresund, and learning from those investments. It also discusses how the learning can be utilized in relation to the new transportation investment over the Fehmarn Belt.

Regionalization Theories

Many theories on regionalization have been developed over the last years. The regionalization theories referred to dealt in this article are mainly theories on transportation corridors *Savelsberg, Eva (2008) and Hanley, Richard E. (2004)* and on the creation of political *(Fitjar, Rune Dahl, 2010 and Hirst and Paul, 2009)* and functional regionalization *(Isard, Walter et al, 1998, and Pomfret and Richard, 2003)*, but also theories on administrative *(Brenner et al, 2003, and Pomfret, 2003)* and cultural regionalization *(Castells, 2000, and Fitjar, Rune and Dahl, 2010)*.

Regionalization Experiences in Relation to the Great Belt Connection

Denmark is a small country with 5.5 million inhabitants and a territory of 43.000 square kilometers. The connection over the Great Belt involved ferry links.

The economic development in Denmark is characterized by EU membership since 1973. This ended the problem for Denmark that two of its main trading partners belonged to two separate trade systems, the EEC and EFTA. Beside trade with the other Nordic countries, agricultural export to the UK and the export of manufactured goods to Germany were the main elements in Danish foreign trade. Since the 1960s, the export of manufactured goods has been exceeding the export of agricultural products. It has implied an urbanization process and a migration of people from the West to the East of Denmark. As a consequence, many Danes from Jutland and from the West of Zealand moved to the Copenhagen area. As a result, many Danes have family both in Copenhagen and in Jutland and thus great demand for crossing the Great Belt. This economic and cultural migration created a pronounced need for more crossings over the Great Belt and also a wish for a replacement of the ferries with a quicker transportation possibility. As a result, there was almost no resistance to the decision to build the bridge.

The bridge has been a success from the start. The income from the bridge has surpassed all the forecasts. 1999 was the first full year for vehicles passing the bridge and 6.9 million vehicles passed. In 2009 close to 11 million vehicles passed the bridge, i.e. an increase from 19.000 to more than 30.000 in 2010 on average per day. *http://www.storebaelt.dk/omstorebaelt/trafiktal/arkiv, November 2010.*

The regionalization process benefitted from all types of region-alization theories: transportation corridors, political -, functional -, administrative -, and cultural regionalization.

Regionalization Experiences from the Øresund Bridge

Øresund is the most frequently crossed sea strait in the World both in north-southerly and east-westerly directions. Until to the middle of the year 2000, ferries provided the only connections, linking Elsinore with Helsingborg and Copenhagen with Malmö and Landskrona respectively, and from Dragør to Lindhamn.

It was a political decision to build the bridge and there was some considerable opposition to the project, revolving primarily around environmental concerns. The question was brought to the court and the project was altered to take more account of environment as impact. In spite of this, there continued to be a remaining resistance against the project.

The project was considered a technical challenge, and it was a perception among the politicians and the CEOs in both Sweden and Denmark, that, when the bridge was built, voters in both countries would demand from their respective governments a reduction in the bridge toll. *(Lyck et al, 2000)*

The bridge was opened on the first of July 2000. During the first months there was a big demand, people wanted to see and pass the bridge, but then the demand decreased, as 'routine' usage for economic purposes set in. Investment calculations were changed and payback period prolonged. Furthermore, the project had been calculateds. Still the financial concerns were not solved and on the Danish side it was decided to establish the corporation Sund & Belt A/S, as a private sector company to take financial and managerial responsibility for both the Great Belt and the Øresund Bridge. *(Lyck, 2002)*

During the upturn of business cycle, prior to the financial crisis in 2008, the economy in Denmark was booming. It implied high price increases on fixed property and a lack of labour. It had a serious impact on regionalization in the around the Øresund. Danes went to Sweden and bought apartments and houses that were much cheaper than in Denmark as well as cars, and they kept their work in Denmark. Swedes got jobs in Denmark. The daily commuting increased. See figure 1 for the development.

Figure 1: Traffic over the Øresund (top, bridge; bottom, ferries)

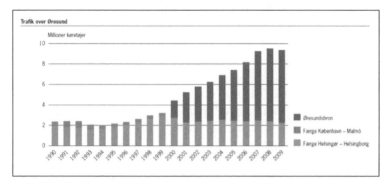

All in all, the Øresund Bridge has been a success story, especially when considering its role as a transport corridor, but also in terms of its political and functional impact. There have been questions about its effect from an administrative and cultural perspectives of regionalization. Furthermore, it should be mentioned that the start of regionalization was characterized by a very successful political governmental regionalization process, together changes to the more recent, question of governance for the Øresund Region has become somewhat more muted. (*Lyck and Nielsen, 2006*).

The main experiences with the regionalisation agenda linked to the the Øresund Bridge are: 1) A regionalization process is not just a technical process. Mental bridges have to be created in advance, and they do not appear just like that. Thus, there needed to be investments in building mental bridges as soon as the decision on constructing the bridge construction is taken. 2) Economic laws are important drivers of regionalization processes. This has become evident from the effects of economic cycles on the regionalisation agenda. (*Lyck, 2009*).

Utilizing the Experiences from the Great Belt Connection and the Øresund Bridge in Relation to the Fehmarn Belt Project

Denmark has gained valuable experiences from the regionalization processes and debates related to the Great Belt Bridge and the Øresund Bridge.

For once, it has become obvious that that regionalization is important for economic development. It is in the light of this that the financing of the Fehmarn-Belt link entirely through the Danish state should be seen.

Secondly, differences on both sides of such a bridging project need to be recognised and addressed through appropriate policies to facilitate cross-border connectivity.

Thirdly, economic rationales matter a lot as drivers of popular behaviour and response to such new connectivity as created by these big bridging projects. Economic rationale is a powerful factor in regionalisation initiatives.

Due to these experiences, the responsible authorities for the Fehmarn-Belt link are working intensively with on policies and projects to tackle the mental divide between the two sides of the Fehmarn-Belt bridge and prepare for the new geographic reality after its opening in 2018. In this respect, tourism is a major driver of a sense of 'being connected' because it has both direct and indirect impacts on the economy lies on either side of the bridge, and influences communication activities. It is for that reason that tourism has a high priority in the activities initiated by the authorities.

Conclusion

This article discussed regionalization processes in Denmark in the wake of establishing two major fixed links across seaways. The main outcome has been that regionalization in the wake of such major projects of establishing new connectivity can be an important driver for economic growth, by overcoming divisions and peripherality. The projects also point to the need of combinig differnt theoretical explanations of regionalisation, as one on its own cannot capture the many aspects resulting from such fundamentsal chasnges to spatial relationships as such major infrastructure projects as a sea bridge. Mental divisions are just as important to overcome. Finally, it became evident that economic rationale prevails over idealistic ambitions and narratives about integration and 'togetherness'.

REFERENCES

Brenner, Neil et al. (2003):"State/space : A reader", Blackwell Publishers, Oxford.

Castells, Manuel (2000) "The rise of the network society", Blackwell Publishers, Oxford.

Fitjar, Rune Dahl (2010):"The rise of regionalism : Causes of regional mobilisation in Western Europe", Routledge, London.

Hanley, Richard E. (2004): Moving people, goods, and information in the 21st century : the cutting-edge infrastructures of networked cities", Taylor & Francis Books Ltd.

Hirst, Paul (2009): "Globalization in question", Polity, Cambridge, 3.Ed.

Isard, Walter et al. (1998): "Methods of interregional and regional analysis", Aldershot: Ashgate Publishing Limited.

Lyck, Lise et al. (2000): "Øresundsregionaliseringen analyseret strategisk og ledelsesmæssigt", Handelshøjskolen i København: Institut for Ledelse, Politik og Filosofi.

Lyck, Lise (2002): "Broens økonomi, ejernes interesser og politiske bindinger, i Öresundsförbindelse med ett hinder mindre" (ed.) Lars Söderström, Øresundsuniversitetet, Lund.

Lyck, Lise and Nielsen, Jens (2006): "Government og governance i Øresundsintegrationen", Copenhagen Business School, TCM, Frederiksberg Bogtrykkeri A/S.

Lyck, Lise (2008): "Interkulturel ledelse i Øresundsregionen", Copenhagen Business School, TCM, Frederiksberg Bogtrykkeri A/S.

Lyck, Lise (2009): "Learning from the Øresund Experiences of Relevance to the Femern Connection", Seminar on the Fehmarn Connection, at Copenhagen Business School, September 9, Room D4.39 arranged by TCM, Copenhagen Business School.

Pomfret, Richard (2003):"Economic analysis of regional trading arrangements", Cheltenham : Edward Elgar Publishing Limited.

Savelsberg, Eva (2008): Innovation in European freight transportation: Basics, methodology and case studies for the European markets", Springer.

Øresundsbro Konsortiet (2010): "10 år – Øresundsbron og regionen." Øresunds Konsortiet, juni.

http://www.storebaelt.dk/omstorebaelt/trafiktal/arkiv; Accessed 5th November, 2010.

JAN ERIK GRINDHEIM – UNIVERSITY OF BERGEN, NORWAY
ADAM MANGA – CORVINUS UNIVERSITY, HUNGARY

Intercity Corridors Restructuring Europe

The need for a common European transport policy was set down already in the Rome Treaty in 1957, to support the freedom of movement of persons, goods and services in the European Community (EC). Until the 1980s, however, transport policies in Europe were formed mainly by national rather than European interests. Hence, in 1985, the European Court of Justice ruled out that the Council of Ministers of the EC had failed to act in accordance with the Rome Treaty, and in 1992, the treaty establishing the European Union (EU), the Maastricht Treaty, reinforced the political, institutional and budgetary foundations for it, including the decision to open up the rail freight market and the introduction of a Trans-European Transport Network (TEN-T), which paved the way for a plan for a European transport infrastructure with the help of EU funding.

In this chapter, we analyse the development of a common transport policy in the European Union from a theoretical perspective developed by the political sociologist Stein Rokkan in the 1960s and -70s. Rokkan differentiated the process of policy-formation into a territorial and functional dimension by using the model of exit, voice, and loyalty developed by economist Albert O. Hirschman in a centre-periphery perspective on the political structuring of Europe and the European Community. What we argue, with the help of Rokkan, is that the development of what we call intercity corridors of transnational transport networks in the European Union is challenging the territorially differentiated economic, social and political boundaries of the European nation-states from a functional perspective which can only be dealt with properly by the development of new multi-level structures of governance across the EU member states and their governmental systems.

Focus is on the regional level of governance and in particular the COINCO North project linking the cities of Oslo, Göteborg and Malmö/Copenhagen in the so called Scandinavian 8 Million City, because this Corridor of Innovation and Cooperation (COINCO) aims at bringing together three major centres and their regions as nodes in a network of communication and interregional development with increased exit opportunities for persons, goods and services across the territorially differentiated governmental systems of political voice and loyalty, that is, Norway, Sweden and Denmark.

Restructuring territoriality in Europe

The territorial differentiation of Europe into its present structure of nationally based democracies and modern welfare states, can be traced back to five macro-developments put forward by Stein Rokkan in his numerous works on European state- and nation-building in the late 1960s and early -70s.[1]

The first was the process of state-building following the Peace of Westphalia in 1648, with its creation of military-administrative, economic and cultural centres under the supremacy of a single set of hierarchically organised territorial institutions. The second was the development of capitalism, transnational in nature, but nourished within the capsule of the state and the formation of national markets. The third was the process of cultural standardisation related to the formation of national communities through the strengthening of boundaries of integration and loyalty following the revolution in France in 1789. The fourth was the process of democratisation by the development of representative political institutions for articulation, recognition and legitimisation of internal voice structuring which followed the radical revolutions across Europe in 1848. The fifth was the development of modern welfare states with the growth of social and economic citizenship rights as a substantive complement to political democracy starting with the closing of Otto von Bismarck's decade of welfare reforms in the newly united Germany in 1889 and fulfilled with the democratisation of the communist central- and eastern-European countries in 1989.[2]

Political scientist Stefano Bartolini adds a sixth major development trend to Rokkan's historical analyses of European state- and nation-building processes to which Rokkan "never devoted much attention", according to Bartolini.[3] That is the process of Europeanisation, which represents a major challenge of boundary disintegration to the territorial processes of border consolidation in Europe – as Rokkan also noted in one of his major works on European state- and nation-building processes in 1973:

This conflict between boundary accentuation and boundary reduction has shaped the history of the European system of states to this day. The current struggles within the Common Market, within the European Free Trade Association, between East and West in Europe, all can be analyzed in terms of these tensions between military-administrative, cultural and economic policies of boundary demarcation vs. boundary reduction.[4]

Bartolini defines Europeanisation as "a process of nation state boundary transcendence, resulting into a process of de-differentiation of European polities,"[5] and sees it as a response to the weakening of the European state system and the pressure of capitalism; yet, it has to come to grip with the other threads of development in Europe's political history:

The relationship between Europeanisation and the features of nation-building, democratisation and welfare developments results problematic and somehow contradictory. Nation-building, democratisation and welfare state development were processes closely linked to the state as a bounded territory and to its internal cultural homogeneity. The mechanisms of democratic decision making and those of redistribution of the material resources

*similarly assume and rest on both strong collective identities and
solidarity ties – that is, high cultural costs of exit – and on the
physical inability or difficulty to subtract resources from the social
obligations contracted on a territorial basis (that is, high material
costs of exit).*[6]

We look upon the development of a common transport policy, and
what we particularly define as intercity corridors of transnational
transport networks in the European Union, as a form of politically
motivated Europeanisation of functional integration across the territorially differentiated economic, social and political boundaries
of the European nation-states, which might also result in a process
of de-differentiation of their polities and political processes insofar
as the transport policy of the EU, according to the European Commission's green paper on this issue from 2009,

*aims to provide the infrastructure needed for the internal
market to function smoothly and for the objectives of the Lisbon
Agenda on growth and jobs to be achieved. It also sets out to help
ensure accessibility and boost economic and social and territorial cohesion. It supports every EU citizen's right to move freely
within the territory of the Member States.*[7]

A cohesion policy to support the single market

The idea of developing a set of Trans-European Networks (TEN)
of functional integration across the territorially defined member states
of the European Union emerged in the 1980s with the introduction
of the single market of the European Community. The argument
behind was that it made little sense to talk about an integrated
market, with freedom of movement for persons, goods and services,
without providing a set of functional networks for transportation,
energy and telecommunications linking the regions making up that
market across the territorial borders of its member states to spur
economic growth and employment.

TENs exist in three sectors of activity, of which our focus is on the first, and within that, in particular on what we call intercity rail corridors:

Trans-European Transport Networks (TEN-T) cover road and intermodal transport, waterways and seaports, and the European high-speed railway network. Intelligent transport management systems also fall into this category, as does Galileo, Europe's satellite radio navigation system.

Trans-European Energy Networks (TEN-E) cover the electricity and natural gas sectors. They help to create a single energy market and contribute to security of energy supply.

Trans-European Telecommunications Networks (eTEN) have as their aim the deployment of telecommunication network-based services. They focus strongly on public services and are at the heart of the initiative 'eEurope – An Information Society for All'.[8]

In the European Commission Communication "Towards a Single Market Act" from 27 October 2010, the need for a common transport policy in the EU was taken a step further, to include a general wish for bringing people together, what in EU terminology is often referred to as day-to-day or people-to-people integration, at the same time as the technical, administrative and regulatory challenges of such a process of functional boundary reduction vs. territorial boundary demarcation were taken into account:

the strategic importance of transport services in reconciling supply and demand is making them play an essential part in economic growth and job creation. At the same time, by improving access to certain areas and bringing people together, they are a key ingredient of a better quality of life. A single, interconnected and efficient European transport system is therefore essential to the smooth movement of goods, people and services – the essential and underlying freedoms of the single market. The creation of a single transport system is still being delayed by a number of technical, administrative and regulatory obstacles that have been hampering the competitiveness of the single co-modal transport market in particular and holding back economic growth in Europe in general.[9]

The legal basis for establishing a set of trans-European networks can be found in Chapter XV (Articles 154, 155 and 156) of the treaty establishing the European Union, the Maastricht Treaty. With this chapter, the Union aimed to promote the development of such networks as a key element for the creation of the single market and for reinforcing economic and social cohesion, including the interconnection and interoperability of national networks as well as access to such networks. Moreover, the European Commission examined the possible synergies between the three categories of networks (transport, energy and telecommunications) along with methods of funding and potential distribution, and the Commission's Communication to the Council of the European Union and the European Parliament "Trans-European Networks: Towards an integrated approach" (2007), highlighted the potential added-value of the combination of infrastructures (more efficient use of space, reduced costs and environmental impact), as well as possible synergies between the three types of networks and potential environmental benefits of integrating them.[10]

Based on the Green Paper issued in February 2009 mentioned above, and the subsequent consultation process, the Commission developed in 2010 a dual layer Trans-European Transport Network (TEN-T), with a core network of the strategically most important nodes and links overlaying the dense comprehensive network. Six expert groups elaborated their recommendations on a strategic network planning methodology, including connections beyond the Union, on supplementary infrastructure measures to integrate other policy fields into TEN-T planning and on legal and financial aspects, and the document "Consultation on the Future Trans-European Transport Networks" adopted by the Commission 4 May 2010, invited stakeholders, European institutions and consultative bodies to express their views in a consultation process ending in September 2010.[11]

During this process, the European Commission together with the Spanish Presidency organized in Zaragoza on 8 and 9 June 2010 a ministerial and stakeholder conference called "TEN-T Days 2010: Trans-European Transport Networks – drawing up the EU Core-Network" for an integrated, efficient and environmentally friendly European transport system. The aim of this conference was to allow the ministers and stakeholders to identify, on the basis of the consultation document from the European Commission, the key elements of the methodology to draw up the future TEN-T planning and implementation framework; including how EU financial instruments can be mobilized more effectively as part of a consistent funding strategy that pulls together European Union and national, public and private funding.

In the public consultation on the Green Paper, more than 300 stakeholders expressed their views and opinions, and, according to the Commission Staff Working Document "TEN-T Policy Review – background papers" (2010), most of them advocated the idea of an integral policy review:

While appreciating the progress and major achievements of 15 years of TEN-T policy development, and at the same time aware of difficulties in policy conception and implementation, they broadly supported the Commission's main directions for the future policy development:
- *meeting new political challenges such as globalisation, climate change, technological innovation and social developments;*
- *a critical review of the TEN-T planning concept with a view to strengthening its Union dimension;*
- *ensuring a strong link between TEN-T and transport policy so as to facilitate efficient, safe, high-quality services across the transport modes;*
- *strengthening the instruments to support completion of the network within the agreed timescale*[12]

As a result of the consultation process and ministerial meeting in Zaragoza, the future planning process in relation to the development of Trans-European Transport Networks (TEN-T) will be subject to a Commission proposal for new guidelines, foreseen to be presented in spring/summer 2011. According to the European Commission's homepage on Mobility and Transport, the ultimate policy objective of the TEN-T is the establishment of:

*a single, multimodal network covering both traditional
ground-based structures and equipment (including intelligent
transport systems) to enable safe and efficient traffic. Increasingly, it also involves the deployment of innovative systems that
not only promise benefits for transport but also have substantial
potential for industrial innovation.*

*The Trans-European Transport Network shall be established
gradually by integrating land, sea and air transport infrastructure
components, and by including the necessary technical instal-
lations, information and telecommunication systems to ensure
smooth operation of the network and efficient traffic management.*

*The transport infrastructure components are road, rail and
inland waterway networks, motorways of the sea, seaports and
inland waterway ports, airports and other interconnection points
between modal networks.*

*Intelligent transport systems include the traffic management
systems for road, rail, air and waterborne transport as well as the
positioning and navigation systems.*[13]

Our focus, however, is on how such transnational transport networks
make it possible to link major centres and their regions across the
European continent functionally as nodes in networks of communication and development, where the logic of increased and easier
exit-opportunities across territorial borders is the driving force
behind the political processes.

Centres as nodes in networks of communication and development

Rokkan defines centres as "sites for the provision of services,
the processing of information, and the control of transactions over
shorter or longer distances,"[14] and presents two models for the
classification of regions surrounding such centres in the European
context: one for regions of "homogeneous land use or resource endowments"; another for "hierarchies of central places and the areas

they serve."[15] Clearly, they feed into each other. Territorial centres cannot be analyzed in isolation: "As soon as you move on to study hierarchies of centres and their surrounding areas, you are forced to pay attention to the characteristics of the overall networks of communication linking them together."[16] In fact, what Rokkan argues, is that any centre has to be analyzed at two levels: firstly, by looking at the components that enter into "the centrality of the single site" and secondly, by reviewing "a variety of indicators of the degree of centralization of the network which it is part."[17]

Building upon an article by geographer Walter Christaller from 1950,[18] Rokkan pays attention to an effort to combine a market model with a transport route model and an administrative model in his historical studies of the development of territorial structures in Europe. We call this combined model a pre-nation-state historical model of Europeanisation, focusing on the economic, social, and political development of Western Europe: "The historical distribution of central cities in Western Europe was heavily influenced by the successive changes in dominant trade routes," says Rokkan,[19] and points out that the Mediterranean Sea helped to orient trade along an East-West axis until the downfall of the Roman Empire and the conquest of Islam, before the decisive trade routes turned northwards, from Italy across the Alps to the North Sea and the Baltic, with the result that a closely knit string of cities developed: "first within the Roman, later within the German-Roman Empire."[20]

This phase lasted until the 15th-16th century, "then the route across the Alps declined in importance and the sea routes along Western Europe and across the world oceans took over."[21] Between the 16th and 18th centuries the medieval trade route belt divided Europe in a western and eastern part, with a continuous strengthening of dominant centres such as London, Paris and Madrid on the Atlantic side and Vienna, Munich, Berlin and Stockholm on the landward side. These city centres controlled larger surrounding peripheries and managed to build up great military-administrative strength and took advantage of economic, social and political resources which counted heavily in the next round of network building: the construction of national railway systems after 1830. "Whether privately or publicly financed," according to Rokkan,[22] "the investments made in the development of rail networks helped to strengthen the established structure of national and regional centres: in fact we may go so far as to say that the railway system "froze" the structure for more than a century".

Whereas Rokkan mainly pays attention to how rail networks in Europe played a vital role in the internal structuring of territories controlled by state- and nation-building elites in the development of modern welfare state democracies, we argue that the establishment of a Trans-European Transport Network (TEN-T) system at the European Union level might lead to what we above have referred to as "a process of nation state boundary transcendence, resulting into a process of de-differentiation of European polities."[23] Because, as long as the logic of increased and easier exit-opportunities across territorial borders is the driving force behind the development of such networks, the territorially differentiated systems of political voice and loyalty so characteristic for the mass democracies of the modern European welfare state system will be under pressure.

From a boundary demarcation vs. boundary reduction perspective, a common European transport policy challenge also the relationship between the European Union and its member states, between the member states as such, and between the EU, its members states and the emerging networks of communication and interregional development linking major centres and their regions in the single market. "Ideally," according to Rokkan,

a centre controls the bulk of the transactions among holders of resources across a territory; it is closer than any alternative site to the resource-rich areas within the territory; and it is able to dominate the communication flow through a standard language and a set of institutions for regular consultation and representation. By contrast, a periphery controls at best only its own resources, is isolated from all the other regions except the central one and contributes little to the total flow of communication within the territory, particularly if its language and its ethnic identity set it apart from the other regions controlled from the centre.[24]

Hence, a much more complex model for the study of boundary transcendence and control has to be developed, to understand how the establishment of a system of trans-European transport networks might restructure the territoriality of Europe. Again, we build upon Rokkan, whom, with reference to Hirschman's model of exit, voice and loyalty, instead of positing three directions of differentiation, argues that there is a need for a model which "posits three sets of boundary transactions and three corresponding sets of control measures: for *goods and services*, for *personnel*, for *messages*."[25]

Europe of networks

According to Árpád Ivány, József Pál and László Tóth, the establishment of a common European transport policy is the result of a complex developing process. To ensure its success, it is necessary to organize cooperation between the economic management system, the scientific, technical development policy, the trade, investment and financial policy, the environmental policy and the regulatory system.[26] If a success, as noted by Ferenc Erdösi, a well structured, coordinated, efficient transport system will promote tourism, facilitate the people and capital flow, increase competitiveness, and help the integration of remote and less-developed areas. It must be taken into consideration, however, that certain modes of transport have different abilities to connect and integrate various areas, according to technological features.[27] Any intervention must therefore be based on a long-term vision of the sustainable mobility of people, goods and services.[28]

As we have already seen, a Trans-European Transport Network (TEN-T) policy was declared an important principle for the process of European integration underlying the single market of the EU in the Maastricht Treaty at the beginning of the 1990s. In Essen, 1994, 14 projects were adopted by the European Council; ten years later, the list contained 30 projects. By 2020, TEN-T will include 89 500 km of roads and 94 000 km of railways, including around 20 000 km of high-speed rail lines suitable for speeds of at least 200 km/h. The inland waterway system will amount to 11 250 km, including 210 inland ports, whilst there are a further 294 seaports and some 366 airports. In order to complete the network, thousands of kilometres of "missing links" have to be constructed and upgraded. The result will reduce travel time for passengers and goods, and decrease of congestions. For inter-regional traffic alone benefits are estimated to almost EUR 8 billion per year.[29] The map below gives an overview of the Trans-European Transport Networks under development in the EU.

Figure 1. Map of the Trans-European Transport Network (TEN-T)

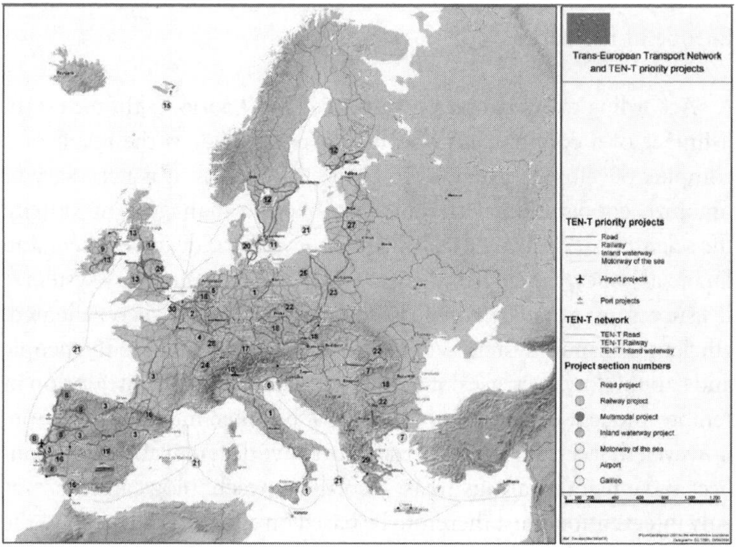

Source: Eurostat 2005.[30]

Financial regulation for TEN-T-support was adopted in 1995. Projects are funded by the member states, public-private-partnerships, the European Investment Bank, the Structural and Cohesion Funds, the European Regional Development Fund, and pre-accession instruments. Total investment on Transport infrastructure for the period 2000-2006 was EUR 859 billion,[31] and in the 2009 European Economic Recovery Plan, 53 percent of the funds connected to TEN-T network supported rail projects.[32]

Political changes in the 1990s led to the spread of a pan-European thought in the sense of transportation. After the first Pan-European Transport Conference in Prague 1991, and the second in Crete 1994, the western, central and eastern European countries identified nine long-distance corridors, which were given priority with regard to infrastructure development. At the third Pan-European Transport Conference in Helsinki 1997, a tenth corridor and the Pan-European Transport Areas for sea regions were added to the existing corridors. These multimodal corridors, the so-called Helsinki corridors, have an overall length of about 48 000 km, 25 000 km of which belong to the rail network and 23 000 km are part of the road network.[33]

The objective behind setting up these corridors was to improve the connection between the western and eastern European countries, but later, decision-makers realized that however they visioned projects to develop the west-east connection, there were no such plans to connect the eastern European countries with each other.[34] This recognition led to the establishment of the Transport Infrastructure Needs Assessment (TINA) network, with the aim of initiating the development of a multimodal transport network within the EU enlargement countries of Estonia, Latvia, Lithuania, Poland, Czech Republic, Slovakia, Hungary, Slovenia, Romania, Bulgaria and Cyprus.[35] The project contained primary and secondary corridors, but after the EU accession of the mentioned states, the secondary corridors had not become parts of the TEN-T-network.[36]

In recent years, some elements of the 30-projects TEN-T list have already been finalised, some are still under construction, and some are waiting for initiation. The Øresund fixed link between Denmark and Sweden (2000), the reconstruction of Malpensa Airport in Milan (2001), the Betuwe railway line in The Netherlands (2007), the Nürnberg-Ingolstadt (2006), Madrid-Barcelona (2008), and the first phase of TGV Est (2007) high speed railway lines, are all completed, and the Paris-Bruxelles-Köln-Amsterdam-London high speed railway project is near completion. The Brenner base tunnel and its access routes, the Lyon-Torino base tunnel, and the Fehmarn-Belt connection, will be completed after 2020.[37]

As we have seen above, however, transport does not stop at the borders of the EU, hence the major Trans-European Network Transport (TEN-T) axes have to be linked up with the transport network of the neighbouring countries, or, transport networks of neighbouring regions have to be connected to the European network. Five transnational axes have been chosen because they will contribute to promoting international exchanges, trade and traffic. As an example, the Northern axis links the European Union with Norway to the north and with Russia and Belarus on the eastern borders of the Union. Another connection is also foreseen, connecting Norway with Russia through Sweden and Finland. These projects are not only about increasing speed and upgrading tracks, they also include the implementation of new technologies, safety and information technology solutions.[38]

In the following, we will introduce some of the priority projects of the 30 elements list of the European Commission, describing the features of the plans of the intercity corridors of Berlin-Palermo; Paris-London-Bruxelles-Amsterdam-Köln, Lyon-Torino-Ljubljana-Budapest; Paris-Germany-Vienna-Bratislava; and the Fehmarnbelt and Nordic Triangle; before we focus our final discussion on the COINCO North project linking the cities of Oslo, Gothenburg, Malmö and Copenhagen in the so called Scandinavian 8 Million City.

Berlin-Palermo

The number one on the list of priority projects in the Trans-European Transport Network (TEN-T) system, is the 2 500 km long rail link Berlin-Palermo, which connects Germany with Italy through Austria, bringing together major cities and regions such as Berlin, Leipzig/Halle, Nürnberg, München, Innsbruck, Bolzano, Verona, Bologna, Firenze, Roma, Napoli, and Palermo in Sicily. The approximate cost of the project is EUR 47.1 billion, and the estimated completion date is 2022. The arguments used to legitimize such a big investment are that they will contribute to environmental protection and boosting the economies of the cities and regions involved, through better freight and passenger transport, reduced travel times, upgrading of tracks and increased capacity. In Germany, one year after inauguration, six million passengers, amongst them 7 000 daily commuters used the Nürnberg-Ingolstadt line.[39] After finalising the Leipzig-Nürnberg part of the high speed rail link in 2015-2016, travel time between Berlin and München will be three hours shorter than the current seven hours.[40] Around München, the Berlin-Palermo line meets with the Paris-Bratislava railway axis, sharing existing infrastructure. The caused bottleneck will be resolved through work progresses on the east-west line.[41]

On the Austrian-Italian section, the project includes an ambitious element, the construction of the 56 km long Brenner Base Tunnel, between Innsbruck in Austria and Fortezza in Italy;[42] the tunnel will be connected to an accession route in Tirol under construction. The New Lower Inn Valley Railway (Neue Unterinntalbahn) will comprise a double track high speed 250 km/h railway, mostly situated in tunnels. Taking into consideration that there are 300 trains running daily on the current railway line,[43] the creation of the Brenner Base Tunnel and its accession route will contribute to improve Alps-crossing rail freight transport and significant reduction of heavy lorry traffic, congestions and environmental load. The Commission decided to grant EURO 903 million for the Brenner Base Tunnel, and both Austria and Italy are taking the necessary decisions to guarantee the financing.[44]

Paris-London-Bruxelles-Amsterdam-Köln

The high speed railway axis Paris-Bruxelles-Köln-Amsterdam-London, „PBKAL", is the first cross-border high-speed passenger rail project in Europe; linking major cities in France (Paris and Lille), Belgium (Bruxelles, Liége, and Antwerpen), Germany (Köln, Aachen, and Frankfurt am Main), The Netherlands (Amsterdam and Rotterdam) and the United Kingdom (London). The network provides a real alternative to air and road transport, the modal share on the Paris-Bruxelles relation, serving 6 million passengers per year[45] with 1h25min journey time, changed in favour of the train significantly since the inauguration of the line, making the share of air transport almost virtually irrelevant.[46]

Following the completion of the high speed section in the United

Kingdom in 2007, between the Channel tunnel and St. Pancras station, journey times decreased to 2h15min to Paris, and to 1h51min to Bruxelles.[47] In the first nine months of 2008, Eurostar trains carried 13.9 percent more travellers, which meant 17.2 percent increase in ticket sales.[48] In 2008, Eurostar trains carried 9 million passengers, a 10 percent growth compared to the previous year.[49] Taking a brief look at air travel data, in 2007, airplanes carried 1.79 million passengers on the London Heathrow-Paris CDG relation.[50] In 2009, number of international travels on the Amsterdam-London relation grew by 30 percent, and further increase is expected after the opening of the international passenger transport market.[51]

Since the inauguration of the high speed line between Liège and the German border (HSL3), Belgium is the first European country where high speed network links its different borders. Thalys and ICE trains use the line between Bruxelles and Köln, reducing the journey time by 29 minutes. Since Thalys switched to use the other new high speed link towards the Netherlands in December, Amsterdam-Bruxelles travel time has been cut by 49 minutes with the use of HSL4 in Belgium and HSL Zuid in the Netherlands.[52] Compared to 2007, the number of international passengers in Belgium increased by 7.4 percent in 2008.[53]

After the delivery of the high speed train sets, NS Hispeed, joint venture of KLM airline and the railways of the Netherlands NS, in cooperation with Belgian railways SNCB, will introduce the Fyra service between Amsterdam, Rotterdam, Antwerpen and Bruxelles. In 2011, NS Hispeed expects to carry 26.4 million passengers. Around 18.4 million of these will be on domestic services.[54]

On the German section, upgrading of the line between Köln, Aachen and the Belgian border is in progress. On the border, a tunnel is also under construction, in order to provide the ability for a better traffic flow, with the expected finalisation date at the end of 2010.[55]

Special for this high speed corridor is that it connects key airports in Europe, such as Paris Charles de Gaulle, Bruxelles National, Amsterdam-Schiphol, furthermore Airport Köln/Bonn and Frankfurt am Main in advance. The airport of Bruxelles will be connected to the link through the Diabolo project, which comprises of a new line between Bruxelles and Antwerpen, and the connecting curves to the airport and the high speed line 3 towards Liége and Germany.[56] Airlines also try to gain advantage of this situation. Air France and service operator Veolia are planning to launch services from Paris to Bruxelles, Amsterdam, London and selected German cities in competition with SNCF, DB, Eurostar and Thalys.[57]

Lyon-Torino-Ljubljana-Budapest

Next project to be introduced is the PP number 6 on the project list, the railway axis Lyon-Torino-Milano-Trieste-Ljubljana-Budapest-Ukrainian border (Záhony). This project involves the construction of high speed lines in France and Italy, and upgraded lines in Slovenia and Hungary. Key elements of the project are the construction of a 52 km long base tunnel and two accession tunnels, each about 20 km, between Torino and Lyon, with expected finalisation in 2023.[58] After the completion of the project, Lyon-Milano journey will take only 1 hour and 45 minutes, instead of the four hours travel time today on the Mount Cenis route. Travel time between Milan and Paris, through Lyon, will be reduced from seven to four hours.[59]

Nowadays, the Fréjus route is extremely overcrowded, with 3 500 lorries passing through every day.[60] Estimates show that this amount will increase in the forthcoming years. Thus, the project is urgent, having an important role in shifting freight traffic from road to rail, protecting the sensitive alpine environment from the unsustainable growth of road traffic.[61]

Paris-Germany-Vienna-Bratislava

West-East corridor "High speed railway axis east" (PP4) and "Railway axis Paris-Bratislava" (PP17), will improve connection between France, Luxembourg, Germany, Austria, Slovakia, and Hungary through the Austrian high speed train sets operating on the Budapest-München relation. The French section of the corridor includes a 300 km long high speed line (LGV Est) designed for 350 km/h operation in the future, where French TGV and German ICE high speed train sets can reach 320 km/h. Since the inauguration of the first phase, travel times between Paris and Luxembourg and Paris and Germany (Frankfurt, Stuttgart) have been reduced significantly. For example, current journey time between Paris and Saarbrücken is less than two hours instead of more than four hours before. After the finalisation of the second phase of the line in 2016, travel time between Paris and Strasbourg will be cut by 30 minutes to 1h50min and in Luxembourg-Strasbourg relation to 1h25min.[62] Only one month after its inauguration in 2007, trains carried one million passengers and in 2008 11.9 million.[63] Besides the construction of the second phase of the high speed line to Strasbourg, the existing line via Forbach and Saarbrücken towards Mannheim and Frankfurt will be upgraded to 200 km/h.

Further sections of „PP17" in Germany are under planning and construction, including an ambitious element, the Stuttgart 21 project. This project includes a 60 km long high speed line between Stuttgart and Ulm, a tunnel under the city of Stuttgart, connecting the high speed lines around the city, the airport, and the new underground Stuttgart Main Station. In the future, travel time between Stuttgart and München will be only one and a half hour, compared to today's two and a half – three hours trip. The project also comprises the unique opportunity to develop the urban area in the heart of the city.[64]

Fehmarnbelt and Nordic Triangle

The next project we want to introduce, is the 20 km long Fehmarnbelt bridge (or an alternative solution, a tunnel), between the German town of Puttgarden and Rødby in Denmark. It is scheduled to be finalised in 2018 and will be the key element of connecting central Europe and the Nordic countries. The link will comprise a double track railway and a four lane motorway, and comparing to the current at least 45 minutes journey, crossing time will be about 12 minutes. Connecting links include upgraded road and rail, with the ability to provide service with speed up to 160 km/h or 200 km/h.

Construction of the link, expected to cost approximately EUR 5 billion, will be financed through loans, guaranteed by the Danish state, and funding from the European Union's TEN-T-programme. The region of the link is made up of flourishing cities such as Hamburg,

Bremen, Lübeck, Copenhagen and Malmö, with a total population of 18.6 million inhabitants, who will become closer in distance and time after the completion of the link, which will not only create faster transport connections but also increased opportunities for trade, business, day-to-day integration and flexibilities in the regional labour market. Connecting links between Germany and the Scandinavian countries (such as Rødby-Puttgarden, Rostock-Gedser and Trelleborg ferries), and existing fixed links (Storebælt, Øresund) experienced traffic growth in the recent years. This increase, particularly in freight transport, is expected to continue in the future.[65] The upgraded rail sections will connect to the German high-speed railway system, and through the Øresund link, the Swedish part of the Nordic Triangle railway axis which is also a TEN-T funded project, a development programme for improving rail transport services, increasing capacity and upgrading of the railway tracks, will reduce travel time between the Swedish cities of Stockholm, Göteborg and Malmö, and to Norway's capital Oslo.[66]

As already mentioned, the Øresund link will connect the Fehmarn axis to the Nordic Triangle network. In 2007, 9.7 million train passengers crossed Øresund via rail – which meant an increase by 25 percent compared to the previous year. Four of five train passengers live in Sweden and one of five in Denmark. The Øresund train serves mainly as a local means of transportation in the region since 90 percent of the train journeys are regional. Approximately six of ten train passengers commute to their studies or to work, and this commuter traffic is the driving force of growth in train traffic.[67]

COINCO North – High speed rail link

Trans-European Transport Networks (TEN-T) high speed rail links are spreading all over the European continent, bringing closer people, regions, countries, businesses, culture, science etc. The vision of the Corridor of Innovation and Coordination (COINCO) North is to promote this progress towards Northern Europe, providing new possibilities for the eight million people living in the three connecting regions of Oslo, Göteborg and Malmö/Copenhagen, by bringing this geographically, and to a certain degree geopolitically speaking, peripheral area of Europe in closer contact with the Continent's central parts and their functionally integrating transport networks. From such a perspective, a high speed revolution will determine a new era of development in Scandinavia.

After inauguration of the high speed line, Oslo and Copenhagen will become closer to each other significantly, at least in time: planned travel time will be 2 hours and 20 minutes. The link will integrate the three labour markets around Oslo, Göteborg and Malmö/Copenhagen,[68] and the COINCO North line will connect not only Norway, Sweden and Denmark, but through Copenhagen and the Fehmarn Belt link, trains from Oslo and Göteborg can reach Hamburg and Berlin. In addition, not only the commuters between Oslo, Göteborg, and Malmö/Copenhagen will benefit from the high speed link, through further railway development projects other parts of Norway could feel as a part of a Euro-Scandinavian corridor too.

From a pure transportation oriented point of view, the aims of the COINCO North project are numerous: everyday commuters and business travellers will gain advantage of the reduced travel time and efficient service. Broad scale ICT-solutions will be developed in favour of providing appropriate environment for current and future passengers, such as on-line booking, paperless ticketing, up-to-date schedule and train information which even can be reached from mobile phones. On-board services will contain wireless internet access and as many laptop plugs as there are seats on the train. Furthermore, the COINCO North link shall not be a separate high-speed line, but part of a complex, efficient transport system. As in many other parts in Europe, the new high speed line is expected to boost the development of new city centres, urban areas, business and residential investments. Along the line, new or reconstructed suburban stations are planned together with shopping centres, and P+R parking, which will be connected to the local mass transit system, creating an important public transport hub. On sections where there will be the possibility of mixed use with conventional speed commuter trains, four tracks are planned instead of two, in order to avoid rush hour congestions.

Our main concern, though, is the future potential for economic development and growth of this region, in particular when seen in the context of the growing knowledge-based economy. As pointed out by the managing director of the regional development agency Oslo Teknopol, Knut Halvorsen: "The most important dynamic effect of this project will be the large and integrated employment market that is created, one that stretches from Oslo in the north to Copenhagen in the south. This will have a magnetic effect for employees, employers, innovators, and investors."[69]

The background of the COINCO North project is that new technology for transport and less regulation in trade and finance have opened up the structure of the global economy, and the future potential for economic growth "is defined by network connectivity and strategic positions in information and trade communication."[70] As put down as the fourth freedom of the European Union's single market, capital can now flow more freely across national borders, and economic activity takes place at a global scale. As a result of this, from a government vs. governance perspective, new strategic areas and networks emerge, "resulting in the development of new organisational structures and cross-border regions,"[71] in which cities are the nodes in networks of communication and development: "City regions have become the engines in developing the knowledge- and information based community. Their performance and competitiveness rely on knowledge, economy, quality of life, connectivity, urban diversity, urban scale, social capital, politics/framework and image."[72]

However, put into the boundary demarcation vs. boundary reduction paradigm of the territorially differentiated economic, social and political structures of the European nation-states, the establishment of functionally integrating Trans-European Transport Networks (TEN-T) such as COINCO North can only be dealt with properly from a political point of view by the development of new multi-level structures of governance across the EU member states and their governmental systems. As emphasised in the COINCO North project, there are a number of key questions to be addressed if we study this interregional network by using the model of exit, voice, and loyalty in a centre-periphery perspective:

- How to achieve a holistic and sustainable planning perspective?
- How to attract knowledge intensive global professionals?
- How to attract knowledge intensive companies, investors and tourists?
- How to achieve a transnational strategy for balanced production and growth?[73]

As pointed out by Floire Nathanael Daub, project manager of COINCO North, "compared to economic centres in Europe and the world, Scandinavian cities have small and somewhat dispersed populations, with concentrations around only the four metropolitan areas of Oslo, Göteborg, Copenhagen/Malmö and Stockholm. In a world were regions are expanding, this is a problem."[74] Stronger economic, social and political ties are therefore required between the Scandinavian city regions, "to build up a leading arena for mutual learning, joint initiatives and exchange of best practice."[75]

COINCO North is one example of a multi-level-governance body which has been set up to spur economic, social and political cooperation across national borders in a European context. It was approved for funding through the European Union Interreg IV A Öresund-Kattegat-Skagerak programme at the end of February 2009, and will run until the autumn of 2011. Norway is not a member of the European Union, but has since 1994 had a special agreement with the EU through its membership of the European Free Trade Association (EFTA) called the European Economic Area Agreement (EEA), which makes Norway a full member of EUs internal market and its supportive policies.

The regional development agency Oslo Teknopol, an inter-municipal public company owned by the Municipality of Oslo and the surrounding County Municipality of Akershus, is both project manager and Norwegian project owner of COINCO North, whilst Business Region Göteborg is the lead partner. In addition, Oslo Municipality, Akershus County Municipality, and Østfold County Municipality in Norway, the cities of Göteborg, Helsingborg and Malmö, plus the regions of Västra Götaland, Halland, Region Skåne in Sweden, and the national planning and executive public agencies

Trafikverket (Sweden), Jernbaneverket (the Norwegian National Rail Administration) and Statens vegvesen (the Norwegian Public Roads Administration) are partners in the project, sharing the same vision for future collaboration:

COINCO North is about thinking networks and coalitions rather than isolated parts of projects, like it has been normally done in the past. This is all in line with the European Union›s new TEN-T strategy, in which the idea has been to establish a model for planning that secures fast construction and linking of national infrastructure systems into a connected European network.

COINCO North wants to be a pioneering project in that, by establishing a collective vision for the whole region. By involving regional and local decision makers, as well as partners in all related areas, as part owners of the project, the aim is to have agreements from the beginning. This will result in faster progress and a common understanding that the whole network as a one is more important than the single parts of the project.[76]

Conclusion

According to Rokkan, "a centre controls the bulk of the transactions among holders of resources across a territory; it is closer than any alternative site to the resource-rich areas within the territory; and it is able to dominate the communication flow through a standard language and a set of institutions for regular consultation and representation."[77] With the introduction of the Trans-European Transport Networks (TEN-T) of the European Union, however, a process of de-differentiation of the territorially structured economic, social and political boundaries of the European nation-states is about to take place. Transactions and the corresponding sets of control measures "for *goods and services*, for *personnel*, for *messages*,"[78] are increasingly coming under the control of larger and centrally located cities and their regions in Europe.

This might be good for the city centres and centrally located regions under investigation here, since it opens up for increased exit opportunities for persons, goods and services across the territorially differentiated governmental systems of political voice and loyalty. But it can become bad news for more peripheral regions, insofar as they are much more dependent on the nationally defined welfare state model of European democracies. A peripheral region at best, controls only its own resources and "is isolated from all the other regions except the central one, and contributes little to the total flow of communication within the territory, particularly, if its language and its ethnic identity set it apart from the other regions controlled from the centre," as Rokkan puts it.[79]

With the establishment of what we have called intercity corridors of transnational transport networks in the European Union, there might also be a need for the development of new multi-level structures of governance across the EU member states to counterbalance the increased exit opportunities for persons, goods and services with systems of political voice and loyalty at the regional level of government, insofar as a strong functional intercity integration in the centre of Europe, will increase the economic, social and not at least cultural differences between centre and periphery and hence the dysfunctionality of the single market of the European Union.

NOTES

1. For an overview, see Peter Flora's edited version of some of Stein Rokkan's most important theoretical works in State Formation, Nation Building, and Mass Politics in Europe. The theory of Stein Rokkan, edited by Peter Flora with Stein Kuhnle and Derek Urwin in 1999. Oxford: Oxford University Press.

2. This argument is further developed in a book about European politics in a comparative perspective by Jan Erik Grindheim: Europeisk politikk i komparativt perspektiv – teorier, modeller, analyser. Oslo: Universitetsforlaget (to be published in 2012).

3. Stefano Bartolini 2006: "A Comparative Political Approach to the EU Formation". ARENA Seminars spring 2006, ARENA Seminar Tuesday 31 January 2006, p. 2. Hereafter Bartolini 2006.

4. Taken from a book published in 1987 in which Stein Rokkan post mortem was credited a chapter on „The Centre-Periphery Polarity" based on his work from 1973: „Cities, States and Nations: A Dimensional Model for the Contrasts in Development". In S.N.Eisenstadt and S. Rokkan (eds.): Building States and

Nations, Vol. I. London: Sage Publications. Here cited from the book Centre-Periphery Structures in Europe. An ISSC Workbook in Comparative Analyis, written by Stein Rokkan, Derek Urwin, Frank Aarebrot, Pamela Malaba and Terje Sande. New York: Campus Verlag. Hereafter Rokkan 1987.

5. Bartolini 2006, p. 4.

6. Bartolini 2006, p. 3.

7. European Commission Green Paper 2009: "TEN-T: A policy review. Towards a better integrated transeuropean transport network at the service of the Common Transport Policy". European Communities: COM(2009) 44 final, p. 3.

8. Downloaded 11 January 2011 from http://epp.eurostat.ec.europa.eu/statistics_explained/index.php/Glossary:Trans-European_networks_(TENs).

9. Communication from the Commission to the European Parliament, the Council, the Economic and Social Committee and the Committee of the Regions 2010: "Towards a Single Market Act. For a highly competitive social market economy. 50 proposals for improving our work, business and exchanges with one another". European Commission: COM(2010) 608 final, p. 12.

10. Communication from the Commission 2007: "Trans-European networks: Towards an integrated approach". {SEC(2007) 374}. Commission of the European Communities: COM(2007) 135 final.

11. Commission Working Document 2010: "Consultation on the Future Trans-European Transport Network Policy". European Commission: COM(2010) 212 final.

12. Commission Staff Working Document 2010: "TEN-T Policy Review – background papers". European Commission SEC(2010) 613 final, p. 3.

13. Downloaded 9 January 2011 from http://ec.europa.eu/transport/infrastructure/networks_eu/networks_eu_en.htm.

14. Rokkan 1987, p. 35.

15. Rokkan 1987, p. 35.

16. Rokkan 1987, p. 35.

17. Rokkan 1987, p. 35.

18. Walter Christaller 1950: "Das Grundgerüst der räumlichen Ordnung in Europa". Frankfurt: Geograf. Hefte 24, 1950.

19. Rokkan 1987, p. 36.

20. Rokkan 1987, p. 36.

21. Rokkan 1987, p. 36.

22. Rokkan 1987, p. 37.

23. Bartolini 2006, p. 4.

24. Rokkan 1987, p. 41.

25. Stein Rokkan 1973: "Entries, voices, exits: Towards a possible generalization

of the Hirschman model". Soc. sci. inform. 13 (1), p. 39-53.

26. Árpád Ivány, József Pál and László Tóth 1987: „Közlekedéspolitika, közlekedés-gazdaságtan" (Transport policy, transport economy). M szaki Könyvkiadó, p. 141.

27. Ferenc Erdösi 2004: "Európa közlekedése és a regionális fejl dés" (Transportation in Europe and regional developement). Dialóg Campus Kiadó Budapest, p. 30.

28. European Commission DG for Energy and Transport 2009: A sustainable future for transport: Towards an integrated, technology-led and user-friendly system. Luxembourg: Publications Office of the European Communities, p. 7.

29. European Commission 2005: Trans-European Transport Network: TEN-T priority axes and projects. Luxembourg: Office for Official Publications of the European Communities, p. 6

30. Downloaded 11 January 2011 from http://epp.eurostat.ec.europa.eu/statistics_explained/images/9/96/Priority_axes_and_projects_of_TEN-T.PNG.

31. Transport infrastructure – What do we want to achieve - http://ec.europa.eu/transport/infrastructure/index_en.htm.

32. European Commission (2009): Trans-European Transport Network: Implementation of the priority projects – Progress report 2009. Luxembourg: Office for Official Publications of the European Communities, p. 68.

33. TINA - Monitoring on the Status of the Pan-European Transport Corridors and Transport Areas - http://www.tinavienna.at/index.php?p_id=1114592820&last_id=1114592820&l_id=en&s_id=42898de6715eebce4dd1ddb3135a25b4 – (2010-03-09).

34. Fleischer Tamás 2008: "Közlekedéspolitika az Európai Unióban" (Transport policy in the European Union). Köz-Gazdaság 2008/04, p. 100.

35. TINA - Monitoring on the Status of the Pan-European Transport Corridors and Transport Areas -http://www.tinavienna.at/index.php?p_id=1114592820&last_id=1114592820&l_id=en&s_id=42898de6715eebce4dd1ddb3135a25b4 – (2010-03-09).

36. Fleischer Tamás 2008: "Közlekedéspolitika az Európai Unióban" (Transport policy in the European Union). Köz-Gazdaság 2008/04, p 101.

37. European Commission 2009: Trans-European Transport Network: Implementation of the priority projects – Progress report 2009. Luxembourg: Office for Official Publications of the European Communities.

38. European Commission DG for Energy and Transport 2007: Building bridges: Extension of the major Trans-European transport axes to the neighbouring countries. Luxembourg: Office for Official Publications of the European Communities.

39. Voller Erfolg: Bayern steigt um auf die Bahn - DB 12.28.2007 - DailyNet Press-

seportal, http://www.dailynet.de/TourismusReisen/11233.php - (2010-03-07).

40. High-speed rail in Germany: Inter-city planes are grounded by faster trains –
guardian.co.uk, 05.08.2009 - http://www.guardian.co.uk/world/2009/aug/05/
high-speed-rail-grounds-city-planes - (2010-03-07).

41. European Commission DG for Energy and Transport 2008: "Better transport
links for Europe - Rail link Berlin-Verona/Milan-Bologna-Naples-Messina –
Palermo". To be found at http://ec.europa.eu/ten/transport/priority_projects_
minisite/PP01EN.pdf.

42. European Commission DG for Energy and Transport 2008: "Better transport
links for Europe - Rail link Berlin-Verona/Milan-Bologna-Naples-Messina –
Palermo." To be found at http://ec.europa.eu/ten/transport/priority_projects_
minisite/PP01EN.pdf.

43. Brenner Eisenbahn Gmbh 2007: „Die neue Unterinntalbahn – Eisenbahntechnik auf höchstem Niveau", p. 2.

44. Karel Van Miert 2009: European Coordinator - Annual activity report Priority
Project 1. Brussels, 17 June 2009.

45. European Commission 2009: Trans-European Transport Network: Implementation of the priority projects – Progress report 2009. Luxembourg: Office for
Official Publications of the European Communities, p. 13.

46. Paris-Bruxelles modal split. UIC High speed rail – Fast track to sustainable
mobility. January 2009, p. 16.

47. European Commission 2009: Trans-European Transport Network: Implementation of the priority projects – Progress report 2009. Luxembourg: Office for
Official Publications of the European Communities.

48. Eurostar sees growth in traveller numbers and ticket sales in third quarter.
Eurostar press release 14.10.08. http://www.eurostar.com/UK/be/leisure/about_
eurostar/press_release/eurostar_sees_growth_in_traveller_numbers_and_ticket_
sales_in_third_quarter.jsp - (2010-03-09).

49. SNCF – Bilan de l'année 2008, Perspectives 2009 – Dossier de presse,
12.02.2009, p. 6.

50. European Commission DG for Energy and Transport 2009: EU energy and
transport in figures - Statistical pocketbook 2009. Luxembourg: Office for Official Publications of the European Communities, p. 130.

51. Eurostar prepares for competition. Railway Gazette International, 02.11.2009
– http://www.railwaygazette.com/news/single-view/view/10/eurostar-prepares-
for-competition.html - (2010-03-09).

52. A star is born – Railway Gazette International, 14.12.2009 - http://www.
railwaygazette.com/news/single-view/view//a-star-is-born.html – (2010-03-09).

53. Le rail en 2009 – Rapport d'Activités 2008 du Groupe SNCB, 1. p. – http://
www.b-rail.be/corp/F/assets/pdf/activity_report_2008_fr.pdf - (2010-03-09).

54. Fyra brand for Amsterdam-Brussels high speed – Railway Gazette International, 07.07.2009 - http://www.railwaygazette.com/news/single-view/view/10/fyra-brand-for-amsterdam-brussels-high-speed.html - (2010-03-09).

55. Deutsche Bahn erstellt neues Gleis im Bereich des Buschtunnels – DB Presseinformation 12.02.2010 – http://www.deutschebahn.com/site/bahn/de/unternehmen/presse/presseinformationen/nrw/nrw20100212.html – (2010-03-09).

56. Diabolo makes the airport more accessible from the north – Infrabel Belgian railway infrastructure manager, mobility project Diabolo - http://www.infrabel.be/portal/page/portal/pgr_inf2_e_internet/mobility_project/le_projet_diabolo - (2010-03-09).

57. Air France-KLM confirms high speed rail discussions - Railway Gazette International, 18.09.2008 - http://www.railwaygazette.com/news/single-view/view//air-france-klm-confirms-high-speed-rail-discussions.html – (2010-03-09).

58. European Better transport links for Europe – Railway axis Lyon-Trieste-Ljubljana-Budapest-Ukrainian border – Directorate-General for Energy and Transport, July 2008.

59. A new rail link between Lyon and Turin – Lyon Turin Ferroviaire LTF – accessible through: http://www.ltf-sas.com/pages/articles.php?art_id=349 – (2010-03-08).

60. A new rail link between Lyon and Turin – Lyon Turin Ferroviaire LTF – accessible through: http://www.ltf-sas.com/pages/articles.php?art_id=349 – (2010-03-08).

61. Priority Project No. 6. - Annual activity report 2008-2009 – Laurens Jan Brinkhorst, European Coordinator – Brussels, 16 July 2009.

62. LGV Est Phase 2 tendering gets underway – Railway Gazette International, 02.09.2009 - http://www.railwaygazette.com/news/single-view/view/10/lgv-est-phase-2-tendering-gets-underway.html - (2010-03-09).

63. 1 million...passengers in just 1 month on the new TGV-Est line (LGV-Est)! – French Embassy – France in the UK, 13.07.2007 - http://www.ambafrance-uk.org/1-million-passengers-in-just-1.html - (2010-03-09); SNCF – Bilan de l'année 2008, Perspectives 2009 – Dossier de presse, 12.02.2009, 5. p.

64. Stuttgart 21 – Das neue Herz Europas - http://www.das-neue-herz-europas.de/en-gb/overview/default.aspx - (2010-03-09).

65. Facts about Fehmarn 2nd edition – Femern A/S 2009.

66. The Nordic Triangle, including Stockholm-Göteborg – http://www.banverket.se/en/Amnen/The-railway/Facts/Future-Plan-for-the-railway-20042015/Passenger-traffic/The-Nordic-Triangle-including-Stockholm-Goteborg.aspx.

67. The overall traffic development across Öresund – TendensÖresund – http://www.tendensoresund.org/en/traffic-across-oresund – (2010-03-09).

68. COINCO North – Transport infrastructure – http://www.coinconorth.com/

EN/vision/intrastructure_and_strategy.html - (2010-03-11).

69. Quotation from "The Scandinavian 8 Million City Guide: Trains, Planes & Automobiles" (no publishing year). COINCO North, p. 8.

70. Quotation from "The Scandinavian 8 Million City Guide: Trains, Planes & Automobiles" (no publishing year). COINCO North, p. 8.

71. Quotation from "The Scandinavian 8 Million City Guide: Trains, Planes & Automobiles" (no publishing year). COINCO North, p. 8.

72. Quotation from "The Scandinavian 8 Million City Guide: Trains, Planes & Automobiles" (no publishing year). COINCO North, p. 8.

73. Quotation from "The Scandinavian 8 Million City Guide: Trains, Planes & Automobiles" (no publishing year). COINCO North, p. 8.

74. Quotation from "The Scandinavian 8 Million City Guide: Trains, Planes & Automobiles" (no publishing year). COINCO North, p. 15.

75. Quotation from "The Scandinavian 8 Million City Guide: Trains, Planes & Automobiles" (no publishing year). COINCO North, p. 15.

76. Downloaded 12 January 2011 from www.coinconorth.com.

77. Rokkan 1987, p. 41.

78. Stein Rokkan 1973: "Entries, voices, exits: Towards a possible generalization of the Hirschman model". Soc. sci. inform. 13 (1), p. 39-53.

79. Rokkan 1987, p. 41.

REFERENCES

Air France-KLM confirms high speed rail discussions - Railway Gazette International, 18.09.2008. http://www.railwaygazette.com/news/single-view/view//air-france-klm-confirms-high-speed-rail-discussions.html – (2010-03-09).

A new rail link between Lyon and Turin – Lyon Turin Ferroviaire LTF. http://www.ltf-sas.com/pages/articles.php?art_id=349 – (2010-03-08).

A star is born – Railway Gazette International, 14.12.2009. http://www.railwaygazette.com/news/single-view/view//a-star-is-born.html – (2010-03-09).

Bartolini, S (2006): "A Comparative Political Approach to the EU Formation". ARENA Seminars spring 2006, ARENA Seminar Tuesday 31 January 2006.

Brenner Eisenbahn Gmbh (2007): „Die neue Unterinntalbahn – Eisenbahntechnik auf höchstem Niveau".

Christaller, W (1950): "Das Grundgerüst der räumlichen Ordnung in Europa". Frankfurt: Geograf. Hefte 24, 1950.

COINCO North – Transport infrastructure. http://www.coinconorth.com/EN/vision/intrastructure_and_strategy.html - (2010-03-11).

Communication from the Commission (2007): "Trans-European networks: Towards an integrated approach". {SEC(2007) 374}. Commission of the European Communities: COM(2007) 135 final.

Communication from the Commission to the European Parliament, the Council, the Economic and Social Committee and the Committee of the Regions (2010): "Towards a Single Market Act. For a highly competitive social market economy. 50 proposals for improving our work, business and exchanges with one another". European Commission: COM(2010) 608 final.

Commission Working Document (2010): "Consultation on the Future Trans-European Transport Network Policy". European Commission: COM(2010) 212 final.

Commission Staff Working Document (2010): "TEN-T Policy Review – background papers". European Commission SEC(2010) 613 final.

Deutsche Bahn erstellt neues Gleis im Bereich des Buschtunnels – DB Presseinformation 12.02.2010. http://www.deutschebahn.com/site/bahn/de/unternehmen/presse/presseinformationen/nrw/nrw20100212.html - (2010-03-09).

Diabolo makes the airport more accessible from the north – Infrabel Belgian railway infrastructure manager, mobility project Diabolo. http://www.infrabel.be/portal/page/portal/pgr_inf2_e_internet/mobility_project/le_projet_diabolo - (2010-03-09).

Erdösi, F (2004): "Európa közlekedése és a regionális fejlödés" (Transportation in Europe and regional developement). Budapest: Dialóg Campus Kiadó.

European Better transport links for Europe – Railway axis Lyon-Trieste-Ljubljana-Budapest-Ukrainian border - Directorate-General for Energy and Transport, July 2008.

European Commission (2005): *Trans-European Transport Network: TEN-T priority axes and projects*. Luxembourg: Office for Official Publications of the European Communities.

European Commission DG for Energy and Transport (2007): *Building bridges: Extension of the major Trans-European transport axes to the neighbouring countries*. Luxembourg: Office for Official Publications of the European Communities.

European Commission DG for Energy and Transport (2008): "Better transport links for Europe - Rail link Berlin-Verona/Milan-Bologna-Naples-Messina – Palermo". http://ec.europa.eu/ten/transport/priority_projects_minisite/PP01EN.pdf.

European Commission (2009): *Trans-European Transport Network: Implementation of the priority projects – Progress report 2009*. Luxembourg: Office for Official Publications of the European Communities.

European Commission Green Paper (2009): "TEN-T: A policy review. Towards a better integrated transeuropean transport network at the service of the Common Transport Policy". European Communities: COM(2009) 44 final.

European Commission DG for Energy and Transport (2009): *A sustainable future for transport: Towards an integrated, technology-led and user-friendly system.* Luxembourg: Publications Office of the European Communities.

European Commission DG for Energy and Transport (2009): *EU energy and transport in figures - Statistical pocketbook 2009.* Luxembourg: Office for Official Publications of the European Communities.

Eurostar prepares for competition. Railway Gazette International, 02.11.2009. http://www.railwaygazette.com/news/single-view/view/10/eurostar-prepares-for-competition.html – (2010-03-09).

Eurostar sees growth in traveller numbers and ticket sales in third quarter. Eurostar press release 14.10.08.

http://www.eurostar.com/UK/be/leisure/about_eurostar/press_release/eurostar_sees_growth_in_traveller_numbers_and_ticket_sales_in_third_quarter.jsp – (2010-03-09).

Facts about Fehmarn 2nd edition – Femern A/S 2009.

Flora, P (1999): "Introduction". In P Flora, S Kuhnle and D Urwin (eds): *State Formation, Nation Building, and Mass Politics in Europe. The theory of Stein Rokkan.* Oxford: Oxford University Press.

Fyra brand for Amsterdam-Brussels high speed – Railway Gazette International, 07.07.2009. http://www.railwaygazette.com/news/single-view/view/10/fyra-brand-for-amsterdam-brussels-high-speed.html - (2010-03-09).

Grindheim, J (2012): *Europeisk politikk i komparativt perspektiv – teorier, modeller, analyser* (European Politics in a Comparative Perspective – Theories, Models, Analyses). Oslo: Universitetsforlaget.

High-speed rail in Germany: Inter-city planes are grounded by faster trains – guardian.co.uk, 05.08.2009. http://www.guardian.co.uk/world/2009/aug/05/high-speed-rail-grounds-city-planes – (2010-03-07).

Ivány, Á, J Pál and L Tóth (1987): "Közlekedéspolitika, közlekedés-gazdaságtan" (Transport policy, transport economy). M szaki Könyvkiadó.

Le rail en 2009 – Rapport d'Activités 2008 du Groupe SNCB, 1. p. http://www.b-rail.be/corp/F/assets/pdf/activity_report_2008_fr.pdf - (2010-03-09).

LGV Est Phase 2 tendering gets underway – Railway Gazette International, 02.09.2009. http://www.railwaygazette.com/news/single-view/view/10/lgv-est-phase-2-tendering-gets-underway.html - (2010-03-09).

1 million...passengers in just 1 month on the new TGV-Est line (LGV-Est)! – French Embassy – France in the UK, 13.07.2007. http://www.ambafrance-uk.org/1-million-passengers-in-just-1.html – (2010-03-09).

Paris-Bruxelles modal split. UIC High speed rail – Fast track to sustainable mobility. January 2009.

Priority Project No. 6. – Annual activity report 2008-2009 – Laurens Jan Brinkhorst, European Coordinator – Brussels, 16 July 2009.

Rokkan, S (1973): "Cities, States and Nations: A Dimensional Model for the Contrasts in Development". In S Eisenstadt and S Rokkan (eds): *Building States and Nations*, Vol. I. London: Sage Publications.

Rokkan, S (1973): "Entries, voices, exits: Towards a possible generalization of the Hirschman model". In *Soc. sci. inform.* 13 (1), p. 39-53.

Rokkan, S, D Urwin, F Aarebrot, P Malaba and T Sande (1987): *Centre-Periphery Structures in Europe. An ISSC Workbook in Comparative Analyis*. New York: Campus Verlag.

SNCF – Bilan de l'année (2008): Perspectives 2009 – Dossier de presse, 12.02.2009.

Stuttgart 21 – Das neue Herz Europas. http://www.das-neue-herz-europas.de/en-gb/overview/default.aspx – (2010-03-09).

Tamás, F (2008): "Közlekedéspolitika az Európai Unióban" (Transport policy in the European Union). *Köz-Gazdaság* 2008/04.

The Nordic Triangle, including Stockholm-Göteborg. http://www.banverket.se/en/Amnen/The-railway/Facts/Future-Plan-for-the-rail-way-20042015/Passenger-traffic/The-Nordic-Triangle-including-Stockholm-Goteborg.aspx.

The overall traffic development across Öresund – TendensÖresund. http://www.tendensoresund.org/en/traffic-across-oresund – (2010-03-09).

"The Scandinavian 8 Million City Guide: Trains, Planes & Automobiles" (no publishing year). COINCO North.

TINA - Monitoring on the Status of the Pan-European Transport Corridors and Transport Areas. http://www.tinavienna.at/index.php?p_id=1114592820&last_id=1114592820&l_id=en&s_id=42898de6715eebce4dd1ddb3135a25b4 – (2010-03-09).

Van Miert, K (2009): European Coordinator - Annual activity report Priority Project 1. Brussels, 17 June 2009.

Voller Erfolg: Bayern steigt um auf die Bahn - DB 12.28.2007 - DailyNet Press-seportal. http://www.dailynet.de/TourismusReisen/11233.php – (2010-03-07).

FRANCISCA HERODES – MID SWEDEN UNIVERSITY, SWEDEN

The Regional Institution dilemma –
How Regional Organisations Adapt to EU Membership

Introduction

Cooperation of the EU is often defined as collaboration between the Member States and the various EU institutions. With reference to EU decision-making, according to the EU Treaty, that collaboration between the Member State and the supra national level is mainly referring to the work carried out by the European Council and the European Parliament. Consequently, EU membership has demanded adaptations at central governmental level inside the Member States' organisations, in order to take part of the EU policy-making and decision-making system. By taking a sub-national perspective of institutional adaptations in response to a changing policy-implementing and policy-making environment over time, which the effects of, or access to, the EU membership may well represent, it is not evident that a similar institutional adaptation process has been taking place internally at the sub-national level. This is spite of a strong direct interplay between the sub-national authorities and the supranational level. The point of departure in the following discussion proposes that the sub-national authorities in the EU Member States contribute to European integration. It is a contribution interpreted in a number of different mobilizations, such as presence in the Brussels arena, strategies for the EU cohesion implementations, constitutional articulations and interregional cooperation. They all embrace a broad view of the institutional formal and informal processes including its practices, customs and norms. The main challenge of the sub-national authority's "European affairs" performance is its dual approach to EU related tasks, theorized by one of the European integration theories called new institutionalism dealing with the impact of institutions' interactions. This chapter will discuss institutional change in view of the new institutionalism,[1] through the lenses of sub-national levels of the South East of England and Stockholm questioning whether the last decade's involvement in EU related tasks and the strong wishes to participate in a more and more intense policy making on the supra-national level has been mirrored in an organisational adaptation of the domestic sub-national organisation? What exogenous variables in the context of European affairs can develop an organisation from one position to another? Further, a relevant issue is also whether this question matters for the outcome of the involvement in the EU activities, in other words: the role of the institutions in their quest to contribute to the European integration.

New Institutionalism

The new institutionalism theory can be applied in the process of finding how organisations relate to their environment. A change of a mode which persists over time is to be considered as institutionalised. In this context the objects of the study, the sub-national organisa-tions, have established structures which are based on both formal as well as informal rules. A way of handling a task is considered being institutionalised when that handling of the task is not called into question, in other words accepted and taken for granted. Another core concept in the new institutionalism is that organisations which have more or less common definitions of their operations do have a common understanding about what constitutes a correct norm to follow in contrast to a less accepted norm. This structural feature of the new institutional theory creates predictability and opportunities to make strategic plans ahead. A non-institutionalised behaviour or process might be less likely to survive in the greater context over time. The new institutionalism can be considered as a modification of the rational choice theory, and proposes that institutions play an important role in shaping the preferences for the participants in the institutional context. Opponents against this view argue that since these priorities are exogenous they cannot be determined by the institution, instead a number of factors play a part in this such as cultural, ideological etc.

Experiences from some regions

The South East of England and Stockholm constitute by size of the population the largest regions in United Kingdom and Sweden respectively. Due to their large size they can serve a broad base for a number of policy implications emerging from the EU membership. Since particular attention is given to the sub-national level, the directly elected parliamentary level below the national parliamentary assembly, often usually referred to as the regional level, we find within this definition a number of counties in the South East of England and in Stockholm the Stockholm County Council which will serve as references to the discussion[2]. To be clear, the sub-national level corresponds to the level in a Member State which is reliant to the national level but has a legitimate government in its own right, which means it has a degree of independent policy making power or limited sovereignty. In this context, the organisations' ability to create and implement policies is crucial. In one respect it is evident that during the last decade, counties in both South East of England and Stockholm have shown many similarities in the development of their task in relation to the EU agenda, similarities that can be shared with many other regions around in Europe. The supra-national level is in many ways gearing the political agenda and indirectly forces the regions to act in one or another way. The fact that sub-national authorities are keen to participate, ambitious and active is unchallenged. However, looking into some cases, we can scrutinize the internal organisational processes and perhaps better understand how to prepare for a durable membership in the EU.

In the aftermath of the strong trend towards regionalism during the 1980s and 1990s, such as strong priorities on the cohesion policy, the introduction of the principle of subsidiarity, the creation of the Committee of the Regions the sub-national authorities have observed that some impact on their own organisations has occurred during the first decade of the 21th century. Experiences from counties in the South East of England show that the handling of European Affairs has not caused any larger modifications on the respective organisations as to the introduction of formal procedures, increase of staff or other organisational adaptations in order to keep up with the EU affairs agenda including both implementing policy but also participation in the policy creation process of EU related matters. Their own estimation is that the counties are not as active as they need to be. The budget lines for European Affairs are very restricted and on top of that in wake of the financial crisis many have shown a decline in resources spent on EU related tasks. Nevertheless, in general the counties have taken a number of pro-active steps securing the monitoring of EU issues. In collaboration with *inter alia* other counties in the same region, a Brussels based office called the Southern England Local Partners representing the organisations has been created. In addition, during the last decade[3] some counties have collaborated to a certain extent with the South East Development Agency in view of positioning the regions on the Brussels agenda on various topics having an impact on the region. Scrutiny of the counties' organisations shows that the work is highly characterized by an ad hoc approach to upcoming EU related opportunities. A typical scenario in the organisational set up is when a very actual situation, e.g. a draft directive considered to threaten a certain issue within the region and the result is foreseeable within a reasonable time frame, and therefore claims its attention, internally in the organisation a broader acceptance of the importance of working with European affairs is momentary gained. If the question has not been processed too far in the EU system the involvement of relevant officers and the political level is often immediate and effective in such a case and can bring a successful result. The challenge appears when proposals have reached a later stage in the process, and interventions are futile. The counties state that unfortunately an early intervention process securing all relevant policy areas is not in place. To overcome the problem, a few policy areas that are of extreme importance bring the sub-national organisation to common lobby groups where many other regions are involved from both the same and other EU Member States. Whether written strategies have an impact on the institutional procedural assignments is a contentious subject. Amongst the counties in the South East of England there are very few EU strategies drawn up by the organisations. During the period of the last ten years, in some cases there has been a strategy on European Affairs in place but after a few years it has been drawn back and the work is no longer based on any written agenda. The EU task neither finds itself within the regular processes of the policy making in the county councils, such as an item on the council meeting.

The Stockholm County Council has in a similar way not adapted its institutions in a formal way to a larger extent but nevertheless seem to have the aspiration on a higher degree of participation in the European affairs work than it has performed so far. The council is serving the organisation with EU related support by an international unit. This task has over time not always been an evident task, although lately a change in the understanding inside the organisation of what kind of impact and effects the supra national level can have on the sub-national authority. Important efforts have been made to strategically spread out the information and assignments to the expertise around in the organisation. The council is explicitly striving for defining EU related tasks as understood as being a horizontal approach and not isolated only to a limited number of staff who should handle the assignments. For instance, this means that an expert on transport should during the daily work also have the European dimension in mind and be able if relevant to take necessary actions. Unlike the organisations of the South East England the Stockholm County Council presents a rather extensive strategy on international affairs including European affairs, which has been in place the last couple of years. One of its objectives clearly expresses that as a consequence of the EU membership is the important task to influence the law making processes and the state of affairs of the EU community. However, this has not been institutionalised in the formal processes, such as for example no EU items are regularly processed on the council meetings. Further, in the same way as the British counties do, the representation in Brussels, the Stockholm Region Office, is secured through a collaborative partnership with other local and regional organisations.

Concluding remarks

The new institutionalism asserts that institutions matter in the creation of political actions and the determination of the result of decisions. Taking the sub-national authority's stand point we have learnt from the examples that European affairs are mainly treated through informal channels. The interplay between the sub-national authority and the supra-national authority has to a limited extent modified formal structures of these types of sub-national authorities. A great deal of the work carried out regarding the sub-national authorities' involvement on EU issues is handled by a third party organisation, which often is a shared stakeholder assignment to the sub-national authority. There are several advantages to these kinds of solutions such as budgetary reliefs but the down side of this construction is the difficulty for the sub-national authority to be able to convey the political will through its own institutional channels and patterns. The institutional constraint will be limited. The consequence will be that the perspective of new institutionalism would describe the outcome of the work, handled by a third party, as being determined mainly by the other institution's influence. Against that view, another angle can be considered; in order to understand organisational changes it is not sufficient to limit our understanding to the institutional constraints set up by each institution. Instead, that critical view suggests that we need to understand where these constraints come from and they should be scrutinized independently from the institutional context where they are put in action. Thus, the reasons why EU tasks have not been able to move the sub-national authority from one position to another in the previously discussed examples, by formalising the handling of EU related tasks, are to be found in factors not related to the 'autonomous entities'; a description of what the institution constitutes according to the proponents of new institutionalism. Representatives of the sub-national authorities discuss that the reasons why there has not been any high impact to modify the institution according to the necessary needs for involvement in European affairs, depends for example on a reluctant view on the EU apparatus amongst the citizens of the EU member states. Through the regional lenses this well-known reluctance is emphasized because of the limited distance to the power of the decentralized parliament dealing with issues that are of a daily relevance. Any EU related issue is automatically perceived as 'none of my concern'. The exogenous factor in this case brought into the institutional frame work places barriers to modify structures and behaviours. Despite these doubts about the possible explanation by the new institutional view, the very same theory seems to be able to explain how institutional changes occur. Analysing the work carried through regarding European affairs, by both politicians and civil servants involved in this specific matter, they can be identified as entrepreneurs exploiting new solutions leading to institutional change. Applying European affairs tasks to a sub-national authority seem to be an introduction of a parallel assignment. A number of informal processes have started and according to the experiences discussed previously over a ten year period these working methods seem to move into a consolidated format, still in an informal shape. However, representatives of the sub-national authorities themselves, in many of the cases, refer to a change of mind set, unfortunately excluding a change of the institution accordingly. The weakness of this reasoning is that when the issue is looked upon in a broader view the voice and involvement in decision-making opportunities remain constant and very low for the sub-national authority. Only to accept institutional change on informal behaviours might probably not progress the sub-national authority to participate in a larger scale of the European integration work. Informal processes are unstable and one should not forget the human being as a main factor. In fact, findings in my study show that enthusiasts in the domain of European affairs drive these issues inside the organisations. A tendency to rely the work on that work force could cause trouble once that particular person is no longer with the organisation. A worrying signal of the new institutionalism perspective suggests that informal processes that have become stable are to be aligned with constraint formal rules, which means that no formal institutional change can take place. As a consequence of that, sub-national authorities would never undergo any change because of factors related to European affairs. It is a worrying development for those who believe that the regions should have a stronger voice in the European integration work as a whole and perhaps less worrying for those who believe that the sub-national authorities do not have the potential to change according to circumstances related to European affairs. The problem is that the people who believe in these two different concepts constitute very often the very same person inside the sub-national organisation. Finally, the constraints on rules suggested in the theory of new institution are legitimized by the need for transparency. Having this view in mind it can be discussed how transparent the vast informal structure the European affairs work is characterised by inside the sub-national authority and for how long that can be accepted, notwithstanding the low interest in EU related issues amongst the general public. It will be interesting to see more future innovative attempts in the name of new institutionalism, to break the circle and transform the informal behaviour into the formal which could open the path to an interesting development of the European integration and regional participation.

NOTES

1. Within the new institutionalism a variety of approaches are at hand. This discussion is based on a the general perspective on the new institutionalism.

2. These sub-national directly elected parliamentary organisations are a selection from the current research work related to my Ph.D. studies

3. Currently a reordering of the British regional development work is taking place

REFERENCES

Adshead, M., *Developing European* Regions, Althenaeum Press, USA 2002

Bullman, *The Politics of the third level*, Le Galès, P. (red), *Regions in Europe*, Routledge, USA, 1998

Cini, M., *European Union Politics*, Oxford, 2003

DiMaggio, P., and Powell, W., *The ironcage revisited: institutional isomorphism and collective rationality in organizational fields*, American Sociological Review 48, p. 147-60, 1991

Green, G., *The New Regionalism in the EU*, Göreborg, 1999

Hill, M., *Policyprocessen*, Stockholm, 2007

Hira, A., and R., *The New Institutionalism: Contradictory Notions of Change*, American Journal of Economics and Sociology, Vol 59, No 2, p. 267 – 282, April 2000

Hooghe, L., Marks, G., *Multilevel governance and European integration*, Oxford, 2001

Hopkins, J., *Devolution in context*, London, 2003

Jeffery, C., *The Regional Dimension of the European Union*, Redwood Books, London, 1997

Keating, M., *The New Regionalism in Western Europe*, USA, 2003

Kohler-Koch, B., *Catching up with change: the transformation of governance in the European Union*, Journal of European Public Policy, Vol 3, Issue 3, p. 359-380, 1996

Le Galès, P. (red), *Regions in Europe*, Routledge, USA, 1998

Lijphart, A., *Patterns of Democracy*, New Haven, 1999

Loughlin, J., Keating, M., *The political economy of regionalism*, Routledge, 1997

Loughlin, J., *Subnational Democracy in the European Union*, Oxford, 2004

Lowndes, V., *Varieties of New Institutionalism: A critical appraisal*, Public Administration, Vol 74, Issue 2, p. 181-197, 1996

Nugent, N., *The government and politics of the European Union*, New York, 2010

Peters, Guy, B., *Institutional Theory in Political Science*, Continuum, London 2005

Rhodes, M., *The regions and the new Europe,* New York, 1995

Rosamond, B., *Theories of European Integration*, St Matrin's Press, 2000

Smith, D. M., Wistrich, E, *Regional Identity & Diversity in Europe*, Federal Trust for Education and research, London, 2007

Wagstaff, P., *Regionalism in the European Union*, Wiltshire 1999

Weatherill, S., *The role of regions and sub-national actors in Europe*, red Weatherill, S., and Bernitz, U., Oregon 2005

MAGDALENA BELOF – WROCŁAW UNIVERSITY OF TECHNOLOGY, POLAND

Quo Vadis Euroregion? – *The Emergence, Present Role and Expected Transformation of Euroregions on the Western Border of Poland: The Case of the Euroregions of Pomerania and Neisse-Nisa-Nysa*

Euroregions in Poland – emergence and role

The meaning of the term "euroregion", as well as their legal construction, vary greatly across Europe. Many studies have examined the typologies and functions, as well as the role the euroregions play in implementation of the European regional policy.

In the majority of cases, euroregions are based on a unique agreement made between particular neighbouring border regions. A key role in their legal establishment is played by documents awarded by the Council of Europe and in particular the European Framework Convention of Cross-border Co-operation between Communities and Local Authorities (so-called Madrid Convention) in force since 1980 and the European Charter of Local Self-Government which is in force since 1989.

In Poland, the term "euroregion" is also associated with an institutionalized form of transborder co-operation. This refers to voluntary associations of territorial-administrative units that straddle national boundaries (Mirwaldt, 2009). However the prerequisites to form euroregions in Poland, and in the other Central and Eastern

European countries, differed from the majority of those found in Western Europe.

Whereas the formalized structures of transborder co-operation in the West (going back to the early 1960s) arose mainly from bottom–up mobilization to address the problems faced by communities divided by national borders, the formation of euroregions in Central and Eastern much more a top-down affair. It was Europe was driven by the political agenda of the early 1990s, when the eastward extension of European Union had already been put on the agenda. The aim was to provide the accession countries with a special institutional framework for cross-border co-operation which would facilitate and support the integration process and thus help adopt EU standards of international co-operation. Particular attention was given to those euroregions designated along the external borders of the EU15-countries. They were to play the role of transferring the know-how of EU policies of cooperation and integration to the adjoining eastern neighbours. They also served as an "observatory room" for the European Commission where the implementation was tested of cross-border policy tools in accession countries.

Between 1991 and 1995, four euroregions were thus established on the Polish-German border, including the first euroregional structure in the whole posts–soviet bloc: the trilateral Euroregion Neisse-Nisa-Nysa, formed at the meeting point Polish–Czech and German borders (1991). The symbolic political significance of its creation reflects the fact, that it followed political memorandum signed by the three eminent political of that time, presidents: Lech Wałesa, Vaclav Havel and Richard von Weizsäcker.

From this moment on, the process of forming similar structures along the national borders of Poland continued, and within a decade the euroregions were packed tightly along the entire length of the Polish border (the most recent Polish Euroregion was established on the border with Russia in 2003, that is some twelve years after Neisse-Nisa-Nysa). Similar processes also took place during the 1990s in the other Central and Eastern European countries as a result of implementing European policy with its support schemes. From 1988, when the Commission launched its first pilot project, until 1999, the number of areas of cross-border co-operation almost tripled, growing from 26 to over 70 (Perkmann, 2003).

Presently, in Poland, there exist 16 euroregions, out of which nine are bilateral, four trilateral, one involves four countries and two even five. According to typology proposed by Perkmann only the Carpathian Euroregion forms a 'Working Community' – a larger structure with regional authorities involved in co-operation, while the rest can be described as "micro Cross-Border-Regions". They are geenerally rather small in geographic extent, but consist of geographically adjacent territories (Perkmann, 2003).

The idea of forming euroregions along the Polish borders appeared to be an exceptional success, although much of it was driven by pragmatic economic interests. Although initially, the euroregions in Poland were financed through membership fees, but soon after (starting in 1995), they were granted EU funds and gained the almost exclusive right to manage the Phare CBC program. This was the pre-accession tool for maintaining transborder co-operation across the then EU external border, and was modelled on the Interreg II, a programme in the (western) EU countries. Worth mentioning here is the Polish innovation developed and implemented within the program – that is the small projects fund – which was later adopted and effectively implemented by the EU in its other cross-border co-operation programs. In contrast to the regular projects within Phare CBC, that had to be worth at least 2 million Euros, the small projects fund facilitated small-scale people-to-people initiatives of up to 50 000 Euros. This went together ,with simplified application and implementation procedures. The euroregions themselves supervised the project selection process and affiliation with them was a precondition to apply for support.

Poland's accession to the EU in 2004, and the introduction of the Community Initiative INTERREG IIIA, brought about significant changes, in scale and organization of transborder co-operation. Firstly, the geographical scope of the program had shifted from euroregions territory to 'regular' NUTS 3 subregions. Secondly, the program management moved to regional self-governing authorities. In consequence, starting from 2006, the euroregions lost the leading role in cross-border programme administration, as well as the preferential treatment in the process of project acquisition. This situation caused at first a serious sense of crisis among euroregions: they lost the position of the "wonder child" and had to fight for retaining their members among local authorities, some of which had second thoughts. Yet, they managed to secure continued role within transborder co-operation programs in the form of managing the small project funds which were continued under the umbrella of Interreg IIIA. Statistical analysis conducted by K. Mirwaldt shows immense activity in this sector: although the overall financial Interreg contribution to small projects was modest, in just four Polish-German euroregions, as much as 2787 projects were processed, that equals an average of 140 projects per year, and 2-3 projects per week in each euroregion (Mirwaldt, 2009).

Nevertheless, euroregions had to seriously revise scope and form of their activity and look for innovative and effective uses of already existing organizational and human potentials. Additionally, the accession to the EU of Central Europe the euroregions located along Poland's western and southern borders into new circumstances From a location along the EU pouter border they became an integral part of the EU's territory. They had to face the question of how to function as "intra-EU transborder region" and utilize new opportunities brought about by accession (Obrycki, 2005). All of the euroregions in Poland survived this radical change (all still exist) and the majority of them has found new impetus for further activity.

Euroregions: Pomerania and Neisse-Nisa-Nysa

As aforementioned, this article focuses in particular on two euroregions located on the border areas between Poland and the Federal Republic of Germany – Euroregion Pomerania and Euroregion Neisse-Nisa-Nysa. Since their location on the western border of Poland, both belong to the "oldest" Polish euroregions, while after Poland's accession to the European Union, they experienced a shift from external to internal European cross-border regions. Out of four Polish-German Euroregions the selected two are the largest and share one additional common feature: they are both trilateral alliances: the Czech Republic is a third partner in the Euroregion Neisse–Nisa–Nysa and Sweden (particularly the Skania region) in the Euroregion Pomerania. Nevertheless, in both cases, it has been the Polish – German relationship that had influenced the nature of co-operation the most.

A characteristic feature of the majority of 'old' euroregions in Western Europe is the existence of communities that have been divided by national borders, but for hundreds of years shared common history, language and traditions. The Polish – German borderland is very far from this model. It presents an exemplary case of the closed border type that prevailed in Central and Eastern Europe, especially (but not exclusively) along the Iron Curtain. The course of history brought about complete replacement of communities in the border areas due to the expulsions of millions of Poles and Germans after World War II. Communities now living next to each other have never before experienced coexistence. What they did share, however, – has been a deep dislike and distrust towards each other, built on the memories of past conflicts, prejudices and lack of knowledge. This all but complete alienation only deepened the impact of shortcomings and problems both sides suffered from, such as heavy devastation of environment, degraded technical infrastructure, non-existing transportation links across the border, language barrier, etc. It seemed obvious that only some kind of institutionalized co-operation, essentially facilitated from the outside, would provide the scope needed to jointly tackle effectively the challenging nature of cross-border relations at the local level. And it was this realisation that paved the way for the euroregions to come into existence.

The Euroregion Neisse-Nisa-Nysa was formally established at the end of 1991 as the first euroregion in Poland; and from the very beginning it represented a trilateral partnership with Czech Republic. The Euroregion Pommerania was put in place almost exactly four years later 1995 as a Polish – German agreement, with of the third party – the Scania region from Sweden – joining in early 1998.

At present, the Euroregion Neisse–Nisa–Nysa is an alliance of:

- The Association of Local Authorities of Euroregion Neisse e.V. (an association of 132 local authorities of the regional state of Saxony, Germany)
- The Association of Local Authorities of the Euroregion Nisa (145 local authorities of the region Liberec, Czech Republic)
- The Association of Polish Local Authorities of the Euroregion Nysa (51 Polish local authorities in the Dolnoslaskie and Lubuskie voivodships, Poland).

Respectively, the Euroregion Pomerania constitutes of:
- The Scania Association of Local Authorities (with 33 communes in Sweden),
- The Association of Local Authorities Europaregion Pomerania e.V. (an association of ywo self-administrated towns and six rural districts in the two regional states of Mecklenburg–Western Pomerania and Brandenburg, Germany),
- Association of Polish Local Authorities of the Euroregion Pomerania city of Szczecin and 114 of the Polish local authorities in the Zachodniopomorskie voivodship.

Both Euroregions share similar missions of improving living standards in the border regions and bringing together citizens from both sides. They are also organized in similar ways with their joint Councils (30–36 people) Presidia (3–6 people), Secretariats and various topical working parties (5–14). Separate national offices are dedicated to everyday matters on either side. The Association of Polish Municipalities in the Pomerania Euroregion and the Association of Polish Local Authorities in the Euroregion Nysa derive their powers and responsibilities from the 1989, Associations Act.

The Euroregion Pomerania covers an area of about 41 000 km² and is inhabited by over 3,4 million people. In this respect, it is nearly three times larger than Euroregion Neisse-Nisa-Nysa with its territory of 12,800 km² and 1,6 million. The latter is spatially contiguous, while Euroregion Neisse–Nisa–Nysa represents consistent geographical terrain and Euroregion Pomerania is divided by the Baltic Sea, which affects the sense of proximity.

Both Euroregions demonstrate many common features, for example: strong division of language and culture between partners, very small number of minorities, welfare gap between Poland and the Czech Republic on one side and (eastern) Germany and Sweden on the other. They also share several structural weaknesses, such as a decline in economic production and employment, insufficient cross-border infrastructure, environmental pollution and population decline, especially on the German side (Mirwaldt, 2009). Both euroregions are relatively attractive as tourist destinations for their recreational landscape and natural and cultural heritage.

Regardless of the many similarities, there are some distinct differences that have clearly influenced extent of, and scope for, cross-border activities in the two Euroregions Pomerania and Neisse-Nisa-Nysa. For once, there is the physical separateness through the Baltic Sea affecting the Euroregion Pomerania. This lack of direct geographical continuity hampers many contacts, and limits the scope for co-operation, especially in areas of spatial planning, building infrastructure connections and local community integration. In this way, there is more a virtual cross-border connectivity. The mountain range of Sudety running through the Euroregion Neisse-Nisa-Nysa also forms a geographical barrier, although it is much less divisive. Secondly, the Euroregion Pomerania shows a rather unbalanced settlement structure. On the Polish side, it has several medium-sized cities and one strong urban centre in the shape of the city of Szczecin – the capital of the Western Pomeranian region (Zachodniopomorskie). With its 408 000 inhabitants, the city holds strong metropolitan ambitions. On the one hand, such an imbalance in functional centrality can be a driving force for euroregional activity in this instance, especially as the German side of the euroregion's territory comprises only rather small settlements, which historically have been part of Szchecin's functional hinterland, and this could now be re-established. However, on the other hand, this causes some difficulties in establishing a balanced partnership. The physical barrier of the Baltic Sea matters, too. Thus, Swedish city of Malmö and the important academic centre of Lund university link up with Szczecin in many activities, but this potential has so far not been fully utilized.

The location of the Euroregion Neisse-Nisa-Nysa is rather peripheral compared to Pomerania. It lies at the far corner of the three participating countries, and away from the three main urban centers: Wroclaw, Dresden and Prague. However, its settlement structure is comparable, all three sides possessing sub-regional centres of similar size (Jelenia Gora, Goerlitz, Liberec) and with a similarly tripolar structure of of towns of the next lower level in the functional hierarchy, (Bogatynia, Hradek, Zittau). In addition, symbolising the borderness of the region, thre is the cross-border city of Zgorzelec-Goerlitz. Such a structure makes cross-border dialog more balanced, without a dominating leader and distrust by the seemingly weaker partners, but also calls for stronger mobilisation, since euroregional matters are perceived as less important for regional capitals.

The third difference between the two euroregions is their position in a broader European spatial context. The Euroregion Pomerania is located within the Baltic Sea Region which is one of the most active European macro regions in terms of joint actions, integration works, formulating common vision and strategies and publicity. By contrast, the location and profile of the Euroregion Neisse-Nisa-Nysa is, and comes across as, as 'peripheral' in terms of socio-economic factors, a sense of marginality created by the mountain ranges, and even mentality. It is distant from economic and decision-making centers, and therefore less competitive and attractive for the influx of new investment and capital.

The first period of euroregional co-operation was devoted mostly to the organization, administration and to promotional issues. The main goals which both euroregions formulated for their activities were similar, and focused mainly on the improvement of transport infrastructure and the condition of the natural environment.

With the introduction of the Phare CBC program (1995) the euroregions became almost exclusively responsible for its management. They benefited from this situation for nearly a decade up until Poland's accession to the EU, and the introduction of the new instrument of Interreg IIIA. The, as a result, secure financial situation and reinfrorced legal status undoubtedly provided the impetus for many new activities and organizational developments in the euroregions.

They turned out to be a laboratory for European project management, with staff training, testing of procedures and implementation of financial rules.

Trilateral euroregions, such as Pomerania and Neisse–Nisa–Nysa also engaged in cross-border operational programs, but such usually resulted in an inevitable division into bilateral sub-programs and a loss of some of the initial spirit of acting jointly. For Euroregion Neisse–Nisa–Nysa some support for trilateral co-operation existed only at the beginning of Phare CBC and for a short period of time. The main flow of activities was based on 3 programs: Poland – Czech Republic, Poland–Saxony and Saxony – Czech Republic with no coordination between them. An even worse situation occurred in the Euroregion Pomerania, where a cross-border program existed neither between Poland and Sweden nor between Germany and Sweden. Some joint actions are still possible within the program of cross-border co-operation for the Baltic Sea Region, this has a wider multi-national context and agenda, involving much larger group of countries and was more popular in the eastern part of the Baltic Region. This situation seriously limited active engagement with partners from Skania.

In the years 1995 to 2003 as many as 469 projects have been completed within the Polish part of the Euroregion Pomerania, costing a total of over 5.7 Million euros, which placed it at the first position in Poland. The second position was taken by the Euroregion Neisse–Nisa–Nysa where 836 projects were completed to the sum of 5.0 Million euros. But it has to be mentioned that the Phare CBC program was not very strict in requiring a real joint dimension for the projects. This allowed their transborder nature and impact to be questioned in the majority of cases.

As previously mentioned, the Interreg IIIA (in the new EU member states from 2004 to 2006) limited the role of euroregions in the management of cross-border co-operation. After the initial shock about this loss of clout, the euroregions have managed to face the new challenge. They have placed their representatives in various managerial bodies of the programs and considerably strengthened their relationship with regional administrations. They provided training programmes for their members about how to make successfully project applications as well as in the promotion of, and lobbying for, the program. They have also searched more vigorously for other forms of activity, not exclusively depended on the financing of cross-border programs. This time of transition towards operating in a 'normal' environment of full EU procedures and competitions can also be considered as a beginning of a serious discussion about the necessity of transforming euroregions into entities based on clear, internationally recognized legal status which would give them greater resilience in responding to, and shaping, future development.

Introducing the Interreg IIIA and later its follow-up programs of European Territorial Co-operation did little to improve the opportunities for trilateral co-operation. The European Commission has offered nothing to the multi-partner cross-border regions, and harmonization of the separate bilateral programs by the euroregions themselves was simply impossible without appropriate legal instruments. Therefore, as in the previous period, co-operation focused on bilateral sub-regional activities.

Out of the two analyzed euroregions, it seems that it has been Pomerania that managed to position itself more successfully within the new structures of the cross-border co-operation programs' structures.However it must be stressed that this applies mainly to co-operation between Germany and Poland (Mecklenburg–Western Pomerania). The activity of the Euroregion Pomerania in the current program (Interreg IVA) is much broader than simply managing micro-projects. It has adjusted itself to act as a 'service agency' for its members, advocating their far-reaching goals and supporting them with know-how. The Pomerania euroregion was also very active in shaping the program document for Interreg IVA, and presently, its representatives are engaged in work of the Common Technical Secretariat and the positive opinion of the special Euroregional Project Committee is meaningful in the application process for larger projects. In reaching such a strong position two 'operational' factors were very helpful: the Polish side of the Euroregion Pomerania, in territorial terms, is identical both to Western Pomerania Region, and to the area eligible for Interreg IV A support. The co-operation with

Scania obviously remains much weaker, because, as has been in the past, the current Interreg IVA does not dedicate special programs to Swedish-Polish or Swedish-German co-operation. Further more, as it was before the current programme, the Southern Baltic facilitates projects across the whole Baltic Sea.

Neisse–Nisa–Nysa region, of course, also offers know-how and support for its members. What is interesting here, is that even in a situation where separate programs create three equally separate bilateral co-operation modes, the euroregion continues efforts to build a common identity in the area through a shared website with equal content in three languages, through issuing an information bulletin and by many actions focused on the collective material heritage.

Euroregions – transform or perish?

For nearly two decades, euroregions on the Polish western border have constituted a very important element of the institutional framework facilitating cross-border co-operation. They played a leading role in the initial stage, where common co-operation goals were formulated by partners, and a recognition of the existing administrative, legal and financial tools took place. Also, their significance is hard to overestimate in the development stage, where co-operation has been stabilized, numerous expert groups have been installed, and various working documents produced and published. Euroregional co-operation has revealed large number of problems hampering a smooth and proper development of the border areas. Some of these problems were specific in particular areas, but the majority were shared, such as different administration structures, legal-financial regulation, socio-economic gaps including the level of spatial development, resulting in rather different expectations among co-operating partners. The latter was reported as a particularly difficult barrier to co-operation between Poland and Sweden. Some of these problems have been vigorously addressed with the help of euroregion activity, and here especially through the use of small project funds, that have supported initiatives more in tune with the community. Other problems – such as social barriers resulting from prejudices, cultivated stereotypes, cultural and language barriers, which are particularly evident along the Polish-German border – will last much longer and take a lot of more time to alleviate. In spite of considerable efforts and financial support, the building of euroregional identities have failed so far, but this is not surprising, when even in the oldest European euroregions such a coalescence is considered as still only partial, and the majority of inhabitants is unaware of the very existence of the euroregions (Markuse, 2004).

It would then seem, that politically-driven structures such as euroregions on the Polish western border have already fulfilled the role they were created for, in the present organizational form have reached their limits of what they can achieve. Their leaders are fully aware of the fact that in the near future, at the beginning of a second decade of the XXI century, the euroregions will have to face the serious question: "what next?".

The first dilemma will concern the transformation of their legal base. For efficient transborder co-operation, there need to be stronger organizational agreements at international level, which would grant the transborder areas a greater degree of strategic capacity. The European Comission's new tool – the European Grouping for Territorial Co-operation, may be a step in the right direction to achieve that. However, there is no general trend across Europe for euroregions to become EGTC. This is vigorously debated in all Polish euroregions. Of course, this touches upon a broader discussion, namely the one on the role of the state in the development of border area and the degree of power and independence delegated to the local and regional levels. This varies considerably from country to country. Also, the shape of the EU policy towards transborder co-operation will play a significant role.

The next two problems are closely associated with the previous one; first, it is about the revision of a partnership, and, second, a revision of goals in view of the current local, national, European and even global challenges.

Should euroregions remain entities with a broad scope of activities, or should they drift towards more specialized functional networks?

What role would the private actors play in the future organizational and economic development of cross-border regions? Would the logic of geographical proximity and mutual interdependence succeed over administrative and political reasoning in the revision of partnerships? European experience demonstrates that common spatial problems and shared resources, such as rivers or protected areas (not to mention transborder towns), are very important in cementing transborder co-operation.

In both analyzed euroregions, the form and scope of the necessary transformation is a core question in an on-going debate regarding future development. In both cases the formation of EGTC is a serious option. This will probably substantially change the partnership of co-operation. In the case of the Euroregion Neisse-Nisa-Nysa, the dialogue is more advanced with the Czech partners, while the German side remains rather hesitant. The example of the Euroregion Pomerania has revealed substantial weaknesses in the co-operation across the Baltic Sea. Thus, for instance, Sweden's future participation in co-operation which aims at stronger institutionalization remains doubtful. In both cases, the role of administrative regions: Lower Silesia (Dolnoslaskie) and Western Pomerania (Zachodniopomorskie) will be, with great probability, substantially strengthened. Current discussions let us presume that possible new structures will be considerably wider and will have more specialized tasks, with the formal, administrative regions playing the leading role. It is too early to predict whether the EGTC model will replace euroregions in the future or both will coexist, forming some kind of double structure for border regions. So far, this remains an open question.

Some dilemmas pointed out above will probably be solved in the near future. Whatever the transformation of trans-border co-operation brings about, one issue remains unchanged: the communities divided by national borders will still need help and support to function better. The initial mission of the euroregions to facilitate the process of their reconciliation should not be underestimated.

REFERENCES

Urzad Mieszkalnictwa i Rozwoju Miast and Bundesministerium für Verkehr, Bau- und Stadtentwicklung (2002), 'Aktualizacja Studium Kierunkowego zagospodarowania przestrzennego obszaru wzdłuz granicy polsko-niemieckiej' [Actualization of the guidance study of spatial development of the area along Polish–German border], Berlin–Warsaw–Dresden.

Anderson, J. and O'Dowd, L. (1999) 'State Borders and Border Regions', special issue, *Regional Studies* 33 (7).

Czernik, L. (2005), 'Integracja regionalna transgranicznego układu Pomorza Zachodniego' [Regional integration on transborder arrangement of Western Pomerania] *Przestrzen i Forma* 1, 45–68, Szczecinska Fundacja Edukacji i Rozwoju Addytywnego SFERA, Szczecin

Despiney, B. (2005), 'Building Entrepreneurial Capacity in Post-Communist Poland: A Case Study', *Human Factors and Ergonomics in Manufacturing*, 15 (1) 109–126

Dolata M., (2008), 'The role of special economic zones in the socio-economic development of Poland's border regions. The case of the Kostrzyn-Słubice Special Economic Zone' [in:] Leibenath M., Korcelli-Olejniczak E., Knippschild R. (ed.) Cross-border Governance and Sustainable Spatial Development. Central and Eastern European Development Studies. Berlin-Heidelberg, 175–183.

Dubeck, K., Schulz, D. (2004) 'German, Polish, and Czech School Cooperation in the Neisse–Nisa–Nysa Euroregion' *European Education*, 36 (3) 70–76.

Duehr, S., Stead D., Zonneveld W. (2007) 'The Europeanization of Spatial Planning through Territorial Cooperation' *Planning, Practice & Research*, 22(3), 291–307

Elworthy, Ch. (2005) 'The Euroregion Pommerania: Structures and Activities' (in): *Polityki i programy Unii Europejskiej [Policies and programs of the European Union], Koszalin: Politechnika Koszalinska*

Euroregion Pomerania (2003), 'Euroregion Pomerania Polska, Deutschland, Sverige', Kommunalgemeinschaft POMERANIA e.V.

Furmankiewicz, M. (2006), 'International co-operation of Polish municipalities: directions and effects' *Tijdschrift voor Economische en Sociale Geografie* 98 (3) 349–359.

Kołodziejski, M., Szmigiel, K. (2004), 'Miedzynarodowa współpraca transgraniczna i miedzyregionalna w kontekscie polityki regionalnej panstwa na lata 2007-2013' [International transborder and transregional co-operation In the view of national region al Policy 2007–2013], Centrum Rozwoju Lokalnego, Warszawa.

Lamour, Ch. 'Perpetuation and changes in the role of public leadership as a feature of the urban management and development process – within and beyond the state', *internal material of "EGTC" URBACT Project (2008-2010)*

Liss-Lepik, K. (2009) 'Euroregions as mechanisms for strengthening cross-border cooperation in the Baltic Sea Region' *TRAMES* 13(63/58), 3, 265–284

Löfgren, O. (2008) 'Regionauts: the Transformation of Cross-Border Regions in Scandinavia', *European Urban and Regional Studies* 15(3): 195–209

Markusse, J. (2004) 'Transborder Regional Alliances in Europe: Chances for Ethnic Euroregions?' *Geopolitics*, 9(3), 649–673

Mirwaldt, K. (2009), 'The Small Project Fund and Social Capital Formation in the Polish-German Border Region: An Initial Appraisal' *European Policy Research*, 68, European Policy Research, University of Strathclyde, Glasgow.

Obrycki, N. (2005, 'Euroregion Pomerania – doswiadczenia pierwszego roku w Unii Europejskiej' [Euroregion Pomerania – the experiences of the first year in the European Union] (in:) Zachodniopomorskie w Unii Europejskiej, Szczecin

OECD Territorial Review, (2009), 'Trans-border urban co-operation In the Pan Yellow Sea Region', OECD

Perkmann, M. (2003) 'Cross-border Regions in Europe: Significance and Drivers of Regional Cross-border Co-operation', *European Urban and Regional Studies* 10 (2): 153–71.

Perkmann M, (2007), 'Policy entrepreneurship and multilevel governance: a comparative study of European cross-border regions' *Environment and Planning C: Government and Policy* 25(6) 861–879

Warych–Juras, A. (2003) 'Euroregiony jako nowa forma współpracy europejskiej' [Euroregions as a new form of an European co-operation], *Informator Polskiego Towarzystwa Geograficznego Oddział w Krakowie,* Polskie Towarzystwo Geograficzne Oddział w Krakowie, Kraków

Wise, M. (2000), 'The Atlantic Arc: Transnational European Reality or Regional Mirage?' *Journal of Common Market Studies* 38(5) 865–890

LISBETH LINDEBORG – MARBURG, GERMANY

The Baltic Sea Region:
A Global Region – No Macroregion

*"For the political scientist the definition of a region is consider-
ably more difficult than the definition of a rose was for Gertrude
Stein. We cannot simply say: A region is a region is a region"*
(Karl Deutsch 1969:93).

Introduction

Over the last few years we could observe a growing and un-
called for confusion in the world of regional terminology. Thus
phenomenologically based classifications like "economic regions",
"administrative regions", "historical regions" etc. have just as much
added to the confusion as new expressions like "soft regions" and
"virtual regions". As all regions have an economy, an administration and a history, this kind of categorization is useless and it has
little to do with regional reality and experience. Furthermore, lofty
concepts like "soft" or "hard", "virtual" or "non-virtual" regions
are most certainly not very useful for politicians and practitioners
wanting to further regionalisation processes.

That the territoriality of regions is an accepted fact and that it is
the only useful *basic* criterion can not be doubted, since the Council
of Europe adopted the concept of regionalisation on its agenda in the
1950ies. In his classic theoretical and principal work," Comparative
Federalism. The Territorial Dimension of Politics", the American

political scientist Ivo Duchacek stated: "Functional interest groups, although dedicated to the promotion of or defense of non-territorial interests can not escape the territorial dimension of any political organization, (...) dividing and subdividing the world according to the territorial principle is probably as old as humanity" (1970:2-3).

When, however, the territoriality – mostly for ideological reasons – is being played down, this "Raumblindheit" (spatial blindness) leads to different problems. One of them is the loss of regional identity. It is common knowledge, that a strong regional identity is a great asset, especially for regional economic development. "Regions cultural identities are building blocks of Europe (...) The role of cultural identity becomes important in promoting economic development. It was a point of debate at the World Economic Forum and is gaining scientific recognition". This Luc van den Brande, former Leader of Government for the Flanders Region, and former President of the Assembly of Europan Regions and the Committee of the Regions stated in a speech in Cardiff in May 1998.

Just as important is how people living in a region conceive of it. The virtualising is but a trend distanced from reality. "Living space remain for most people limited to a few geographical points of reference that will never be interchangeable in the same way as products and services are" (Savy/Husson 1995:1).

But the way the dividing and sub-dividing of territories is being handled and how "new" territories are to be defined is also a matter of controversy. This can be seen when the concept of macroregion is being attached to the Baltic Sea Region (BSR). Lately both in EU-context1) and in some new research 2)the Baltic Sea Region (BSR) is being called a "macroregion". A so called "BSR-strategy" is being outlined as conceptual framework for making the BSR a "pilot case for other macroregional strategies to come". 3)

But neither the Baltic Sea Region, nor its southern counterpart, the Mediterranean Region, do represent macroregions in their original meaning being defined by the Assembly of European Regions (AER). 4) Their very names ought to be allowed to speak for themselves. They do not have to be subsumed to any kind of category. If necessary – they could be defined as global regions.

Branding the Baltic Sea Region as a macroregion – in comparison with other and older established macroregions – may be counterproductive and lead to its losing some of its realness. Thus you have to make clear what the concept of macroregion implies and why the suggestion to make BSR a kind of macroregional model is not correct.

Definition of macroregion as a concept

Macroregions could be described as larger crossborder regions, which are mostly *transnational,* although they also exist in *national* contexts. They are made up of more than two regions and / or microregions in two or more neighbouring states, or in the case of *national macroregions* within the same state. Most of them are transnational, for example the Barents Region in the most northern part of Europe (Barents Euro Arctic Region – BEAR with regions in Sweden, Norway, Finland and Russia). Another example would be the Grand Region or the SaarLorLux-Wallonien-Rheinland-Pfalz region in the so called "blue banana"5) with regions in Germany, Belgium, France and the State of Luxemburg participating. (As a general rule there are no states within a macroregional context but in two or three cases the membership of European miniature states are the exceptions to confirm this rule.) (Weihe-Lindeborg, 2001/2005:65-66; Lindeborg and Tallberg: 2010).

Compared to the many European crossborder regions (as fulfilments of crossborder cooperations) as still another type of region within the regional taxonomy, and which are more tightly defined and generally smaller in size, macroregions are being conceived as more loose constellations at least at the beginning of their coming into being. Whereas crossborder cooperations and crossborder regions develop into bodies characterised of a more and more intense and formalised cooperation within a legal framework, the macroregions tend to be more informal. Now and then they start out their cooperation around one common single issue; when the cooperation around this issue stops, it can well happen that the macroregion disappears from history. The experiences in Europe, however, most of the time show an opposite development. The recognition of the many benefits a cooperation on a large scale is offering, leads to further cooperation around other issues. Thus the "content" of the macroregion is widened and it grows stronger.

Among the earliest macroregions, which are also the most well known, is Arge-Alp, with the participation of eleven regions from four countries in the Alps. When Arge-Alp was founded in 1972 the expressed purpose was the common responsibility for the vulnerable alpine area. Since then Arge-Alp has developed further and today the cooperation includes all political issues with an extensive ecologic, economic and social cooperation. (Weihe-Lindeborg 2001/2005:196). Another macroregion dating back to 1972 is made up of nine regions from three states around the Bodensee also including the miniature principality of Lichtenstein (Internationale Bodenseekonferenz – IBK). Around the Bodensee the first common issue was the sea border, the responsibility for the water reservoir and the fairways at sea. (Lindeborg 1995: 306-316). As with the case of Arge-Alp, the Bodensee macroregional cooperation has been further developed as regards more issues and higher intensity. Today it has a legal framework in parts.

This, however, is not the only way for a macroregion to emerge. A macroregion can also develop from one or more crossborder cooperations within a defined territory. In such cases the crosssborder regions attract other neighbouring regions and microregions to join in. This was the case with SaarLorLux, which started out as a crossborder cooperation between the regions of Lorraine och Saar plus the state Luxemburg. Later Wallonie and Rheinland-Pfalz joined and the Grand Region (La Grande Région, die Grossregion) SaarLorLux-Wallonie-Rheinland-Pfalz became a reality.(Lindeborg 2010: 416-422).

Among national macroregions within the same state are the Lega Nord in northern Italiy. and Grand-Est in eastern France made up of five regions: Champagne-Ardenne, Lorraine, Alsace, Bourgogne and Franche-Comté.

Regional diversity

In order to better understand the concept of macroregion the best thing is to start out with the basic concept of region. An overview of the main regional categories makes it clear:

- Region
- Microregion
- Crossborder region
- Macroregion
- Trajectory

The basic territorial concept of a region is to be seen on the excellent map "Tabula Regionum Europae" with the 500 regions in Europe mapped out – from the Atlantic in the west to the Caspian See in the east, from the Polar Sea in the north to the Mediterranean in the south.6) As regards a written definition of a region, the best and most recognised one is from the AER: "A region is the first substate formalised entity – an administrative territory directly under the level of the state – with an established public rule of law and an elected political representation".

(From Article 1, Declaration of Regionalism in Europe, AER 1996)7 (Lindeborg 2008:18).

It should again be emphasised that territoriality is a first criterion. Beside the basic regions there also are *microregions*. A a rule they are geographically smaller regional contexts – although larger than local authorities – either within a region, or they are crossbordering between smaller parts of two or more regions always ,however, in the same state. Compared to the basic region the territory and the existence of a microregion is being determined by geographic-topographic, historic-cultural, economic or administrative factors, which give each microregion its specific character. Sometimes microregions are called subregions.

A third category are the *crossborder regions* emerging from intensified crossborder cooperations with regions and/or micro regions and/ or local authorities in neighbouring states participating. One criteriion determining the change from crossborder cooperation to crossborder region is a common rule of law and certain common institutions. (Lindeborg 2008: 24).

Beside the fourth category, *macroregions*, there is a fifth one – the so called *trajectories*, which could be described as corridors or belts. Being of different width and length a trajectory has the double task of both being a territory in its own right and to connect other surrounding territories. Since the concept of "territorial cohesion" was established, their importance is growing. (Lindeborg 2008:25).

As we can observe this basic establihed regional taxonomy is simple to understand and logic. The latest attempts to turn the Baltic Sea Region into a macroregion does complicate the issue of regional terminology in a way which is not very constructive. As we can see, there are no states (except for the few miniature states) in all the above mentioned and generally accepted regional contexts.

A muddled concept

In Nordregio's Electronic Working Paper 2009:4. we find one typical example of giving new meanings to an existing concept based on real experience. According to the referred literature on the subject, the authors of the paper mainly use Nordic sources, although Regional Science in the Nordic countries were never in any way leading or pioneering in European Regional Science. Thus the Swedish researcher Björn Hettnes anachronistic and ambigiuous regional concepts are uncritically being used as basic facts.8) Other referred sources come from the EU Council of Ministers, e.g EU state government level. Missing is literature from the European regional organisations with their long experiences and many publications and books. Just as strange is the reference to some essays published and edited by the United Nations, an organization, which has never shown itself to be in the forefront of regional science.

It adds to the confusion in their paper, that the Nordregio authors do not differ between European versus American Regional Science (Weihe-Lindeborg 2001/2005: 48-49; Lindeborg 2008: 18-19). Whereas the region according to the European concept denotes the first substate entity, American science defines the region as a limited amount of states, which in one way or other are loosely connected – it is a global area like NAFTA, OAS, OAU, ASEAN. MERCOSUR etc.9) Very often the common denominator for these states is a common market-factor. (Jfr. Nye 1968/1971; Haas 1975; von Bredow 1994:12-13; Hoffmann 1995: 293; Fawcett-Hurrell 1995:3f.; Telo 2001).

When using this conception it becomes evident, that both the Baltic Sea Region and the Mediterranean Region with states (including regions and local authorities) as main participants are regions on a global level.

From a systems analytic approach a concept of the Baltic Sea Region as a macroregion with its mixture of regional and global contexts leads to a disturbance effecting the regional substate system. It is not very helpful. One consequence is that it becomes hard for the region to keep the important border line to the state level above and the local authority level underneath. Too much confusion is counterproductive and will not ease the political regionalisation process. *"There is a systematic relationship between words and concepts to be explored"* (Skinner 1995:8) Any one concept is not only a mirror of political reality, but the concept itself is also influenced and developed by the way terms are being used.

For any one scientist the terminology is the platform to stand on. The haphazard throwing away of concepts based on long experience in real life and still the best ones to have, is to change a *win-win-situation* to a *lost case*.

NOTES

1. See Baltic Sea Region, Programme 2007-2013, Newsletter, March 2010; see EU, Forum at the Committee of the Regions, Brussels: "Europe's Macro-Regions. Integration through territorial co-operation". Conference Programme, 13 April 2010

2. Nordregio Electronic Working Paper 2009:4: "EU macro-regions and macroregional, strategies. A scoping study", by Alexandre Dubois, Sigrid Hedin, Peter Schmitt, José Sterling

3. Ibid. p. 7

4. Assembly of European Regions (AER) is an NGO with its headquarters in Strasbourg; it was founded in 1985. At the most more than 300 European regions were members. The AER is being described as a "first school for new regions".
  · See in German: Weihe-Lindeborg, Lisbeth, 2001/2005: Zum regionalen System. Stellenwert der Versammlung der Regionen Europas (VRE), Marburg

5. The "Blue Banana" is the early name of an area stretching from Paris to London, considered to be one of Europe's foremost growth areas

6. "Tabula Regionum Europae" is the first map of the regions of Europe. It was made by the Greek professor Kormoss at the Europe College in Brügge and was first published by the AER in 1995. Since then the map has been updated another eight times; the latest version dates from 2009

7. The Declaration, which is no doubt a milestone, was signed by the former two presidents of the AER, Jordi Pujol, former governor of the region of Catalonia and Luc van den Brande, former governor of the region of Flanders, at the AER General Meeting in Basel, 6.12.1996

8. As note 2, p.17

9. NAFTA (North American Free Trade Area), OAS (Organisation of American States), OAU(Organisation of African Unity), ASEAN (Association of South East Asian Nations), MERCOSUR (Mercado Común del Cono Sur or Common Market of the South)

REFERENCES

Bredow, Wilfried von, 1994: *"Regionale Grossmächte in der Entwicklung des internationalen Systems"* in Bredow/Jäger, Thomas (eds.), Regionale Grossmächte, Opladen, p. 7-21

Deutsch, Karl, 1969: *Nationalism and ist alternatives*, New York

Duchacek, Ivo, 1970: Comparative Federalism. The Territorial Dimension of Politics, New York

Fawcett, Louise/ Hurrell, Andrew (eds.), 1995: *Regionalism in World Politics. Regional Organization and international Order*, Oxford

Haas, Ernst, 1975: *The obsolence of regional integration theory*, Berkeley

Hoffmann, Stanley, 1995: *The European Sisyphos. Essays on Europe 1964-1994*, Boulder

Lindeborg, Lisbeth, 1995: *Regionalt samarbete i Europa – med tyska erfarenheter, ERU* (Expertgruppen för forskning om regional utveckling), Rapport 87,· Stockholm (Weihe)–Lindeborg, Lisbeth, 2001/2005: *Zum regionalen System. Stellenwert der Versammlung der Regionen Europas*, Marburg

Lindeborg, Lisbeth, 2008: *"Regional mångfald. Semantiska och realpolitiska apekter på regioner i Europa"*, in, Tallberg, Pontus (red.), Regioner i Europa,

Hässleholm, p. 16-37

Lindeborg, Lisbeth, 2010: *"Med kulturen som ledstjärna. Europeiska städer och regioner i förvandling"*, i Lindeborg, Lisbeth/Lindkvist,Lars (red.): Kulturens kraft för regional utveckling, SNS, Stockholm, p. 400-455

Lindeborg, Lisbeth/Tallberg, Pontus, 2010: *Makroregioner "Europas nya superregioner"*, paper, presented at the Europa-Forum, Hässleholm, 14.4. 2010

Nordregio Electronic Working Paper (Dubois, Alexandre, Hedin, Sigrid, Schmitt, Peter, Sterling, José), 2009:4: *EU macro-regions and macro-regional strategies. A scoping study*, Stockholm

Nye, Joseph (ed.), 1968: *International Regionalism: Readings, Center for International Affairs*, Harvard University, Boston

Savy, Robert/ Husson, Claude, 1995: *Regions and Territories in Europe*, AER, Limouin/Strasbourg

Skinner, Quentin, 1995: *"Language and political change"*, in Ball, Terence/ Farr,

James/ Hanson, Russell (eds.), Political Innovation and Conceptual Change, Cambridge and New York, p. 6-24

Telo, Mario, 2001: *European Union and New Regionalism*, Aldershot, Ashgate

CECILIA JOSEFSSON, REGION SKÅNE, SWEDEN

Database: *Regions of Europe*

Region Skåne has during the past year worked to develop a database of regions in Europe. The database is supposed to serve researchers as well as practitioners who want to compare regions and establish contacts in regions similar to their own in order to gain knowledge and share information.

Which regions?

The database includes regions at the level immediately below the state; hence a mixture of NUTS 1, 2 and 3 regions. As for now, all EU member states are included as well as Norway, Iceland, and Canada. Contacts are initiated with other non-EU member states such as Russia and Ukraine in order to develop the database further. The long-term goal is to include all European countries. However, this calls for cooperation from representatives in these countries since statistical data and other information often are scarce and difficult to find in countries outside the European Union. Below is a list of the regions included. Some of these regions have quite extended political responsibilities while others more or less lack a political mandate and function more as statistical regions.

Regional self-government
   Austria *9 states*
   Belgium *3 regions + 3 communities*
   Czech Republic *13 regions*

Denmark 5 *regions*
France 26 *regions*
Germany 16 *states*
Hungary 19 *regions + Budapest*
Italy 20 *regions*
Netherlands 12 *provinces*
Norway 19 *counties*
Poland 16 *provinces*
Romania 41 *counties*
Slovakia 8 *regions*
Spain 17 *regions + two cities (Ceuta and Melilla)*
Sweden 21 *län*
Switzerland 26 *cantons*
United Kingdom 4 *nations*

Canada 10 *provinces + 3 territories*

No regions or limited regional self-government:
Bulgaria
Estonia
Finland
Greece
Iceland
Ireland
Latvia
Lithuania
Luxemburg
Malta
Portugal
Slovenia
Cyprus

Indicators

The indicators included in the database is a mixture of descriptive and statistical indicators as well as indicators describing each region's political responsibilities. As of today the following descriptive/statistical indicators are included:

Type of state the region belongs to (federation, regionalized state, unitary state)

Directly elected region or not
Number of provinces
Number of municipalities
Region area
Region population
Population density
GDP/capita
GDP
Employment rate
Unemployment rate
Physicians/1000 inhabitants
Life expectancy at birth for men and women
Employed in agriculture as a share of total number of employed

The above list of indicators is not a finite list of possible indicators. However, they proved to be relatively easy to find information on and they are fairly good in order to compare regions since they give quite a bit of information. The statistics are largely drawn from the OECD regional statistics and Eurostat. Since neither of these two includes all countries that the region database aims to include, national statistical databases have also been used to find the information needed.

Apart from the descriptive/statistical indicators, the database also takes into account the regions' political mandates. The political indicators chosen are policy areas that commonly are included in European regions' political responsibilities. With regards to the policy areas, each region is coded as to weather they have extended responsibilities in the given area, some responsibilities, no responsibilities or if it is unclear. The following political indicators are

currently included:
    Legislation powers
    Taxation powers
    Regional development policy
    Labor-market policy
    Environment policy
    Culture policy
    Infrastructure policy
    School policy
    Health care policy
    Police tasks
    Regional political parties

Problems and ways ahead

The database is still in its infancy and it will continue to develop in dialogue with researchers and practitioners. Below follows a few points worth considering and discussing in order to improve the database.

First of all, which regions should be included? Maybe our purpose is better served if we include more regions of similar size, for example more NUTS 3 regions. As of today some regions, for example the German bundesländer, stand out both in size and in their extensive political responsibilities. Other regions are not directly elected and lack a political mandate all together. This is a point worthy of consideration. Furthermore and as stated above, work to involve regions outside of the European Union is intitiated.

A second point that needs consideration is what statistical indicators we shall include. Here, one should keep in mind that it is desirable to have as few indicators as possible so that the database is easy to manage and update. At the same time we want as much information as possible about the regions in different aspects. Thus, the ideal is a few but informative indicators that need little update and that are easy to find information on.

A third point connected to which statistical indicators to include is weather it is actually possible to find the information we need. For example it is difficult to find statistics on new EU-member states whose regional level might be newly formed and where statistical information thus is still lacking. There is also a difficulty to use national statistical databases as a source since the states still differs in their way of measuring a given indicator.

A fourth and last point is how to measure the regions' political responsibilities. First of all we need to consider what type of policy areas we shall include. Secondly, we also need to discuss weather the current classification with no, some, or extended political responsibilities in the given policy area is a good way to describe regions' political responsibilities or if there might be some other more informative way to indicate this.

The database will be available at Region Skåne's webpage: www.skane.se

Notes on Contributors

Jørgen Amdam is rector (from 2007–) and professor at Volda University College, Norway. His main academic interests and research fields are planning theory and methods, local and regional planning and development, communicative and collaborative planning and regional policy and planning. He was leader of the Norwegian Regional research program from 1998 to 2003 and has been president of the International Society for the Study of Marginal Regions (ISSMR) and other national and international academic organizations. He has written more than 200 publications, mainly in Norwegian.

Magdalena Belof is an Assistant Professor at the Faculty of Architecture, Wroclaw University of Technology (Poland). Her research interests include the European spatial planning, cross-border cooperation, planning theory, urban design and regeneration. Also, for over 10 years she has been active in the field of regional planning in Lower Silesia region, presently holding the position of the deputy director of the Regional Bureau of Spatial Planning in Wroclaw. Her field of activity covers mainly the transnational and transborder dimension of regional spatial planning and development. She has been managing and serving as an expert in numerous international co-operation projects. She coordinated the elaboration of international document: Spatial Development Study for Polish-Czech Borderland (2005).

Petter Boye is Econ. Dr. specialized in strategy and business development in regional contexts. Since the early 1990-ties he has, as researcher and consultant worked with strategic development processes of regional and transnational competence platforms. This work spans from internationalization of SMEs to industrial organization and regional policy issues. As a researcher and program coordinator at the Scandinavian Academy of Management Studies in Copenhagen, Boye started in the late 1990-ties to study the strategic development of the Öresund region. In the mid 2000, he began as researcher and Director of the Baltic Business Research Institute in Sweden to focus on strategy processes in the Baltic Sea region and the expanding EU. He has also been an active researcher and lecturer at Copenhagen Business School in Denmark, Lund University in Sweden, Stanford University and currently at Linnaeus University in Sweden.

Jan Erik Grindheim, Cand. Polit. and PhD in Comparative Politics, is Associate Professor of European Integration at University of Agder and Associate Professor II of Comparative Politics at University of Bergen. Grindheim has also been EU Adviser to the University of Oslo and he has worked for the regional development agency Oslo Teknopol for more than ten years with comparative statistics of regional development. His main research interests are European integration, Europeanisation and regional development.

Francisca Herodes is a Ph.D. student of political science at the Mid Sweden University. She is currently writing a theses on how various European sub-national authorities have adapted their organisations to handle tasks related to the interplay between the sub-national level and the EU supra-national level. Francisca has 15 years experience both from the private and public sector working with Swedish organisations, businesses, local and regional authorities and their linkage to European affairs within *inter alia* political monitoring, lobbying and strategic development. Between 2004 and 2007 she held the position as Director of the regional office Mid Sweden Office in Brussels and after that she worked as Practice Director of Public Affairs at Hill & Knowlton, Stockholm. Recently she joined the Swedish Government as a civil servant in the Unit for Regional Growth, Ministry of Enterprise.

Eve Hepburn is Senior Research Fellow in Politics and Depute Director of the Academy of Government at the University of Edinburgh. Her research explores party responses to multi-level governance, dynamics of regional party systems, regional governance, citizenship and immigration, and decentralization in the UK, Italy, Germany, Spain and Canada. She has published widely in the field, and is the author of Using Europe: territorial party strategies in a multi-level system (Manchester University Press, 2010) and editor of New Challenges for Stateless Nationalist and Regionalist Parties (Routledge, 2010).

Cecilia Josefsson is a master student in political science at Uppsala University. She has written a thesis on cross-border cooperation between regions in the European Union and constructed a database of regions in Europe.

Joerg Knieling holds the Chair for Urban Planning and Regional Development at HafenCity University Hamburg (HCU) and is Vice-President for Research Affairs of HCU. He graduated in urban and regional planning, holds a master's degree in political sciences and sociology and a Ph.D. from the University of Hanover. From 1992 until 2001 he was managing director of a private planning agency, then member of the Office of the Senate of the Free and Hanseatic City of Hamburg. In 2003 he was appointed Professor for Spatial Planning at Dresden Technical University. His main research fields are sustainable regional and metropolitan development, territorial governance, and planning theory. Current publications have been "Planning Cultures in Europe. Decoding Cultural Phenomena in Urban and Regional Planning (2009). Furnham: Ashgate", and „Metropolregionen. Innovation, Wettbewerb, Handlungsfähigkeit" (2009), Hannover. For further information see www.hcu-hamburg.de

Anders Lidström is professor in political science in the Department of Political Science, Umeå University, Sweden. He carries out research in the field of local politics and government, comparative politics and education policy. This includes studies of local democracy and self-government, both within Sweden and in a comparative perspective. Among recent publications are *The Oxford Handbook of Local and Regional Democracy in Europe* (co-edited, Oxford University Press, 2011). He has also recently published books and articles on for example comparative local government, regionalization of northern Sweden and municipal reforms in Sweden and Finland.

Anders Lidström is convenor for the LOGOPOL network of local government researchers in the European Consortium of Political Research. Since 2007 Lidström is the substitute member from Sweden of the Group of Independent Experts on the European Charter of Local Self-Government, Council of Europe.

Lisbeth Lindeborg has a PhD in Political Science from the J.W. Goethe-university in Frankfurt/Main and a BA in Culture and Arts from the University of Lund. She is working as a freelance author, writer and journalist and has written extensively on regional and cultural issues.Her main research interests are regional theory, regional cooperation and the significance of culture and identity for regional development. In 1995 she was one of the first to write a comprehensive 500 page report on regional cooperation, Regionalt samarbete i Europa – med tyska erfartenheter (ERU, Sweden) (Regional cooperation in Europe – with experiences from Germany). In 2001 (updated 2005) she wrote Zum regionalen System. Stellenwert der Versammlung der Regionen Europas (Tectum Wissenschaftsverlag). In 2010 she co-edited and co-authored Kulturens kraft för regional utveckling (The Power of Culture for Regional Development), SNS, Stockholm.

Lise Lyck is Centre Director at the Center for Tourism and Culture Management at Copenhagen Business School, Denmark. Lyck is conducting research within the fields of tourism, transport, service management and experience economy plus regionalization.

Lyck has made the first national account for Greenland and been active in Arctic research and in regionalization at the national, cross-border and EU level. Recent focus has been on the EU project AGORA 2.0, which seeks to create a common identity and strengthen the tourism industry within the Baltic Sea Region, and on a book about the Danish museum sector. Concerning publications see the CBS library (http://uk.cbs.dk/bibliotek/). The latest books are: *Intercultural Leadership in the Øresund Region,* Copenhagen Business School, Frederiksberg Bogtrykkeri, 2008, and *Service- og Oplevelsesøkonomi i Teori og Praksis,* Academica, (ISBN: 9788776752064), 2008, *Museer: Hvorfor og hvordan?,* Frederiksberg Bogtrykkeri, (ISBN: 9788792019097).

Nicola McEwen is Co-Director of the Institute of Governance at the University of Edinburgh. A political scientist, she specialises in research on devolution, nationalism and territorial politics, and has published widely in these fields. Her monograph, Nationalism and the State: Welfare and Identity in Scotland and Quebec (PIE/ Peter Lang) was published in 2006 and she co-edited (with Luis Moreno) The Territorial Politics of Welfare (Routledge) in 2005. More recent publications include articles on elections, voting behaviour and intergovernmental relations. She is Director of an Msc programme in Multi-level and Regional Politics.

Adam Manga is a graduate of International Relations and European Studies at University of West Hungary and ISES-Corvinus University. His main research interest is the transport policy of the EU, mobility, connection of transportation and society.

Joakim Nergelius is professor of law at the University of Örebro. He has written extensively on Swedish, comparative and European constitutional issues. Previously, he has also worked at the European Court of Justice and the EU Committee of Regions, where his interest in regional issues grew. His most recent publications include The Constitutional Dilemma of the European Union (Europa Law Publishing, Groningen, 2009).

Jefferey M. Sellers is Associate Professor of Political Science, Geography and Public Policy at the University of Southern California. He is author of *Governing From Below: Urban Regions and the Global Economy* (Cambridge: Cambridge University Press, 2002), and co-editor of *Metropolitanization and Political Change* (Wiesbaden: VS Verlag, 2005) and The *Political Ecology of the Metropolis* (forthcoming, ECPR Press). He has also authored or co-authored dozens of articles, book chapters and papers on comparative urban politics, decentralization, law and society, urban geography, territorial identity, legal studies and public policy.

Malin Stegmann McCallion is Senior Lecturer in Political Science at the Department of Political and Historical Studies, Karlstad University, Sweden and she holds a PhD from Queen's University, Belfast (QUB). Before joining Karlstad University she was a Research Fellow at Institute of Welsh Studies, Department of International Politics, Aberystwyth University, Wales on a project Paradiplomacy in Post-Devolution Wales' together with Dr Elin Royles and Professor Richard Wyn Jones; she has also held lecturing posts at University College Dublin, Ireland and Limerick University, Ireland. Her research has been published in, for example, Regional and Federal Studies (2007) and Regional Studies (2008) and joint research with her colleagues at Karlstad University by Nordregio (2009).

Elvira Uyarra is a Research Fellow at the Manchester Institute of Innovation Research (Manchester Business School). Elvira holds a Ph.D in Science and Technology Policy (Manchester), an MSc in Technical Change and Regional Development (Cardiff) and a BSc ('licenciatura') in Economics (University of the Basque Country). Elvira has worked in the field of regional technology, innovation and development since 1998 first as an industry-based economist and then as academic researcher. Elvira's research and teaching activities centre mainly on: regional science and innovation policy; spatial dimensions of knowledge and innovation; evolutionary approaches to public policy, universities and regional development, and the innovation impact of public procurement. Her recent work has been published in Research Policy, the Journal of Evolutionary economics, Environment and Planning C, European Planning Studies, as well as chapter contributions in edited books volumes for Palgrave and Edward Elgar Publishers.

EDITORS

Tassilo Herrschel is a Reader (Associate Professor) in Urban and Regional Development and co-director of the Centre of Urban and Regional Governance (CURG) at the University of Westminster, London, where he is based in the Department of Politics and International Relations. His main research focus, on which he has published widely, is on city-regional economic governance and policy, city regions, regionalism. multi-level governance and 'transition' societies in Europe and North America. His publications include 'Governance of Europe'sCity Regions' and 'Geographies of Post-Socialist Transition' (both published by Routledge). He is a board member of the Regional Studies Association with the remit for knowledge transfer between academia and policy practice.

Pontus Tallberg is the responsible manager in Region Skåne for analysing regional self-rule in sweden. He has a broad experience from the Swedish Tax Authorities. He focuses especially on the relations between municipalities-regions and the national level. He has been the editor of many antologies concerning municipalities and regions in Sweden as well as other other parts of the European Union.